9.00

73 - 445

D0992362

The Conditions of Learning

ROBERT M. GAGNÉ
The Florida State University

The Conditions of Learning

SECOND EDITION

HOLT, RINEHART and WINSTON, Inc.
*New York   Chicago   San Francisco   Atlanta   Dallas
Montreal   Toronto   London   Sydney*

Preface

The first edition of this book was intended to answer the question, What is known about the process of learning that can be put to use in designing better education? This aim has not changed in the present edition, and the answer I give continues to have the same basic structure.

The point of view of this text is that learning must be linked to the design of instruction through consideration of the different kinds of capabilities that are being learned. In other words, the external events that are called instruction need to have different characteristics, depending on the particular class of performance change that is the focus of interest. The book describes eight distinguishable classes of performance change (learning) and the corresponding sets of conditions for learning that are associated with them.

Additional studies and sources of evidence are cited in this volume for areas that in the last edition depended upon observations of a less systematic nature. An attempt has been made to provide a somewhat more complete and contemporary view of the process of learning by the inclusion of a more adequate treatment of contingency-of-reinforcement theory, a chapter describing common features of learning events, and description of a number of other relevant findings of modern learning research. In addition, I have attempted to fill gaps, wherever these have been pointed out to me by students and instructors, and to clarify the meaning of such difficult terms as "concept" and "rule."

The topic of learning hierarchies has been given increased prominence in this edition, including additional description and, I hope, clarification. This conception, which in its fundamental form proposes that the types of learning are dependent upon each other in a prior learning sense, may be viewed as a theory. Chapter 9 treats learning hierarchies primarily as tools for instructional technology, particularly in connection with the design of sequences of instruction, courses, and curricula. The relevance of these hierarchies to questions of learning readiness and intellectual development is described in Chapter 10.

The book is intended for students in psychology and education who have gained some acquaintance with the phenomena of learning in an earlier course of study. I am told that the book in its first edition has seemed particularly appropriate for students who have had such a background, and I trust this will continue to be the case. Use of the book in courses in psychology, as well as in education, is gratifying for an author who identifies firmly with the former discipline. The orientation of the book toward educational problems is, of course, deliberate, but the demonstration of its applicability to fundamental research in learning is a task that may well require the efforts of many bridge builders. As for the relation of the ideas contained in this text to educational planning and practice, I have had many heartwarming examples described to me, frequently accompanied by helpful criticisms, and I am most grateful for them.

Tallahassee, Florida   R.M.G.
February 1970

Contents

1 Introduction

Few things are so intriguing to wonder about as the development of human behavior. The adult human being becomes a marvelously adaptable, competently functioning person within a complex society. How he progresses to this point from a beginning as a highly dependent, relatively noncapable, newborn infant is a question of great intellectual interest and importance. One part of the answer to this question, to be sure, lies in an understanding of the processes of growth and development, characteristic properties shared by all living things. The other part, relating to a different set of circumstances in the life of the individual, is learning. The human skills, appreciations, and reasonings in all their great variety, as well as human hopes, aspirations, attitudes, and values, are generally recognized to depend for their development largely on the events called learning.

One may, if one wishes, cease to wonder about learning at this point, having confirmed to one's own satisfaction that human development in all its manifestations must depend on the twin factors of growth and learning and their interactions with each other. One can say about a child, "He'll learn," just as one says, "He'll grow into it (or out of it)," and such a statement is difficult to deny. But to equate

1

learning and growth as natural events is to overlook the one most important difference between them. The factors that influence growth are to a very large extent genetically determined, whereas the factors that influence learning are chiefly determined by events in the individual's living environment. Once the individual's genetic stock has been chosen at the moment of conception, his growth cannot be altered very much, except by rather extreme measures. But members of the human society, which itself is responsible for the care of a developing person, have a tremendous degree of control over those events that affect his learning. Experience, we are told, is the great teacher. This means that the events the developing individual lives through—in his home, in his geographical environment, in school, and in his various social environments—will determine what he learns and therefore to a large extent what kind of person he becomes.

This enormous dependence of learning on environmental circumstances implies a great responsibility for all members of human society. The situations in which the developing child is placed, whether deliberately or otherwise, are going to have great effects on him. In fact, there is not a very clear understanding at present of what the limits of these effects may be. Are the situations in which the growing person is nowadays customarily placed the sort that will encourage the development of disciplined thinkers, of great artists and scientists? Or are they such as will discourage such development and inhibit the full exploitation of human thought and intellect?

The realization that learning is largely dependent on events in the environment with which the individual interacts makes it possible to view learning as an occurrence that can be examined more closely and understood more profoundly. Learning is not simply an event that happens naturally; it is also an event that happens under certain observable conditions. Furthermore, these conditions can be altered and controlled; and this leads to the possibility of examining the occurrence of learning by means of the methods of science. It becomes possible to observe the conditions under which learning takes place, and to describe them in objective language. It is possible to detect relations between these conditions and the changes in human behavior that occur in learning, and thus to make inferences about what has been learned. It is also possible to construct scientific models and theories to account for the changes observed, just as it is with other types of natural events.

Learning and Its Conditions

This book is about the *conditions of learning*. It attempts to consider the sets of circumstances that obtain when learning occurs, that is, when certain observable changes in human behavior take place that justify the inference of learning. It will deal with a number of varieties of these changes, and accordingly with a number of relationships between them and the situations in which they occur. It will stop short of a theory of learning, although the raw materials from which one or more theories may be constructed will hopefully become apparent. Its major concern is to find a reasonable answer to the question, What is learning? This answer is to be phrased mainly in terms of an objective description of the conditions under which learning takes place. These conditions will be identified, first of all, by reference to the situations of ordinary life, including those of the school, in which learning occurs. Their identification will also be aided in certain instances by reference to experiments from the psychological laboratory.

Learning is a change in human disposition or capability, which can be retained, and which is not simply ascribable to the process of growth. The kind of change called learning exhibits itself as a change in behavior, and the inference of learning is made by comparing what behavior was possible before the individual was placed in a "learning situation" and what behavior can be exhibited after such treatment. The change may be, and often is, an increased capability for some type of performance. It may also be an altered disposition of the sort called "attitude," or "interest," or "value." The change must have more than momentary permanence; it must be capable of being retained over some period of time. Finally, it must be distinguishable from the kind of change that is attributable to growth, such as a change in height or the development of muscles through exercise.

The Elements of the Learning Event

On one and the same day, a child may learn to tie his shoelaces and may also learn to call the mailman by his name, "Mr. Wells." Somehow, the events in the child's environment, whether deliberately arranged or not, conspire to bring about these changes in his performance. The changes are also in his capabilities, as shown by the fact that he can now tie his shoelaces or call the mailman "Mr. Wells" any time he is asked to. What are the elements in either or both situations that can be abstracted as having to do with learning?

1. First there is a *learner,* who is a human being. (It would be possible for the learner to be an animal, but that is another story.) For the events considered here the most important parts of the learner are his senses, his central nervous system, and his muscles. Events in his environment affect the learner's senses, and start chains of nervous impulses that are organized by his central nervous system, specifically, by his brain. This nervous activity occurs in certain sequences and patterns that alter the nature of the organizing process itself, and this effect is exhibited as learning. Finally, the nervous activity is translated into action that may be observed as the movement of muscles in executing responses of various sorts.

2. The events that stimulate the learner's senses are spoken of collectively as the *stimulus situation.* When a single event is being distinguished, it is often called a *stimulus.*

3. The action that results from stimulation and subsequent nervous activity is called a *response*. Responses may be described more or less specifically; for example, one can speak of the movement of a particular muscle, or of the action of the whole body in walking. For this reason and others, responses are often described in terms of their effects rather than in terms of their appearances. When so classified, they are called *performances*. For example, a response might be "moving the finger rhythmically over a small area of the scalp." But it may often be more useful to refer to the performance of "scratching the head."

A learning event, then, takes place when the *stimulus situation* affects the learner in such a way that his *performance* changes from a time *before* being in that situation to a time *after* being in it. The *change in performance* is what leads to the conclusion that learning has occurred.

At the level of general description, the child's learning to tie his shoelaces came about in the following way. Before the learning, his performance was such that he could not tie his shoelaces. (Perhaps he could do certain parts of this performance, but not the whole thing.) Then a stimulus situation was introduced, which may have included a parent who used verbal communication to get the child to make certain responses. Still another kind of stimulus that may have been employed is a picture or drawing. At any rate, a sequence of stimulus events was made to occur. At the end of this sequence, the child succeeded in producing a tied shoelace (much to his satisfaction, no doubt). The parent then verified to himself, and to the child, that learning had taken place by asking the child to tie the lace on his other shoe. The performance was again exhibited successfully, and the inference was made that learning had taken place. It had produced in the child a new *capability*.

Learning to call the mailman "Mr. Wells" likewise involves these same elements. The child's initial performance indicates that he does not say "Mr. Wells" when he sees the mailman, but perhaps calls him "man," or simply points to him. Assuming that the child has a certain verbal facility by this age, the stimulus situation might be as simple as the statement by a parent "That's Mr. Wells." The child then makes the response "Mr. Wells." When the mailman is next seen again, the child once more exhibits the performance, saying "Mr. Wells." At this point, one concludes that the child has learned; his performance has undergone a change; he has acquired a new capability.

Each of these examples is somewhat oversimplified, of course. But the framework for the events of learning exhibits a constant set of elements. As our discussion of the *conditions* of learning proceeds, there will be many occasions that call for reference to these elements of the learning event.

What is the nature of new capabilities established by learning? It should be recognized that there are as many different kinds of capabilities as there are performances. But there are also different levels of complexity of these capabilities. With the simplest kind of learning that can be observed or even imagined, there is an unvarying relation between the stimulus and the response. The learning change is from

$$\text{Stimulus} \rightarrow (\text{nothing})$$
$$\text{to}$$
$$\text{Stimulus} \rightarrow \text{Response.}$$

This basic kind of learned capability is called an *association*. Suppose a child of suitable maturity does not originally respond when the parent says, "Smile!" Following a suitable learning situation, he now *does* smile invariably to the same spoken stimulus. One can say he has acquired an association. If an adult who previously could not supply the English word "horse" for the French word "cheval" now does so, it is similarly appropriate to call this newly learned capability an association. There will be many references to learned associations in the following pages. It will also be seen that the learning of *single* associations is a rare event. Most investigators of learning, however, are of the opinion that the association is the simplest form of learned capability, and also that it constitutes a fundamental "building block" for other more complex performances. This trend of thinking can clearly be seen in the development of ideas about learning in American psychology.

LEARNING IN AMERICAN PSYCHOLOGY

How people learn, and the conditions under which they learn, are questions that have been investigated by several generations of American psychologists, as well as by those in other parts of the world. But learning has always been a favorite problem for American writers and researchers, partly no doubt because of a philosophical tradition that tended to place great emphasis on experience as a determiner of knowledge. It is of some value, therefore, to spend a little time in describing what these historically important ideas about the nature of learning have been, since they will point the way to the influences that have shaped current learning theory, and that will undoubtedly affect future developments as well.

Research on learning has generated several typical models, or *prototypes*, which are frequently referred to by writers on the subject. There are the conditioned response, trial-and-error learning, insight, and others, which are often used to communicate basic similarities and contrasts among situations in which learning occurs. It is important for an understanding of the varieties of learning, as discussed in subsequent chapters, to become acquainted with these prototypes of learning and the situations in which they have typically been observed.

The Associationist Tradition

One of the oldest lines of thinking about learning in American psychology derives from the British associationist psychologists, who formulated a number of theories about how ideas are associated. These theorists were primarily concerned with the question of how complex ideas like flower or number are constructed in the human mind from elementary sense impressions. In other words, they were interested in the question of how such "complex ideas" were learned in the first place. On this latter point, they were generally agreed that acquiring a new idea necessitated (1) *contiguity* of the sense impressions or simple ideas that were to be combined to form the new idea, and (2) *repetition* of these contiguous events. Some of these psychologists also discussed "mental concentration" (which is now usually called attention) as an important condition for the learning of new ideas by association (Mill, 1869).

American psychologists like William James and John Dewey added some distinctly new interpretations to this associationist tradition. The ideas of Darwin concerning the functions of living phenomena in adaptation exerted a considerable influence on these American scholars. Accordingly, they sought to discover the *functions* of behavioral events like learning and thinking, rather than simply the composition of these events. A most important characteristic of learning was considered to be its function in the life of the organism. This view led them to place the *nervous system*, rather than "the mind," in a position of central importance to an understanding of how sense impressions get connected with behavior. And perhaps most significant of all, they assigned a critical role to *action* as a factor in learning. Action did not simply follow ideas, as British associationists had proposed, but became an essential feature of the process of behavioral organization called learning.

Animal Trial and Error

Another direction taken by American psychology in its treatment of learning established perhaps the most important trend of all. This was the use of animals for the performance of experiments on learning. Edward L. Thorndike (1898) was a pioneer in these efforts to understand the learning of animals by performing experiments rather than by collecting anecdotes about animal behavior. From his controlled observations of cats, dogs, and chickens escaping from problem boxes, he concluded that many previous accounts of animal thought were erroneous in that they attributed greater power to animal intelligence than actually existed. His investigations suggested the possibility that all that was necessary to explain animal learning were specific bonds between "sense impressions" and "impulses to action." These associations he considered to be stamped in by the consequences resulting from the completed act (such as escape from the problem box). Thorndike believed that associations of this sort also made up a large part, although not all, of what human beings learned and remembered.

A hungry animal, such as a cat, is placed in a box with slatted sides and a door that can be opened by pressing a wooden lever to release a latch, allowing the animal to reach food placed within his view outside the box. At first, the cat is observed to engage in a variety of acts, including scratching at the sides and door of the box. Sooner or later, these various activities lead by chance to the depression of the latch that opens the door. The animal then immediately leaves the box and eats the bit of food. When placed in the box again, the animal's behavior is obviously changed. He spends less time scratching at the sides of the box, and more time making movements in the region of the latch. On this second trial, it takes him much less time to release the latch and get to the food. Subsequent trials reduce the time still more, until he is releasing the latch only a few seconds after he is placed in the box.

The view of learning that is represented by this prototype situation may be described briefly as follows. When confronted with a novel situation, the motivated learner engages in various "tries" to attain satisfaction. Sooner or later, largely by chance, he makes a set of responses that lead to motive satisfaction. The particular responses that are immediately followed by motive satisfaction (eating the food, in this case) become "stronger" in relation to others. Thus, when the animal is placed in the box a second time, the latch-pressing responses occur sooner, whereas the other responses (like scratching the floor of the box) tend to be shorter in duration or entirely absent. On subsequent trials in the box, these "errors" progressively weaken and disappear. The correct responses, in contrast, are progressively strengthened by being followed immediately by motive satisfaction. This generalization was called the "law of effect" by Thorndike. The learning situation does not differ in basic characteristics from that of the rat pressing a lever, employed later by Skinner (1938). "Reinforcement" is the term Skinner uses to identify the events that Thorndike called the law of effect.

Is the animal trial-and-error prototype representative of human learning? The answer is clearly in the negative. It is, in fact, rather difficult to relate it to the learning that might occur in a human being. If a person is put in a problem box, we know that he is likely to adopt a strategy of searching for a way out. He recognizes latches, knobs, or other devices as having certain functions. He "thinks out" the consequences of his actions before he takes them, and chooses the most likely alternative. Once he finds his way out, he will under most circumstances remember it, and there will be no gradual error reduction on subsequent trials. How can such behavior be in any sense comparable to "trial and error"? The strategies, the recalling, the recognizing, the thinking, the choosing are all there in his behavior; they can readily be observed if the proper experimental conditions are provided.

By searching hard, one can probably find some degree of comparability between the trial-and-error prototype and the acquisition of a motor skill by young children, such as balancing blocks, making a simple knot, or learning language sounds. Insofar as the prototype helps us to understand such learning, it is useful. But this is, of course, an extremely circumscribed usefulness for the field of learning in general.

A number of more modern learning theorists have made the individual association, as seen in animal behavior, the basis of their ideas on learning. Among these are Edwin R. Guthrie (1935), Clark L. Hull (1943), and B. F. Skinner (1938), each of whom has proposed somewhat different interpretations of the basic idea that the *association*, as observed in animal learning of simple acts, is the typical form of learning. Other investigators of animal learning opposed this tradition, however. Chief among these was Edward C. Tolman (1932), whose experiments convinced him that Thorndike and those who followed him were wrong in asserting that nothing but an "association" existed between a situation and the response that followed it. Tolman's theory maintains that association is an internal matter, between a representation (within the animal's nervous system) of the stimulus situation, and a representation of the alternatives of action to be taken. He thus attempted to restore to animal behavior the "ideas" (although this was not his term) that had been considered unnecessary by Thorndike.

One modern theorist, Neal Miller (1967), has provided evidence to indicate that strong and lasting single associations can be learned by rats in a single trial as rapidly as they often are by human beings. Thus there is good reason to believe that the speed of forming such associations does not differ in man and the lower mammals. Differences in capacities of learning between men and animals must presumably be sought in the greater complexity of intellectual processing, and perhaps in the size of the memory store, rather than in the basic mechanism for learning.

The Conditioned Response

I. P. Pavlov (1927) found that when a signal such as a buzzer was sounded at the time food was shown to a hungry dog, and this set of events was repeated several times, the dog came to salivate at the sound of the buzzer alone. Whereas the salivation at the sight of food could be considered a natural (or unconditioned) response, salivation to a buzzer had to be acquired as a conditioned response. This learning occurred when the new signal (the buzzer) was presented together with the food in a number of trials. A new signal-response connection was thereby established.

John B. Watson (1919) championed the view of learning suggested by the work of Pavlov in his studies of conditioning in dogs. In Watson's writings, learning was viewed as a matter of establishing individual associations (conditioned responses) firmly based in the nervous system. More complex human acts were considered to be chains of conditioned responses.

Most investigators of Pavlovian conditioning now believe it to be a very special kind of learning, representative of the establishment of *involuntary,* "anticipatory" responses such as the startled eyeblinking that may follow a threatening gesture (Kimble, 1961). It is likely, of course, that human beings acquire many conditioned responses of this sort in the course of their lives. One may find oneself, for example, waking with a start at the slight click the alarm clock makes before it actually rings. Hearing an automobile horn from an unexpected direction may evoke a tensing of muscles in the hands on the wheel and in the foot on the brake. In the schoolroom, the teacher's pointing to an object to be described may become a conditioned signal for students to be alert for other stimuli to come from that direction. It is even possible that learned anticipatory responses may be largely what is meant by "paying attention" to something. Conditioned emotional reactions of an involuntary sort may be involved in reactions to snakes, spiders, or other events that are accompanied by unexpected signals. Perhaps they also play a part in the determination of attitudes.

Despite the widespread occurrence of conditioned responses in our lives, they remain unrepresentative of most of the events we mean by the word "learning." Voluntary acts can be conditioned only with difficulty, if at all. If a child wants to learn to ride a bicycle, he will get no help in this activity by arranging the pairing of a conditioned and unconditioned stimulus, because voluntary control of his actions is not acquired in this way. The same is true, needless to say, for most other kinds of things he must learn, beginning with reading, writing, and arithmetic. There can be little doubt that Watson's idea that most forms of human learning could be accounted for as chains of conditioned responses is wildly incorrect; and this has been pretty generally conceded for many years.

The Learning of Verbal Associates

Hermann Ebbinghaus (1913) carried out an ingenious set of experimental studies of learning and memorization. He used himself as an experimental subject, and as materials, series of nonsense syllables of the sort NOF-VIB-JEX, and so on. These constructed syllables were employed in the attempt to gain control over the unwanted variable of previous practice, since it was immediately apparent to Ebbinghaus that an association like BOY-MAN was already more or less well learned. In committing to memory these series of nonsense syllables, he was able to study the effects of such variables as length of series, order of presentation, and many others. Later investigators saw in the nonsense syllable a versatile tool for the study of *verbal association*.

An important and productive line of investigation of the learning of nonsense syllables and other verbal units was carried on by Robinson (1932), McGeoch (1942) and down into the present day by Melton (1940, 1964), Underwood (1964a), Postman (1964), and many others. Generally speaking, investigators in this tradition have championed empirical research rather than the development of comprehensive theory.

For a period of some years, investigators of verbal associate learning apparently believed that their findings could account for the learning of *single* associations. But even Ebbinghaus' results showed that committing one syllable to memory was strongly influenced by the presence of other

syllables. During the many years of research following
Ebbinghaus, the number of factors that have been found
to affect the learning of nonsense lists has constantly increased, and the difficulty of experimental control has similarly become greater. The learning of any single association
in a sequence has been shown to be markedly affected by
the *interference* of other associations both within the list
and outside it. A great many of the characteristics previously
thought to describe the learning of single associates are now
attributed to the effects of interference.

The verbal associate prototype must also be considered to
represent a very limited range of actual learning situations.
The differences in learning and retaining logically connected prose and poetry, as opposed to nonsense lists, have
been apparent for many years (see Ausubel, 1968), and
it is doubtful whether the interference that occurs within
these two types of material follows the same laws. There
may be a limited number of instances in which human
beings engage in the learning of material whose members
are arbitrarily related, as in learning the alphabet, or π to
ten places. But the vast majority of verbal learning that
occurs must be affected strongly by its meaningfulness, as
experiments on verbal associates have themselves demonstrated.

Insight

Opposed to these associationist trends in studies of learning has been the *Gestalt* tradition, reflected in the writings
of Max Wertheimer (1945), Wolfgang Köhler (1929), and
Kurt Koffka (1929). As conceived by these writers, learning
typically takes the form of an *insight*, which is a suddenly
occurring reorganization of the field of experience, as when
one "has a new idea" or "discovers a solution to a problem."

Köhler used a variety of problem situations to study insightful learning in chimpanzees (1927). For example, a
banana was suspended from the top of the animal's cage,
out of his reach. Several wooden boxes were available

within the cage, but the animal could not reach the banana by standing on any one of them. A great variety of restlessness and trial and error was exhibited. On occasion, however, an animal was observed to act suddenly, as though he were carrying out a plan, by placing one box on top of another, then immediately climbing on this structure to reach the banana. As another example, one chimpanzee was observed, again after much trial and error, to put together two jointed sticks, which he then used as a single long stick to reach a banana placed outside his cage. Köhler called such learning *insight*, and emphasized the discontinuity it had with the previous trial-and-error behavior. The total successful act was put together and exhibited suddenly, without error and as if by plan. Köhler's interpretation was that insight involved a "seeing" of relations, a putting together of events that were internally represented.

This form of learning by human beings has also been described by other Gestalt writers like Wertheimer (1945) and Katona (1940). For example, Wertheimer describes solutions to a geometric problem by children, insightful and otherwise. Children who knew the "formula" for the area of a rectangle as $h \times b$ were asked to derive a means of finding the area of a parallelogram. Some proceeded in a "rote" fashion to multiply the length of the base times the length of the side, which, of course, is incorrect. Others were able to see the correct solution by cutting a right triangle from one side of the parallelogram, and attaching it to the other side, thus reconstructing a known figure, the rectangle. Still others were able to see the problem as one of dividing up the entire parallelogram into little squares (a very sophisticated solution). Although a child may have tried several wrong approaches, a "good" solution was arrived at, according to Wertheimer, when the child could see the essential structure of the problem situation.

The most frequent criticism of the "insight" explanation of these learning events is, however, a very serious one. This is to the effect that animals and children solve these problems by *transfer from previous learning*. The chimpanzee is able to pile boxes one upon another because he has previously learned to do this, although not necessarily in this particular situation. The child is able to identify the triangles as similar because he has previously done this with other right triangles. It cannot be said that such an explanation is not true, because in fact in these Gestalt examples the factor of prior learning has not been controlled. Despite the neatness of a theory that accounts for insight on the basis of the structure of the observed situation, the phenomena of insight have in one instance after another been shown to be affected by previous learning.

One of the most impressive modern evidences of the effects of prior learning on insightful behavior occurs in Harlow's studies of *learning set* (1949). Harlow trained monkeys to solve problems in which the correct choice among three objects was the "odd" one, the object dissimilar to the others. By trial-and-error learning, monkeys learned to choose the odd one of three objects when they were consistently rewarded for doing so. In the next problem, three new objects were presented, including an odd one, and the monkeys again learned to choose the odd one, somewhat faster this time. A third problem, again with a new set of objects, was solved faster than the second. After solving a few more oddity problems of this sort, the animal was able to solve oddity problems (involving objects he had not previously encountered) at once, without any hesitation. He had acquired, Harlow said, a learning set that enabled him to solve oddity problems correctly without trial and error.

This evidence implies that previous learning, acquired through a number of encounters with similar problems, can establish a kind of internal capability that makes the animal quite different from naïve monkeys of the same age and strain. He becomes an "oddity-problem solver" monkey, who displays insight when given an oddity problem to solve. Obviously, this capability for insight did not arise because of a "structuring of the situation." It came, rather, from accumulated experience based on many individual trials of previous learning.

What can be said about the representativeness of insight as a prototype of learning? On the one hand, it does appear to represent some common learning occurrences that are rather easy to identify. When children are led to "see" relations, such as those between addition and multiplication or between weight and the "pull" of gravity, they often display insight. On the other hand, it is difficult to find insight in the learning of a great variety of other things. A child cannot learn the names of plants or stars in an insightful manner. He cannot learn to read by insight, nor to speak a foreign language. A student of biology does not learn the structures and functions of animals by insight. In short, insight cannot be a prototype for a vast amount of learning that human beings ordinarily undertake. Perhaps it occurs when we learn by "solving problems," but we also learn many, many things that are not problems at all. They may simply be facts, or propositions, or principles.

Reinforcement Theory

The term "reinforcement" has played a prominent role in determining the prototype situations studied by learning investigators. It is important to note, first, that reinforcement has several different meanings, and it is doubtful at the present time that these can be conceived as similar to each other. Thorndike's classic statement of the *law of effect* has already been mentioned. Learning was thought to be influenced positively when the animal attained through its activity a "satisfying state of affairs." One direction of theory that represented a somewhat more precise statement of reinforcement was proposed by Hull (1943) and also by Spence (1956) and Miller (1959). In this type of theory, reinforcement is typically considered to occur when a motive is directly satisfied—for example, when a fundamental drive like hunger undergoes a reduction in intensity. The effects of such reinforcement may be to strengthen a learned association or its recall or both. This general conception of motivation may be called *reward theory*. Obviously, the prototype learning situation to which it leads has the newly acquired response of the learner followed as immediately as possible by a reward. In the case of an animal, the reward may be something that reduces the intensity of a drive, as a bit of food reduces hunger. With human beings, however, various kinds of symbolic rewards may be equally effective.

Skinner's (1968) conception of reinforcement, which constitutes a central part of his theoretical view of learning, is really quite different from that of Hull and Miller. It does not depend necessarily on the notion of reward. To Skinner, reinforcement is the name for a particular arrangement of stimulus and response conditions that bring about the learning of a new association. Specifically, a response that one might want the individual to learn must be made *contingent* on the occurrence of certain stimulus conditions, which in turn bring about another response. This theory may appropriately be called the *contingency of reinforcement* theory. Typically, in the learning situation a response that the individual makes is deliberately made contingent upon the occurrence of some other response which precedes it and which has a high probability of being made. Thus the cat's obtaining food (as in Thorndike's puzzle box) is made contingent upon his pressing the lever. Various kinds of arrangements of contingencies (some of which will be referred to later) are possible. They all involve the common characteristic that the activity to be learned is made to be preceded systematically by the occurrence of some chosen event. Shortly this event comes to exert control over the activity, and one can thus say that learning has occurred.

Modern ideas of reinforcement are thus by no means unitary in their meaning. Yet it seems likely that the concept of reinforcement will continue to play a prominent part in learning theory. If there is anything in common about the idea, it is its emphasis on the *after-effects* of the response that is to be learned. To Thorndike, the satisfying after-effects strengthened the association. To Hull and his associates, learning was influenced by after-effects of a sort that brought about drive reduction (or motive satisfaction). To Skinner, the activity to be learned must be made to take place in such a way that after-effects are made contingent on its occurrence.

The Significance of Learning Prototypes

Thus we see that learning in American psychology has usually been considered a problem of understanding the *association*. To the British associationists, the association of interest was between sense impressions and ideas, or between simple and complex ideas. Following James and Dewey, Watson, Thorndike, and others set out to study the association between sense impressions and impulses to action, or, in more modern terms, between stimulus and response (S and R). Tolman believed that the essential kind of association in learning was an internal event connecting "significates" and "expectations." And then there have been those who, all along, have denied that association is a central event in learning at all.

Throughout the period of scientific investigation of learning, there has been frequent recourse to certain typical experimental situations to serve as *prototypes* for learning. Most prominently, these have been derived from animal learning studies, the conditioned response, the learning of verbal associates, or insight studies. Actually, the choice of these prototypes has had considerable influence on the course of learning research. When contrasting predictions are made by theories, it is these prototypes that are appealed to as concrete ways of settling the issue. And it is from these prototypes that experiments are designed to test theoretical predictions. They have become, in other words, the concrete models that investigators of learning think about when they set out to study learning experimentally.

As examples, the prototypes themselves represent a variety of kinds of learning. It has not been found possible to "reduce" one variety to another, although many attempts have been made. In addition, there are many instances of learning that these prototypes apparently do *not* represent. There seem, in fact, to be a number of varieties of learning that are not considered at all by these standard examples; their representativeness of all the varieties of actual learning phenomena is not at all comprehensive.

These learning prototypes all have a similar history in this respect: each of them started to be a representative of a particular variety of learning situation. Thorndike wanted to study animal association. Pavlov was studying reflexes. Ebbinghaus studied the memorization of verbal lists. Köhler was studying the solving of problems by animals. By some peculiar semantic process, these examples became prototypes of learning, and thus were considered to represent the domain of learning as a whole, or at least in large part. Somehow, they came to be placed in opposition to each other: either all learning was insight or all learning was conditioned response. Such controversies have continued for years, and have been relatively unproductive in advancing our understanding of learning as an event.

THE VIEW OF LEARNING PRESENTED IN THIS BOOK

How can one determine what learning is? The plan to be followed in this volume is to classify some everyday observations about learning, and thus to identify and distinguish some varieties of situations in which learning occurs. Once these varieties of learning have been identified, an account can be given of the *conditions* that govern the learning occurrences. This will lead to a description of the factors that determine learning, derived insofar as possible from available evidence in controlled experimentation. By this means it will be possible to differentiate several kinds of learning, each requiring a different set of conditions for its occurrence.

From this naturalistic viewpoint, it will be possible to show that there are eight kinds of learning, not just one or two. The traditional prototypes described in the previous section are considered to represent only parts of the situations in which learning occurs, and therefore to depict the generation of mere fragments of the human capabilities that are acquired. The kinds of questions to be raised and answered by subsequent chapters are suggested by the following set of contrasted ideas:

1. The conditioned response prototype is used to account for the fast alerting reaction of an automobile driver to a flashing red light. What about the subsequent actions requiring skilled control of the car?

2. An infant's first words may be acquired as simple associations. Is it possible also to understand how the child learns to construct meaningful sentences?

3. A traditional prototype may be used to represent learning the name of a particular dog. Can one also account for the differentiation of dogs from cats?

4. Learning the names of the numerals 7, 8, and 9 can be represented by a simple learning prototype. How does an individual learn to use these numerals as numbers to express quantity?

5. Verbal association can represent the memorizing of a particular expression of Newton's first law. Is it possible to understand how an individual learns to apply this law to an actual situation involving the motion of bodies?

6. Insight is often used as a prototype for the solution of a mathematical puzzle. How does a learner acquire knowledge of the structure of mathematics?

All these human activities are learned. To suppose that there is one set of conditions that govern their occurrence is to ignore the facts of common observation. A serious attempt to describe learning must take all these varieties into account. Naturally, it must make differentiations among

them, and classifications of them, if these are possible. But
to begin with the premise that "all learning is the same"
would be quite unjustifiable.

The Conditions of Learning

The occurrence of learning is inferred from a difference
in a human being's performance as exhibited before and
after being placed in a "learning situation." One may, for
example, think of designing some conditions of learning
to teach a child how to form the plurals of nouns. The child
could then be placed in the learning situation, and following
this, his performance in making plural nouns could be observed. But it would be embarrassing to discover that his
performance in making plurals was no better than that of
a child of equivalent age and ability who had *not* been placed
in the same learning situation. The presence of the performance does not make it possible to conclude that learning
has occurred. It is necessary to show that there has been
a *change in performance*. The incapability for exhibiting
the performance *before* learning must be taken into account
as well as the capability that exists after learning.

It is in fact the existence of prior capabilities that is
slighted or even ignored by most of the traditional learning
prototypes. And it is these prior capabilities that are of crucial importance in drawing distinctions among the varieties
of conditions needed for learning, as will be seen in later
chapters. The child who is learning to tie his shoelaces does
not begin this learning "from scratch"; he already knows
how to hold the laces, how to loop one over the other, how
to tighten a loop, and so on. The child who learns to call
the mailman "Mr. Wells" also does not begin without some
prior capabilities: he already knows how to imitate the
words "mister" and "Wells," among other things. The theme
is the same with more complex learning. The student who
learns to multiply natural numbers has already acquired
many capabilities, including adding and counting and recognizing numerals and drawing them with a pencil. The

student who is learning how to write clear descriptive paragraphs already knows how to write sentences and to choose words.

The initial capabilities of the learner play an important part in determining the conditions required for subsequent learning. If one has determined that a child does not have the capability of saying the words "mister" and "Wells," obviously the conditions of learning represented by a parent saying, "That's Mr. Wells" will not succeed in teaching the child the mailman's name. One must, instead, begin this learning with quite a different set of conditions. For an individual who has one kind of prior capability, the printed sentence, "When glucose sugar ferments, alcohol is formed, and carbon dioxide is given off" may serve to bring about in that individual the learning of a principle, at least as readily as the child learns to name the mailman. But for another individual without the prerequisite capabilities such a printed statement is likely to accomplish nothing at all.

The set of initial capabilities possessed by the learner may be spoken of as conditions *internal* to the learner. But there is also a second category of learning conditions that are *external* to the learner, and that are independent in their action. Let us suppose an individual possesses all the prerequisite capabilities needed for learning the English equivalents of ten foreign words. Another individual possesses all the prior capabilities for learning how to multiply two negative numbers. Ignoring the differences in content, there is no particular reason to suppose that the external conditions needed for learning in one case are the same as the external conditions needed for learning in the other. In the first case, common observation would lead us to expect that the pairs of words would need to be repeated a number of times in order for learning to occur. But in the second case it is not at all apparent that similar amounts of repetition would work very well. The differences between these two sets of external conditions, among others, will be discussed more completely in the chapters to follow. At this point, the important thing to note is that the conditions are not the same.

Two different kinds of capabilities are being learned. They require not only different prior capabilities, but also different external conditions for learning.

The point of view to be expanded on in this book will probably be apparent from previous paragraphs. In brief, it is this: there are as many varieties of learning as there are distinguishable conditions for learning. These varieties may be differentiated by means of descriptions of the factors that comprise the learning conditions in each case. In searching for and identifying these, one must look, first, at the capabilities internal to the learner, and second, at the stimulus situation outside the learner. Each type of learning starts from a different "point" of internal capability, and is likely also to demand a different external situation in order to take place effectively. The useful prototypes of learning are those delineated by these descriptions of learning conditions.

EDUCATIONAL IMPLICATIONS

The identification of varieties of learning in terms of the conditions that produce them obviously has some definite implications for education and educational practices. Some of these may be immediately evident to the reader as he becomes acquainted with the conditions of learning for each variety. Others, however, need to be separately specified and more extensively discussed, since they are so fundamentally related to educational procedure.

It will be apparent from the discussion of educational problems in later chapters that the fewest possible assumptions are made about the mechanics (or "logistics") of education. None of these logistic elements is assumed as a "given." Quite to the contrary, the point of view is presented that these features of the educational process should be determined by the requirements of getting students to learn efficiently. In discussing implications, therefore, it is not assumed that a school building is necessarily needed, nor a set of books, nor desks, nor chalkboards, nor even a teacher. Insofar as these components of the educational system are shown to be necessary because of the requirements of learning, well and good. The only thing that must be assumed is the existence of a student who is capable of learning. This is the starting point.

Limitations of Learning Implications

The reader needs to be made aware, also, that there are some problems of great importance to education which *cannot* be solved by applying a knowledge of the principles of learning as they are here described. For example, there are many aspects of the personal interaction between a teacher and his students that do not pertain, in a strict sense, to the acquisition of skills and knowledges that typically form the content of a curriculum. These varieties of interaction include those of motivating, persuading, and the establishment of attitudes and values. The development of such human dispositions as these is of tremendous importance to education as a system of modern society. In the most comprehensive sense of the word "learning," motivations and attitudes must surely be considered to be learned. But the present treatment does not attempt to deal with such learnings, except in a tangential sense. Its scope is restricted to what may be termed the intellectual, or subject matter content that leads to improvement in human performances having ultimate usefulness in the pursuit of the individual's vocation or profession.

Another kind of limitation needs to be mentioned. Regardless of how much may be known about how to *begin* the process of establishing competence through learning, it is clear that no one knows very much at present about how to *continue* the process to its highest levels. It does not seem possible at present to specify all the conditions necessary to attain the highest and most complex varieties of human performance such as those displayed in invention or esthetic creativity. How does one produce an Albert Einstein or a Leonardo da Vinci? Certainly there are distinct limits to currently available knowledge bearing on such questions. The most that can be said here is that the production of genius is not based on "tricks," but on the learning of a great variety of specific capabilities.

To understand how learning operates in everyday situations of the school is a most valuable kind of understanding. But it does not unlock all the mysteries of education. What it can do is to illuminate some of the activities of the curriculum planner, the course designer, and the instructor. Specifically, an understanding of the conditions of learning is of value in the kinds of activities mentioned in the following paragraphs, which are to be discussed more extensively in the later chapters of this book.

Planning for Learning

One important implication of the identification of learning conditions is that these conditions must be carefully planned *before* the learning situation itself is entered into by the student. In particular, there needs to be planning in terms of the student's capabilities both before and after any learning enterprise. From where does the student begin; and where is he going? What are the specific prerequisites for learning, and what will he be able to learn next? The needed specificity of such planning is suggested by the following: what is meant by "prerequisite" is not that fourth-grade social studies must precede fifth-grade social studies. Rather, the meaning is that learning to pronounce foreign words must precede learning to use them in sentences; or that learning to count numerically must precede learning to add numbers.

The planning that precedes effective design for learning is a matter of specifying with some care what may be called the *learning structure* of any subject to be acquired. In order to determine what comes before what, the subject must be analyzed in terms of the types of learning involved in it. The acquisition of knowledge is a process in which every new capability builds on a foundation established by previously learned capabilities. The convenient escape mechanism that the student is not "mature" enough to learn any particular content needs to be studiously avoided, since it is valid for only the very earliest years of life. A student is ready to learn something new when he has mastered the prerequisites; that is, when he has acquired the necessary capabilities through preceding learning. Planning for learning is a matter of specifying and ordering the prerequisite capabilities within a topic to be learned, and later perhaps among the topics that make up a "subject."

Managing Learning

The learning conditions to be described also have implications for the management of learning. How can the student be motivated to begin and to continue learning? How should the direction of his interest and effort be guided? What can be done to assess the outcomes of learning? These are questions that pertain to the *management* of learning and the learning situation. They are questions which are general, in the sense that their answers are independent of both the content to be learned and the particular conditions of learning required for that content.

Clearly, these functions are among the most important that a teacher performs. A student cannot ordinarily do these things by himself (although, to be sure, he tends to improve constantly as he gains experience in taking over these functions). Getting the student interested in what he is doing, in the capabilities he is going to acquire, is a task that takes great skill and persuasiveness by a person, usually a teacher, who represents the adult world of experience and wisdom. Determining and advising on the branches of knowledge, the directions of further learning, the possibilities of additional topics and areas to be explored are important activities of learning management that again demand a great deal of knowledge and broad experience of the sort that may be possessed by a good teacher. Finally, the outcomes of learning, the achievements of the learner, need to be assessed by an agent "external" to the student, in order to ensure that they are objective and unbiased. Such assessment needs to be undertaken for the primary purpose of informing the student of what he has been able to achieve through learning, and is therefore likely to be intimately connected with his motivation.

The needs for these various functions of learning management are clearly implied for any system whose purpose it is to accomplish learning in an effective manner. They are required regardless of what particular conditions of learning may be appropriate at any given time. The proper exercise of these functions in an educational setting by a teacher requires that he understand the conditions of learning. Knowing these conditions makes it possible for the teacher to reach the proper decisions about what achievements the student is being motivated for, and to give suitable guidance concerning the possible directions of future learning that may be available to the student. In addition, the teacher must know the conditions of learning that have entered into any new attainment of the student in order to assess such achievement realistically.

Instructing

The function of *instructing* derives in a specific sense from a description of the required conditions of learning. Instructing means arranging the conditions of learning that are external to the learner. These conditions need to be constructed in a stage-by-stage fashion, taking due account at each stage of the just previously acquired capabilities of the learner, the requirements for retention of these capabilities, and the specific stimulus situation needed for the next stage of learning. As a consequence, instruction is seen to be a very intricate and demanding activity.

Sometimes instruction is predesigned, as in the case of a well-constructed textbook or workbook, or, more typically, in the programmed instruction of teaching machines. Sometimes it is extemporaneously designed by a teacher. In any case, instruction very often involves communicating verbally with the student for the purposes of informing him of what he is going to achieve, reminding him of what he already knows, directing his attention and actions, and guiding his thinking along certain lines. All these events are instituted for the purpose of establishing the proper external conditions for learning. Assuming that the necessary internal capabilities have been previously learned, a suitable arrangement of instructional events will bring about efficient learning.

Instructing is an activity that is at the heart of the educational process. It is extremely difficult to do well with a group of students. It is easier to accomplish under the rare conditions in which a single teacher communicates with a single student. Alternatively, it can be largely if not wholly predesigned and used in programs of self-instruction. There is reason to suppose that an instructional mode which requires self-instruction may be very efficient, when properly designed, and may also help to establish valuable habits of independent study on the part of the student. Obviously, the mature student (for example, the university graduate student) is a person who has developed his own very efficient habits of self-instruction.

One aspect of instructing, however, deserves special mention because it takes a special form. This pertains to the function of *knowledge generalization* (or *knowledge transfer*), which is to be contrasted to the initial learning of knowledge. Knowledge transfer is frequently emphasized as a purpose of education. It is said that education should be concerned not simply with the acquisition of knowledge, but more importantly with the use and generalization of knowledge in novel situations. First of all, it is evident that knowledge transfer cannot occur if the knowledge itself has not been initially mastered. But beyond this, there is an important question of what conditions of instruction are required to encourage generalization of knowledge. For a number of reasons, the instructional mode of organized *group discussion* is one that appears to be well designed to accomplish this function. When properly led, such discussion not only stimulates the production of new extensions of knowledge by students but also provides a convenient means of critical evaluation and discrimination of these ideas.

Selecting Media for Instruction

Still another implication that derives from a specification of the conditions of learning concerns the choice of media for instruction. Media are here to be considered in a broad and inclusive sense, including such traditional instructional media as *oral* and *printed verbal communication,* and such relative newcomers as *motion pictures* and *television receivers.*

The required conditions for learning can be put into effect in different ways and to differing degrees by each medium. Some media are much more broadly adaptable for instructional purposes than are others. For example, the concrete objects that may be needed to convey the distinctions among a solid, a liquid, and a gas can obviously not be successfully supplanted by a mere verbal description in print. Conversely, though, examples of a solid, a liquid, and a gas, or even pictures of them, have extremely limited functions in instruction when compared with verbal communication. By themselves, the objects or pictures cannot instruct in the varieties of solids, liquids, and gases, nor in the principles that relate them to each other. There are, then, some positive characteristics and some limitations of each instructional medium that become evident when they are examined in the light of their learning functions.

As has often been said, instructional media constitute the valuable "resources for learning" that an educational system has to draw on. When these resources are put to use, they are usually placed in some particular arrangement called a *mode of instruction.* Some of these, like the lecture, are very widely and frequently used, but others, like the tutoring session, are employed rather infrequently (at least in this country). The various modes of instruction are employed for the purpose of getting the greatest instructional usefulness from media and combinations of media. Thus the choice of modes is also a matter of aiming for optimal functioning in generating the proper conditions for learning. As will be seen in later chapters, these conditions provide the immediate instructional purposes on the basis of which correct decisions can be made about media and modes of instruction.

GENERAL REFERENCES

Learning and Learning Theories

Deese, J., and Hulse, S. H. *The psychology of learning,* 3d ed. New York: McGraw-Hill, 1958.

Hilgard, E. R., and Bower, G. V. *Theories of learning,* 3d ed. New York: Appleton-Century-Crofts, 1966.

Hill, W. F. *Learning: A survey of psychological interpretations.* San Francisco: Chandler, 1963.

Kimble, G. A. *Foundations of conditioning and learning.* New York: Appleton-Century-Crofts, 1967.

Melton, A. W. (ed.). *Categories of human learning.* New York: Academic Press, 1964.

Travers, R. M. W. *Essentials of learning,* 2d ed. New York: Macmillan, 1967.

Points of View about Learning

Hull, C. L. *Principles of behavior.* New York: Appleton-Century-Crofts, 1943.

Keller, F. A., and Schoenfeld, W. N. *Principles of psychology.* New York: Appleton-Century-Crofts, 1950.

McGeoch, J. A., and Irion, A. L. *The psychology of human learning.* New York: McKay, 1952.

Pavlov, I. P. *Conditioned reflexes.* (Transl. by G. V. Anrep.) London: Oxford University Press, 1927. (Also available in paperback; New York: Dover.)

Skinner, B. F. *The behavior of organisms; an experimental analysis.* New York: Appleton-Century-Crofts, 1938.

Thorndike, E. L. *Animal intelligence.* New York: Macmillan, 1911.

Thorndike, E. L. *Human learning.* New York: Appleton-Century-
    Crofts, 1931.
Tolman, E. C. *Purposive behavior in animals and men.* New
    York: Appleton-Century-Crofts, 1932.
Wertheimer, M. *Productive thinking.* New York: Harper & Row,
    1945.

2 | Varieties of Learning

This chapter contains brief descriptions of the varieties of learning that are distinguishable from each other in terms of the conditions required to bring them about. There are some old friends here, in new dress, who will be recognized from the previous chapter. There are also some new characters, who should be quite familiar from common experience, but whose names no one, perhaps, has been very confident about.

In discussing the various kinds of learning, it is necessary to refer to the components of the situation that are used to establish its presence, and occasionally also to employ simple diagrams to represent these components. These are a stimulus situation, represented by S, a set of responses, R, and the inferred connection between them, often shown by a set of connecting lines. These are simply convenient descriptive terms, and should not be considered to imply any of the varieties of "S-R theory," or other inferences concerning the mechanisms of behavior. The present consideration of the conditions of learning makes no attempt to evaluate the usefulness of these theories; it does not attempt to deal with them in any systematic fashion.

An observer of learning must deal with an input, an output, and a functioning entity in between. The input is a *stimulus situation* (*S*), which includes the varieties of changes in physical energy that reach the learner through his senses. Sometimes these stimuli are described in a shorthand way, for convenience, as when one describes a stimulus situation as "a projected slide image of the letter E," rather than specifying the brightness, size, and shape of this stimulus in physical terms. The stimulus situation is in general (except for the special instance of stimulation from the muscle sense) *outside the learner* and can be identified and described in the terms of physical science.

The output, *R*, is also in a real sense outside the learner. It is a response or a set of responses that produces an identifiable product. The *R* that is the focus of interest here is not muscular movements, although it is well known that these are necessary for it. The output may be something like a "wave of the hand," but strictly speaking, it is not the muscular movements that underlie this event. Rather, it is the external, observable effect of these movements. The learner may produce a spoken output, which may leave no permanent record unless the observer of learning has used a recording machine; speaking the words is what is meant by *R*. Alternatively, the learner may write some words, and thus incidentally produce a permanent record. But the *R* is "writing words," as this may be seen by an observer. However, the record of these words may frequently be employed in judging the adequacy of this output.

The nature of the connection between an *S* and an *R* cannot be directly observed. Studies of nervous system functioning may some day provide a much greater understanding of these mechanisms than is now available. But in the meantime, it is desirable and necessary to make some immediate inferences (see Northrop, 1947) about the kind of transformation that must occur. To speculate about *how* such mechanisms work would be to construct a theory, as Pavlov, Hull, and other investigators have done, and which is not intended here. But simply to describe what the requirements must be in order for an observed transformation between S and R to occur is not constructing a theory, in the strict sense of the word. It may, however, be thought of as a description of what theories of learning have to explain, now or in the future. The kind of immediate inference that is based on observations of learning consists, then, of a statement (or diagram) indicating *what capability of the learner exists following the events of learning that was not there before.*

A simple example may be useful. A *reflex* is the inferred capability one is accustomed to make in describing the transformation between an S of a light shining on the retina and an R of pupil contraction. In a diagram, such a simple transformation may be represented as a line:

$$S \underline{\qquad} R$$
light   pupil contraction

Obviously, the reflex is neither the S of the light nor the R of the contracting pupil; instead, it is the immediate inference we make about the nature of the transformation that occurs, the capability for which resides within the individual. This particular capability is of the sort that some authors have described as a one-to-one correlation; that is, whenever light (of specified brightness) shines on the retina, pupil contraction occurs. Of course, the reflex capability used here as an example is an unlearned one. But there are transformations of similar simplicity that are learned, and can therefore be represented in the same way. Also, as will be seen, there are more complex transformations that occur as a result of learning.

EIGHT TYPES OF LEARNING

Subsequent chapters are devoted to descriptions of eight sets of conditions that distinguish eight types of learning, called *signal learning, stimulus-response learning, chaining, verbal association, discrimination learning, concept learning, rule learning,* and *problem solving.* A preview of these varieties is given here in order to set the stage for later discussion.

Learning Type 1: Signal Learning

Learning to respond to a signal is a kind of learning quite familar to everyone. Guthrie (1935, p. 48) gives this example of it:

> Two small country boys who lived before the day of the rural use of motor cars had their Friday afternoons made dreary by the regular visit of their pastor, whose horse they were supposed to unharness, groom, feed and water and then harness again on the departure. Their gloom was lightened finally by a course of action which one of them conceived. They took to spending the afternoon of the visit re-training the horse. One of them stood behind the horse with a hay-fork and periodically shouted "Whoa" and followed this with a sharp jab with the fork. Unfortunately no exact records of this experiment were preserved save that the boys were quite satisfied with the results.

This is, of course, a description of a set of conditions appropriate for the establishment of a *conditioned response*. It is customary to represent what has been learned here in the following way:

$$S \frac{}{\text{``Whoa!''}} R_{\text{pain response}}$$

In other words, a capability has been acquired by the horse that was not previously present: making a response typical of that to pain (including struggling, shying, running) to the sound of "Whoa!" It is as if the horse had learned to anticipate the painful stimulus; the verbal command has become a *signal* for pain. Some authors, notably Mowrer (1960a), propose that the response signaled in such situations as this is one of fear.

The conditions for establishment of this form of signal learning seem fairly clear. There must be nearly simultaneous presentation of two forms of stimulation: (1) the stimulus producing a generalized reaction of the sort one is interested in establishing, and (2) the stimulus providing the signal. If the "Whoa" comes after the painful stimulus by a fraction of a second, it cannot become a signal; if it comes too many seconds before the painful stimulus, it also fails to produce the desired learning. The number of times this pairing of stimuli must occur is a question that has no single answer. There are many instances of signal learning of this type that have occurred in one trial, and there are many others that seem to require several pairings of the proper stimuli.

Obviously, such learning represents a somewhat specialized type, although it is not exactly rare in the occurrences of everyday existence. People who have peeled onions may feel tears at the sight of one. The young child may learn that a shout by one of his parents signals pain to come. The military command "Attention!" is designed to signal a condition of alertness. Involuntary fears of many sorts, such as fear of the water and fear of heights, may be engendered in individuals as children when these signals have been accompanied by painful or frightening stimulation. Presumably, pleasant emotions may also be involved in signal learning. The sight of the mother's face may become a learned signal to the infant for various pleasurable events associated with the presence of his mother. The sight of one's old high school after many years of absence may evoke pleasant feelings of nostalgia that are quite independent of the recall of any specific events.

All these examples, however, merely serve to emphasize one important characteristic of this type of signal learning (that is, the Pavlovian conditioned response): *the responses are general, diffuse, emotional ones.* This is learning that has a truly "involuntary" character, and applies to responses that are not typically under voluntary control (see Kimble, 1961, pp. 44–108). A fear response, involving general, diffuse activity, including speeded heartbeat, constriction of blood vessels, and other internal involuntary behavior, may readily acquire a connection with a signal under the conditions we have described. But precise voluntary responses, such as kicking a football or writing one's name, cannot be acquired in this way.

Learning Type 2: Stimulus-Response Learning

Another type of learning to respond to a signal is probably much more important than the classical type we have just described. This is a kind of learning that involves making very precise movements of the skeletal muscles in response to very specific stimuli or combinations of stimuli. In the human being, we often speak of "voluntary responses" as constituting the observed output. In other words, this kind of learning makes it possible for an individual to perform an action when he wants to; so far as we know, the same is probably true of animals also.

A simple and well-known example of such learning occurs when a dog learns to "shake hands" in response to a vocal stimulus supplied by his master, or by another friendly person. The events that take place in such learning, as Mowrer (1960a, p. 215) describes them, are somewhat as follows: While playing with the puppy, the master says, "Shake hands!" At the same time, he gently raises the dog's paw and shakes it, then pats the dog's head, or gives him a piece of dog biscuit. He then repeats this entire procedure on several subsequent occasions, perhaps using progressively lighter force to raise the paw. After several occasions of this sort, the dog raises his own paw when his master says, "Shake hands," and is patted or fed as usual. Eventually, the dog comes to perform this act promptly and more or less precisely whenever the proper signal is given. It can then be said that the dog has learned what may be called a *stimulus-response* capability.

Obviously, this kind of learning is distinguishable from *signal learning* in terms of its outcome. The response acquired by this means is a fairly precise, circumscribed, skeletal muscular act, far different from the generalized emotional responding that characterizes the Pavlovian kind of signal-responding.

Returning to stimulus-response learning itself, it is important to take note of certain other conditions that attend the acquisition of this kind of capability. First, there appears to be a typical gradualness to the learning of this act. The dog does not suddenly shake hands, all at once; at least a few occasions of repetition appear to be necessary. Second, the response that the dog makes becomes more and more sure and precise throughout these several occasions. (The response is said by Ferster and Skinner (1957) to undergo "shaping.") Third, the controlling stimulus also becomes more and more precise—whereas initially the dog may respond to other commands than "Shake hands!" these other vocalizations eventually lose their control over the outcome. And finally, a point that many learning theorists would consider of utmost importance, there is *reward* or *reinforcement*. The dog is rewarded for responses that are "correct" or that approach being so in his master's view, and he is not rewarded for those that are incorrect.

The capability that has been acquired in this kind of situation ought to suggest this *differential* characteristic of the learning, by implying that a particular S-R is established, and at the same time other S-R's, equally probable at the beginning of learning, are disestablished. We can show this by using an arrow rather than the line between the S and the R, as S → R, to emphasize that a *process of discrimination* is an integral part of this kind of learning. A degree of precision has been established in the response, which can easily be distinguished from similar although "wrong" responses. In like manner, there is precision in the stimulus, which is a particular complex of stimulation differing from other stimuli that may be present at the time the response is made.

Still another characteristic of stimulus-response learning must be noted before the description is complete. Every uncomplicated example of $S \rightarrow R$ learning indicates that it is *motor learning*. The implication of this statement is not simply to the effect that muscular movements are involved in the outcome, because this may be true of other varieties, including signal learning (as when an animal learns to struggle or run at a signal originally paired with shock). In $S \rightarrow R$ learning, though, an important component of the *stimulus itself* is generated by muscular movements. While the act is being established, the external stimulus "Shake hands!" is accompanied by proprioceptive stimulation from the muscles that raise the dog's paw. Even when the act is fully learned, some parts of this stimulation are still present. For example, the dog often raises his paw "as if voluntarily," even when no one has said "Shake hands." He may now "invite" his master to shake hands! Presumably, this portion of the total stimulation plays an important role in the learning process, as Mowrer (1960a) has emphasized. As will be seen, it is a very essential part of the capability that is learned.

This kind of learning can accordingly be represented in complete fashion as follows:

$$Ss \longrightarrow R$$

where the S refers to an external signal, s the accompanying internal proprioceptive stimulation, and R the response. The arrow, rather than a line, is used to indicate the precise, discriminated nature of the capability; other potential $Ss \rightarrow R$'s are disestablished (or *extinguished*) by the events of learning.

In the descriptive language used by Skinner (1938), this capability is called a *discriminated operant*. A common example from the animal-learning laboratory is the rat learning to press a lever in the presence of a light (the external S), and at the same time extinguishing this response when the external S is darkness. The conditions for establishment are essentially the same as those we have described: (1) the lever is initially baited with food so that the rat will press it, and thus the presence of a proprioceptive s is ensured; (2) correct lever-pressing responses are reinforced by delivery of bits of food, while incorrect responses including those made in the absence of the light go unreinforced; (3) several repetitions are required to establish the capability.

This form of learning appears to govern the acquisition of a new vocalization habit by a young child and *can* be employed to teach an adult the pronunciation of an unfamiliar foreign word. The young child, being petted by the admiring parent, receives reinforcement for many of the responses he makes, including such things as smiling, gurgling, cooing, and vocalizing. The process of discrimination has already begun because some kinds of responses (such as crossing his eyes) are not likely to be rewarded. The parent may frequently introduce the desired signal, such as, "Say mama," and eventually the child does say, "Mama," more or less by chance, immediately following this signal. Suitable reinforcement follows, and the learning of this new capability is then well launched. It is noteworthy that nothing exactly comparable to lifting the dog's paw for him occurs here; the parent cannot directly manipulate the child's vocal cords. But the parent comes as close to this as he can by cleverly choosing the occasions for the stimulus "Say mama" to correspond with those times when the child is making (or about to make) movements of opening and shutting his mouth while breathing out and vocalizing. The learning conditions for this particular example are therefore somewhat inefficiently arranged, and the parent must make up for this by his astuteness in *selecting* the occasions when an appropriate internal s will occur.

Of course, teaching an adult to pronounce a new foreign word is a somewhat easier process, although much the same set of events is involved. The adult, though, begins with an *approximate* capability already established. When the signal is given, "Say *femme*," he can immediately say something that is almost correct. Subsequent trials in his case, therefore, are largely a matter of bringing about discrimination. He must receive reinforcement for responding to a narrow range of correct external sounds of *femme*, and also for a narrow range of internal stimuli from his muscles in pronouncing the word. The adult learner also reinforces himself, by recognizing a match between his vocalization of *femme* and that of his French teacher. If he is going to do this effectively, he must, of course, have previously adopted a suitably precise set of matching criteria.

Learning Type 3: Chaining

Another extremely simple and widely occurring learning situation is called *chaining*. In brief terms, it is a matter of connecting together in a sequence two (or more) previously learned $Ss \rightarrow R$'s. Our language is filled with such chains of verbal sequences, as is well known to students of linguistics, and is also revealed by studies of word association. "Horse and buggy," "boy meets girl," "never again" are three of the hundreds of examples that could be given in which the first member of the sequence seems firmly tied to the second.

It is relatively easy to arrange a set of conditions in which a dog who has learned to shake hands offers his paw after he barks, or, alternatively, offers his paw and then barks. But perhaps one of the simplest human examples is that of a child learning to ask for a specific object by name.

Many a fond parent has attempted to teach his infant to call for an object, say a doll, by its name. After a number of parental tries at presenting the doll and saying "doll," distributed perhaps over several months, the child eventually achieves success. In fact, he appears to acquire such a capability "suddenly," and without there being an entirely clear relationship between his calling for a doll and the events that have gone before. Of course, growth factors are at work during this period: one cannot expect the nervous system of a newborn child to be ready to learn such a chain. But there are other aspects of readiness that are even more relevant to our present discussion, and probably also more important for an understanding of this kind of learned behavior.

Obviously, if the child is going to learn to ask for a doll, he must first know how to make this verbal response. This is a matter of stimulus-response learning (type 2), as we have seen. The sight and feel of the doll accompanied by the spoken word "doll" becomes the stimulus situation that is connected by learning with the child's saying "doll." Thus there is established the stimulus-response sequence:

$$Ss \xrightarrow[\text{doll}]{} R \text{ "doll"}$$

Another $Ss \to R$ connection has also been learned, perhaps even earlier. The child has picked up the doll, handled it, hugged it, shaken it, and so on. Thus in a fundamental (and nonverbal) sense he "knows what a doll is." A doll is the particular set of stimuli connected with hugging, and is thus distinguished from other stimuli, like a ball or a wagon, that cannot be hugged. Perhaps the hugging of the doll has been associated particularly with lying in his bed, preparatory to going to sleep. There is, then, some such connection as the following:

$$Ss \xrightarrow[\text{lying down}]{} R \text{ hugging doll}$$

If both $Ss \to R$ connections are present, the chain of asking for the doll is a relatively simple matter to establish. First, the child is placed in his crib. Perhaps he makes the movements of hugging the doll that is not there. But now his mother shows him the doll; perhaps she also says, "Do you want your doll?" These events establish a sequence that sets the occasion for learning that may be depicted as follows:

$$Ss \xrightarrow[\text{lying down}]{} R \underset{\text{hugging doll}}{\sim} \underset{\text{doll}}{Ss} \xrightarrow{} R \text{ "doll"}$$

The capability that has been learned is simply this: The child, on lying in his crib and seeing the doll outside the crib, "asks for" it by saying "Doll." He may even come to do so without actually seeing the doll, since the hugging responses he makes may generate internal stimuli (small *s*'s that are a part of the stimulus situation of feeling the doll) that have themselves been previously connected with the vocalization "doll."

In a similar manner, the chain can be extended. Perhaps the child is initially placed in his crib in an upright position. His mother now says, "Lie down," and he has previously learned to respond to this stimulus in an S-R manner. Having lain down, the next connection in the sequence comes into play: he makes the incipient hugging movements toward his absent doll, and this in turn sets off the next link in the chain—he asks for his doll.

Now all these events are likely to occur in a very natural manner in the natural world. They occur so naturally, in fact, that it may not be apparent that any learning has occurred at all. Yet, at one period in time these chains are not there, and in a subsequent period, as if by magic, they *are* there! The magic, though, may be made to happen deliberately if we want it to, as may be true in teaching a child a chain like tying a knot or printing a letter. These are the conditions that appear to be necessary:

1. The individual links in the chain must have been previously established. The child must already have learned to say "doll," to hug the doll, to lie down when his mother tells him to. (Of course, one *can* attempt to establish all these links at a single time, but that is not an efficient procedure.)

2. There must be *contiguity* of each link with the next following one. The hugging responses must be followed in a brief period by the stimulus leading to the child's vocalization "Doll," or the chain will not be established. Often such contiguity is "built into" the chain of events, as is the case, for example, when the response of lying down (link 1) is immediately followed by the stimulus situation for link 2, which is the "lying down" situation.

3. When the two previous conditions are fully met, it appears that the acquisition of a chain is not a gradual process, but one which occurs on a single occasion. (Of course, if

these prior conditions are *not* met, the occasion may have to be repeated for the purpose of establishing the links themselves. This would be the case, for example, if the child had not fully yearned the $Ss \rightarrow R$ connection of saying "doll.")

Learning Type 4: Verbal Association

In view of the amount of attention devoted to the learning of verbal associates and nonsense lists since the time of Ebbinghaus, it would be unusual if we did not find a place for this type in a list of learning varieties. However, verbal association might well be classified as only a subvariety of chaining. There are short chains, such as that of a single pair of associates, like GUK-RIV, and long ones like ten- or twelve-syllable lists that have been so extensively studied. But because these chains are verbal, and therefore exploit the remarkable versatility of human processes, verbal association has some unique characteristics. For this reason, it is described here as a fourth form of learning, to be established by a distinguishable set of learning conditions. It should be possible to discern what kind of chaining is involved, and what the links are.

One learns to translate an English word into a foreign one by acquiring a chain. For example, the French word for "match" is *alumette*. In order to learn this equivalent most expeditiously, something like the following set of events occurs. One examines the combination "match-*alumette*" and notices that something already known connects the two: the syllable "lum," which occurs in the word "illuminate." One then runs through the sequence, not necessarily out loud, "a match illuminates; lum: *alumette*." For many people, the chain is most readily established by means of an image of a match bursting into flame, so that the entire chain would be something like this:

The internal parts of this chain, denoted by s's and r's, are likely to be highly individualistic, since they depend on the previous learning history of the individual. Thus, if a person does not know the word "illuminate," it is obvious that the chain he acquires must be an entirely different one. It may be a longer one or a shorter one; and it may involve a visual image or some other kind of internal representation.

The conditions for the learning of verbal chains of this sort would appear to be as follows:

1. An $Ss \rightarrow R$ connection must have been previously learned that associates the word "match" with the image of a burning match (or with whatever other internal response may be employed). In simple terms, the individual must "know what a match is."

2. Another $Ss \rightarrow R$ connection must have been learned that enables the individual to associate the key syllable "lum" with the response *alumette*. In other words, response differentiation must have previously taken place. The individual must know how to say the word *alumette* with sufficient accuracy to be considered correct (whether or not he sounds like a native Frenchman).

3. A "coding connection" must also be available, that is, must previously have been learned, if the chain is to be established with ease. In this case, the code is represented by the association of the image of the flaming match and the word "illumination." As we have said, the selection of this code by the individual depends on his own previous history. A highly verbal person may have many codes available, whereas an individual who ranks low in such ability may have very few. Probably, the code we have depicted here would serve adequately for a large portion of the adult population.

4. The chain must be "reeled off" in a sequence, so that each $Ss \rightarrow R$ is contiguous in time with the next; in other words, contiguity is necessary for learning. Under these circumstances, the chain, like other learned behavior chains, is probably acquired on a single occasion.

It is noteworthy that a young child may have few "codes" available to him. Thus he may have considerably greater difficulty in acquiring a verbal chain of this sort. If the words "match" and *alumette* are repeated together frequently enough, the child eventually will find a code that will enable him to learn the chain. If one wants him to learn it rapidly, however, presenting a distinctive code (perhaps in a picture) would seem to be an important aspect of the process. The efficacy of using pictures in the learning of foreign word meanings is well known.

What about the nonsense chains that connect the stimulus GUK with the response "riv"? There is no particular reason to believe that these require any different conditions for learning. The optimal conditions may, however, be more difficult to achieve. For example, $Ss \rightarrow R$ learning must be established, both for the stimulus member GUK and for the response member RIV. Then a coding connection must be selected, and there may be only a few available to the individual, depending on the "meaningfulness" (to him) of these syllables. He may have to resort to a somewhat lengthy chain, as would be the case if he said to himself "GUK suggests gook (engine sludge), which may affect the engine when you 'rev' it, or RIV."

Learning Type 5: Discrimination Learning

Considered as isolated acts, the learning of single $Ss \rightarrow R$'s and the learning of chains of $Ss \rightarrow R$'s represent fairly simple events. Each seems easy, and in fact *is* easy, just so long as each instance of learning is carefully distinguished and insulated from other instances that may tend to occur at the same time, or from other instances of a similar sort occurring at different times in the same individual. But we also know that, practically speaking, making a permanent change in behavior by means of learning is not always so easy. The reason at once comes to mind: people readily *forget* what they have learned. The marvelous plasticity that characterizes the nervous system and makes possible these fundamental varieties of modification is counterbalanced by another characteristic: what has been learned and stored is readily weakened or obliterated by other activities.

When an individual acquires a chain that makes it possible for him to say *alumette* to "match," and then goes on to learn to say *fromage* for "cheese," he may by so doing weaken the first chain; he may forget the French word for "match." By experiment, it may also be shown that it is harder for him to remember *fromage* (for "cheese") than it would have been had he not first learned *alumette* for "match." If he tries to learn four French words at once, rather than two, the process will be more than twice as difficult; six at once will be more than three times as difficult; and so on. Obviously, some new kind of process has entered the picture. Short chains are easy to learn but hard to retain. Increasing the number to be learned does not change the basic nature of the learning process, but it highlights the effects of another process—*forgetting.*

Many an American boy undertakes to learn to identify all the new models of automobiles produced in this country in any given year. He does not learn this in school, but it is surely as marvelous an accomplishment as many that do take place there. Each year there are changes in appearance of body, fenders, grill, lights, and insignia, some of them large and others quite small. Within a few weeks after all the new cars appear, a boy may be able to distinguish correctly the scores of new models that are adding to road congestion, as well as the ones he learned last year or the year before. His father, in contrast, may never get them straightened out—he has given this up long ago.

What the boy has acquired is a set of *discriminations*, obviously a multiple set of them. Each single identifying connection he learns is, in this case, a chain. As a stimulus, each automobile must be discriminated from other stimuli, like trucks and buses, as the intial $Ss \rightarrow R$ connection in the chain that has as its terminal response the model name.

But then something else is added to the situation. Each individual model, with its distinctive appearance, must be connected with its own model name and *with no other*. How is this ever possible, thinks the adult, when they all look so much alike? It is possible because the models are in fact physically different, and they can be identified when one learns to make different responses to these physical differences. Twin headlights and a vertical grill, with chrome trim around the windshield, may constitute a stimulus combination that can invariably be connected with a single model name; a distinctive body shape may serve to identify another; and so on. In order to acquire multiple discriminations that identify all of them, the individual must first acquire a distinctive set of $Ss \rightarrow R$'s that differentiate the stimuli and set off the chains leading to the responses that are the model names.

If one starts out to acquire these multiple identifications, however, the process takes longer than one would expect from a simple summing of the occasions for the chaining of each identification. As we have said, the reason is that some get forgotten and have to be re-established. The new chains *interfere* with the retention of those previously learned, and vice versa. The phenomenon of *interference*, which presumably is the basic mechanism for forgetting, is therefore a prominent characteristic of the learning of multiple discriminations. In fact, it may be said that the question of how to arrange the conditions for the learning of discriminations becomes mainly a matter of reducing or preventing interference.

In brief, then, the conditions for learning discriminations are as follows:

1. Individual chains connecting each distinctive stimulus with each identifying response must be learned. This, of course, implies that the individual $Ss \rightarrow R$'s that differentiate the *stimuli* must have been previously learned, as well as the *response* names themselves. (For American cars, these

are usually chosen to be both highly familiar and distinctive.)

2. In order to ensure retention, measures must be taken to reduce interference. A number of methods, to be described in a later chapter, may be employed. Generally speaking, they have the purpose of making the stimuli as highly distinctive as possible. (A highly distinctive appearance of a car model virtually ensures that its name will be easily remembered.)

/Discrimination is the type of learning the teacher undertakes in order to be able to call each of her pupils by his correct name. It is the type that applies when a student learns to distinguish plants, animals, chemical elements, or rocks and to call them correctly by their individual names. In the young child, it is the kind of learning that happens in learning colors, shapes, common objects, letters and words, numerals and operation symbols. In the student of foreign languages, it occurs in the distinguishing of new words, as the sounds of *fin, femme,* and *faim,* as well as others that are less likely to be confused, that is, less subject to interference. It is, therefore, a kind of learning that is remarkably prevalent in all of formal education/

It may be noted that in its simplest form discrimination may involve differentiating stimulus-response connections. The child may learn a discrimination between the responses "puh" and "duh." Perhaps more frequently discrimination is between two or more chains, and the conditions that apply to such learning differ in essential respects. Is discrimination "rote learning"? Perhaps yes, perhaps no; it depends on what is meant. As we have pointed out, the prominent characteristic of discrimination is not the acquiring of new entities as such, since these are simply chains, each of which is readily acquired in isolation. Insofar as "rote" implies "committed to memory," the emphasis is surely correct: the important factor in multiple discrimination is the interference that must be overcome if retention is to be assured.

But if "rote" implies repeated practice as an optimal method of learning, then this is not necessarily the case. A later chapter will deal more extensively with this question.

Learning Type 6: Concept Learning

We turn now to a kind of learning that appears to be critically dependent on internal neural processes of *representation* for its very existence. In man, this function is served by language. Although it has been demonstrated that a number of animals possess the capacity to make internal representations of their environments, present evidence suggests that this capacity is extremely limited even in the higher apes. Human beings, in contrast, employ this capacity freely and prodigally; they are highly inclined to internalize their environment, to "manipulate" it symbolically, to think about it in endless ways.

Learning a concept means learning to classify stimulus situations in terms of abstracted properties like color, shape, position, number, and others. A child may learn to call a two-inch cube a block and also to apply this term to other objects that differ from it somewhat in size and shape. Later he learns to classify an object of a particular shape as a cube, and is able to identify a class of objects by this name that differ from each other physically in a great variety of ways. A cube may be represented concretely by objects made of wood, glass, wire, or almost any material; the object may be of any color or texture and of any size. Considering this great variety of physical stimulation that may correctly be identified as cubical, perhaps it is not surprising that it takes some very precise language on the part of geometers to define what is meant by cube. But, of course, a person does not have to understand such a definition in order to identify correctly a cube under most ordinary conditions of his existence. Except for some very special purposes of mathematical theory, an individual identifies a cube "intuitively," that is, on the basis of an internalized

representation that does not employ the words of the geom-
eter's definition. Whatever the process may be, there can
be little doubt that a concept like cube is learned, and that
its possession enables the individual to classify objects of
widely differing physical appearance. His behavior comes
to be controlled, not by particular stimuli that can be identified in specific physical terms, but by abstract properties
of such stimuli.

As an example, we may consider how a child learns the
concept *middle*. Initially, he may have been presented with
a set of blocks arranged like this: □   □   □ . If previous $Ss \rightarrow R$ learning has enabled him to receive reinforcement for a request such as "Give me a block," he can then
readily learn the simple chain of picking up the middle block
when his parent says, "Give me the *middle* one." Similar
chains can then be established with other objects, such as
balls arranged in the same configuration ○   ○   ○ , or
sticks | | | . One might want to make certain that the
chains were generalizable over a range of separations, like
| | | and | | | . In other words, the deliberate at-
tempt is made to establish a number of chains applicable to
a *variety* of specific physical configurations. Continuing this
effort, the spoken word "middle" might be applied to various
other arrangements of objects, including such situations as
these:

(1)   (2)   (3)   (4)   (5)
 □ | ○ | ○
 □ | □   △
 □ | ○   □
                       ○   □

By this means, the child comes to respond correctly to
"middle" as a concept meaning "an object between two
others." (Other meanings of "middle," such as the "center
of an area," are, of course, different, but may be similarly
learned.)

How does one know whether the child has in fact learned the concept *middle*? The crucial test is whether he will be able to respond correctly, not by chance, to some new configurations of objects he has not previously used in the course of learning. For example, these might be:

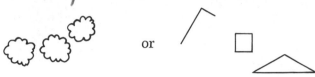

If the child can now respond properly when told "Give me the middle one," it may be concluded that he has learned a concept, and that his behavior is *not* controlled by specific stimuli.

Of course, it should be understood that a concept, once acquired, may also be associated by chaining with responses other than lifting. The response may be pointing, or pushing. No new events are involved in such instances; they are simply further examples of chain learning. It may also be noted that an essential part of the chain is the internal response "middle," which is the internal representation that permits discrimination of the correct final response from any incorrect response. This representational $s \rightarrow r$ may be spoken out loud as an overt verbal response "middle," or it may not be. In any case it functions as a word does. The individual must have a name for what he is about to select, even if the "name" is no more than an "ugh!" It is this name that selects and directs the final response, in the face of the varying stimulus situations encountered. A resemblance may also be noted between this naming response and the coding response that occurs in verbal association. Again, a similar function is being served.

The conditions for concept learning that are apparent in the preceding example are as follows:

1. The stimulus portion of the chain, by means of which a *middle block* is differentiated from the two others in the

set, must have been previously learned. Likewise, the internal coding portion of the chain must have been previously acquired, which enables the individual to verbalize the word "middle" (or some other word serving the same function). And the response portion must also be available (saying "middle," or pointing to it).

2. A *variety* of stimulus situations must be presented incorporating the conceptual property to be learned, in order that this property can become discriminated in its internally represented form.

3. Because of the necessity for this process of discrimination in a variety of different stimulus situations, the learning of a brand-new concept may in some circumstances be a *gradual* process.

One may expect that a child acquires many important concepts by means of this procedure. This is how he first learns what a circle is, or a square, or, for that matter, a cat (the class cat as opposed to a particular animal), or a tree. Presumably, he learns concepts like *up* and *down* this way; *near* and *far; right* and *left; larger* and *smaller; outside* and *inside;* and many others. Initially, the mistakes he makes, as in correctly identifying a saucer as circular, but not a dime, result from his having responded to an inadequate variety of stimulus situations. The concept may become more nearly adequate when he has a greater number of experiences in the course of everyday existence. Alternatively, it may become equally comprehensive as a result of a deliberate instructional process carried out over a much shorter period of time.

It is quite important to note, however, that adults do not always, or even frequently, learn new concepts in the manner previously described. Adults can take shortcuts because they have a greater fund of language. If an adult does not happen to know what *middle* means, he can learn it by acquiring a chain linking this word with another concept he already knows, such as *in between.* Suppose an adult were presented with the situation of three cubes in a row: □   □   □ . He is told, "Give me the middle one." Now suppose he responds incorrectly. Assume also that he possesses the concept *in between* from previous learning. In order to learn this new and strange concept *middle,* it is simply necessary for another person to say, "*Middle* means in between." As a result of this communication, the adult acquires a verbal chain (type 4 learning) that becomes a part of the longer chain leading to the correct response.

This example of adult concept acquisition is instructive for two reasons. First, it illustrates how *verbal instruction* can function to remove the necessity for the gradual process of experience with a variety of stimulus situations necessary for concept learning in the child. By means of verbal chaining, an adult can acquire a new concept (at least a fairly adequate one) in a single trial. Second, the example emphasizes the difference between the genuine learning of a truly novel concept, as in a child, and the verbal generalization of an already learned concept, as in an adult. In some experimental studies, the second type of event has been identified as concept learning, whereas it might better be called *concept generalizing* or *concept using,* and distinguished from the concept learning that may be observed most clearly in the child.

It is important to mention here, also, that whereas concepts of the *concrete* variety (such as the object properties used as examples) provide good prototype examples, another common kind of concept is *defined* and is often learned entirely by means of verbal cues rather than by reference to directly observable objects. The human being also learns to classify such entities as fathers, mothers, uncles, aunts, means of transportation, tools, obstacles, and many more that cannot be learned by exhibiting a variety of concrete examples to the learner. These defined classifications are learned by means of verbally stated definitions, for example, "An uncle is the brother of a parent." There are, then, both concrete concepts and defined concepts (see Gagné, 1966). It will be pointed out in a later chapter that the capabilities to be inferred in these two instances are also somewhat different.

Learning Type 7: Rule Learning

The kind of learning that can be identified as most broadly applicable to the content of formal education is somewhat easier to describe than the simplest kinds of learning, perhaps because we must be particularly careful to keep our descriptions of the latter simple. A kind of learning like *rule learning* has some well-known conditions for its establishment which all of us employ very frequently. Continuation of the basic theme of the argument—that different varieties of learning can be distinguished by the conditions required to bring them about—leads to the view that rule learning is not only a highly familiar kind of learning but also a readily understandable one. As is true with certain other forms, the most important conditions are the prerequisites for learning.

Rule learning may be exemplified by the acquisition of the "idea" contained in such propositions as "gases expand when heated"; "the pronoun *each* takes a singular verb"; "the chemical expression for salt combines the elements Na and Cl"; "$xa + xb = x(a + b)$"; "the definite article *die* goes with a feminine (German) noun"; and many others. Surely there can be little doubt that human beings must learn large numbers of such rules, from simple ones to highly complex ones, along the road to attaining the status of being considered educated.

Possibly the immediate objection will be raised, "Why, these are simple verbal facts to be memorized!" Not so; and that is why the word "idea" has been employed to describe these rules, inexact as that word may be. From our previous discussion, it is apparent that each of these statements *can* be learned as a verbal chain. If we want to teach a five-year-old to memorize them in that way, this surely can be done. But the only kind of performance that would be possible following such learning would be something like this: "Complete the statement, 'The pronoun *each* takes _____.' " Such a performance is by no means what is established when one has learned a rule. In fact, one may learn the rule about "each" and its verb without being able to verbalize such a statement at all. What *is* meant by learning such a rule is the ability to use the singular form of the verb in a variety of sentences or clauses having "each" as a subject. If an individual is able to demonstrate this capability in a number of instances of representative sentences and clauses, one is justified in concluding that he has learned a rule.

In a formal sense, a rule is *a chain of two or more concepts*. (Recall that concepts result from classification learning.) Some people would say a rule is a *relation* between concepts; but it seems preferable to state the nature of this relation. The simplest type of rule may usually be cast in the form, "If A, then B," as in the example, "If a feminine noun, then the article *die*." The principles of chaining are essentially those that have been described for type 3 learning, except, of course, that concepts resulting from classification are being linked rather than being simply $Ss \rightarrow R$'s. Accordingly, the conditions for the learning of rules appear to be these:

1. The concepts to be linked must have been previously established. Thus for an effective capability to be acquired in using singular verbs with the pronoun "each," the relevant classifications should be learned as prerequisites. The learner must have previously learned to classify "each" as having a particular function in a sentence, and as different from other pronouns such as "they" or "all." In addition, he must have previously learned to classify singular verb as different from singular noun and from plural verb. (Again, it is necessary to emphasize that we do not imply simply the acquiring

of verbal chains by such learning, but rather true concept learning described as type 6, leading to the capability of identifying the concepts correctly in a variety of specific examples.) In simple terms, when a rule is to be learned, the individual must already have learned to classify the concepts being chained.

2. Assuming that the first condition has been fulfilled, the process of chaining is a very simple matter. Usually one simply states the rule verbally: "The pronoun 'each' takes a singular verb."

3. Under these circumstances, the learning of a rule takes place on a single occasion.

Some writers have suggested that rules need to be *discovered,* meaning that examples of the rule should be presented and the learner left to do his own chaining, without the help of verbal statements. The evidence is not particularly one-sided that this is the better method. After all, one should not forget that man is a verbal animal, and there are marvelous shortcuts in learning to be achieved by the use of language. The chances are that, provided condition 1 has been fully realized, telling the learner the rule verbally is much quicker than any other method and may well be as effective (see Ausubel, 1968). Discovery of rules *can* certainly be made, however. In this case, the individual selects his own idiosyncratic representations of the concepts to be chained.

The danger in using verbal statements as a kind of shortcut to learning is that sheer *verbal chains* may be acquired rather than truly *conceptual chains.* All teachers are acquainted with the student who can *say* the rule without being able to *do* it. But this is an example of ineffective instruction. It implies that the student really has not previously acquired the concepts (condition 1); therefore he reacts to the verbal statement as a verbal chain to be memorized. If one makes certain that the concept "each" is known, and the concept singular verb, then the statement, " 'each' takes a singular verb" should in fact represent an optimal condition for learning. Of course, to test this one must determine whether the learner can use the rule.

Learning Type 8: Problem Solving

Once the human being has acquired some rules, he can use them for many purposes in dealing with and controlling his environment. He can also do something else that is most important—he can think. Basically, this means that he is able to combine the rules he has already learned into a great variety of novel higher-order rules. He may do this by stimulating himself and also by responding to various forms of stimulation from his environment. By means of the process of combining old rules into new ones, he *solves problems* that are new to him and thus acquires a still greater store of new capabilities. The problems he solves are new to him, but they may not be new at all to other people. Of course, every so often a scientist or other creative person may arrive at a problem solution that is new to society in general.

Problem solving, by which is meant "thinking out" a new rule that combines previously learned rules, is a process that is very familiar to most adults. There is nothing very special about such events, since they are likely to occur ten or twenty times daily in the life of an average man. When a driver maps his route through traffic (as opposed to simply being swept along by it) he is solving a problem. When a man replans his luncheon schedule as a result of a new appointment, he is solving a problem. When a housewife decides to shop selectively for certain items on the basis of differential prices, she is solving a problem. These everyday examples bear a close formal resemblance to the problems that are solved by students in composing reports and themes, in marshaling arguments to present a point of view, in performing laboratory experiments, and in reading a properly written textbook.

Suppose that a student of physics encounters this situation in reading his textbook:

Power is defined as the work done divided by the time during which this work is done. That is,

$$Power = \frac{Work}{t}.$$

Suppose we have a body doing work on another body, acting with force F and velocity v. Can you show that the power delivered to a body is the product of the force acting on it and its velocity?

The solution of such a problem requires thinking, which might go somewhat as follows: first, the student formulates to himself that he wants an expression relating power to force (F) and velocity (v), in other words, containing these symbols on one side of the equation. He then recalls a "substitution rule" to the effect that the expressions which are equivalent may be substituted. Searching for such an equivalence rule, he recalls that work is related to force and the distance through which it moves; that is,

$$Power = \frac{Work}{t} = \frac{Fs}{t},$$

and he is therefore able to state that

$$Power = Fv.$$

Using still another rule, he is able to check and recognize that this formulation fills the requirements of the expression he is seeking.

When these steps have been accomplished, it is reasonable to suppose that the student has learned something new. He has not learned simply that $Power = Fv$, because he could readily have learned that as a verbal sequence (type 4). Rather, he has learned how to demonstrate in concrete terms the relation of power to force and velocity, beginning with the definition that power is work done per unit time. In other words, he has learned how to *use* this definition and how to generalize it to some considerable degree to situations in which a force acts against a body with a known velocity. This act of problem solving, then, has resulted in some very substantial learning. The change in the individual's capability is just as clear and unambiguous as it is in any other variety of learning.

A number of conditions can be identified as apparently essential for this act of learning:

1. The learner must be able to identify the essential features of the response that will be the solution *before* he arrives at the solution. (Some writers on problem solving have said that the learner must have a *goal.*) This particular condition appears to be important because of the lengthy chains involved and the steplike character of the problem-solving act. In the present example, the student knows he needs an equation relationg to power, force, and velocity. Presumably, the function of this identification is to provide direction to thinking. By checking his successive responses against those of this simple chain, each step of the way, the learner is able to "keep on the track" and also to "know when to stop."

2. Relevant rules, which have previously been learned, are recalled. In the example given, the learner recalls specifically the rules (1) $Work = F \cdot s$ and (2) $v = s/t$, as well as mathematical rules such as $(ab)/c = a(b/c)$ and if $a = b$ and $b = c$, then $a = c$. (It should be noted that in all probability these mathematical rules would be highly recallable for the student of physics, because they have already been frequently used.)

3. The recalled rules are combined so that a new rule emerges and is learned. It must be admitted here that little is known about the nature of this "combining" event, and it cannot now be described with any degree of completeness. Simply writing down in a sequence the "logical steps" followed in the act of thinking does not answer this question. These steps are the intermediate responses made by the learner, that is, they are *outcomes* of his thinking. But they provide few clues as to the nature of the combining process itself.

4. The individual steps involved in problem solving may be many, and therefore the entire act may take some time.

Nevertheless, it seems evident that the solution is arrived at "suddenly," in a "flash of insight." Repetition has very little to do with it. Nor is repetition a very powerful factor in the prevention of interference, or forgetting, as is the case with multiple discrimination learning. A "higher-order" rule resulting from an act of thinking appears to be remarkably resistant to forgetting.

/ Problem solving results in the acquisition of new ideas that multiply the applicability of rules previously learned./ As is the case with other forms of learning, its occurrence is founded on these previously learned capabilities; it does not take place in a vacuum, devoid of any prior knowledge. The major condition for encouraging the learner to think is to be sure he already has something to think about. Learning by problem solving leads to new capabilities for further thinking. Included among these are not only the "higher-order" rules we have emphasized here but also "sets" and "strategies" that serve to determine the direction of thinking and therefore its productiveness. More will be said about these capabilities in a later chapter.

LEARNING TYPES AND LEARNING THEORY

Eight different classes of situation in which human beings learn have been distinguished, that is, eight sets of conditions under which changes in capabilities of the human learner are brought about. The implication is that there are eight corresponding kinds of changes in the nervous system which need to be identified and ultimately accounted for. Each of these may involve different initial states or different structures, or both. From the standpoint of the outside of the human organism, however, they seem to be clearly distinguishable from one another in terms of the conditions that must prevail for each to occur. Might there actually be seven, nine, or ten rather than eight? It is quite possible that as research is continued it will become necessary to make new formulations of these conditions, to separate some or—what appears less likely—to collapse some. The distinctions made here are simply those that appear to be consistent with present evidence, much of it based on simple observation.

In brief, the varieties of learning that can currently be distinguished are as follows:

Type 1: Signal Learning. The individual learns to make a general, diffuse response to a signal. This is the classical conditioned response of Pavlov (1927).

Type 2: Stimulus-Response Learning. The learner acquires a precise response to a discriminated stimulus. What is learned is a connection (Thorndike, 1898) or a discriminated operant (Skinner, 1938), sometimes called an instrumental response (Kimble, 1961).

Type 3: Chaining. What is acquired is a chain of two or more stimulus-response connections. The conditions for such learning have been described by Skinner (1938) and others, notably Gilbert (1962).

Type 4: Verbal Association. Verbal association is the learning of chains that are verbal. Basically, the conditions resemble those for other (motor) chains. However, the presence of language in the human being makes this a special type because internal links may be selected from the individual's previously learned repertoire of language (see Underwood, 1964b).

Type 5: Discrimination Learning. The individual learns to make *n* different identifying responses to as many different stimuli, which may resemble each other in physical appearance to a greater or lesser degree. Although the learning of each stimulus-response connection is a simple type 2 occurrence, the connections tend to interfere with each other's retention (Postman, 1961).

Type 6: Concept Learning. The learner acquires a capability of making a common response to a class of stimuli that may differ from each other widely in physical appearance. He is able to make a response that identifies an entire class of objects or events (see Kendler, 1964). Other concepts are acquired *by definition*, and consequently have the formal characteristics of rules.

Type 7: Rule Learning. In simplest terms, a rule is a chain of two or more concepts. It functions to control behavior in the manner suggested by a verbalized rule of the form, "If *A*, then *B*," where *A* and *B* are previously learned concepts. However, it must be carefully distinguished from the mere verbal sequence, "If *A*, then *B*," which, of course, may also be learned as type 4.

Type 8: Problem Solving. Problem solving is a kind of learning that requires the internal events usually called thinking. Two or more previously acquired rules are somehow combined to produce a new capability that can be shown to depend on a "higher-order" rule.

To distinguish a number of varieties of learning is not, of course, a completely novel idea. Learning types have been distinguished by many other writers. One of the most widely accepted distinctions is that between the classical conditioned response (here called type 1) and trial-and-error learning (type 2). Thorndike believed that this was a valid distinction, and Skinner (1938) considers it a basic and essential one. Hull (1934) considered the distinction between these two learning types to be one of different experimental conditions rather than of different underlying mechanisms. Several learning theorists have further distinguished chaining (type 3) as a separately identifiable form of learning; these include Skinner (1938) and also Hull (1943) in his treatment of habit-families hierarchies. Some investigators of learning describe a number of different types of distinctive learnings; Tolman (1949) distinguished six kinds; Woodworth (1958), five. Modern writers have tended to pay increasing attention to the more complex forms of learning. For example, Mowrer (1960b) discusses discriminations (type 5) and concept learning (type 6), as well as the simpler varieties. Harlow (1959) has studied the acquisition of concepts in comparison with simpler discrimination in monkeys. A detailed analysis would reveal many ideas within the present volume that are derived from these writers.

Prerequisites to Learning

Throughout many years of experimental investigation of learning, there have been those who have contended that *all learning is basically the same.* Thorndike (1931, p. 160), for example, says essentially this, and there have been many others who have espoused this view, explicitly or implicitly. It should be perfectly clear from the present chapter that it is this viewpoint about learning which is categorically rejected. The attempt is made to show that each variety of learning described here begins with a *different state of the organism* and ends with a *different capability for performance.* It is believed, therefore, that the differences among these varieties of learning far outweigh their similarities. Furthermore, great confusion can arise—and has arisen— through believing that these varieties are somehow alike. To equate the responding of an animal to a warning signal with the learning of a child asking for a doll, or the learning of a student to identify a chromosome or the learning to predict inheritance with the laws of genetics is considered to be a matter of gross disregard for some obvious and simple observations.

The most important class of conditions that distinguishes one form of learning from another is the initial state of the learning—in other words, its *prerequisites.* The conditions for chaining, for example, require that the individual have previously learned stimulus-response connections available to him, so that they *can* be chained. If this condition is not met, one finds oneself dealing with conditions for establishing these prerequisite $Ss \rightarrow R$'s, and thus one is likely to draw incorrect conclusions about chaining itself. This gen-

eralization, applied to the varieties of learning we have
discussed, may be briefly stated as follows:

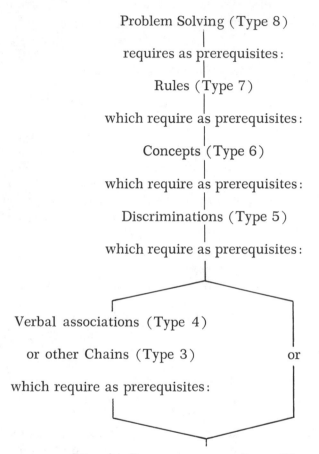

Problem Solving (Type 8)

requires as prerequisites:

Rules (Type 7)

which require as prerequisites:

Concepts (Type 6)

which require as prerequisites:

Discriminations (Type 5)

which require as prerequisites:

Verbal associations (Type 4)

or other Chains (Type 3)   or

which require as prerequisites:

Stimulus-Response connections (Type 2)

It is tempting to agree with Mowrer (1960a) that Ss → R
connections (type 2) require signal learning (type 1) as
a prerequisite. This may be true, but it does not seem
possible to draw this conclusion with complete confidence
from presently available evidence; it remains as a proposition to be further illuminated by experimental research.

LEARNING TYPES AND INSTRUCTION

Do all these varieties of learning apply to school instruction? The answer is yes, but some of them in rather specialized ways. It will not come as a surprise to the reader, perhaps, to learn that most instruction in school subjects is concerned with the learning and use of concepts and rules and with problem solving. The applicability of other learning types is also important, however, and needs to be stated briefly here.

Signal learning is thought by some investigators to be involved in very fundamental attitudes toward the school and the teacher. For example, Jensen (1968) has speculated that the early environment of some individual children may condition them to dislike the school environment, books, and other familiar appurtenances of the schoolroom. As a further possibility, initial learning experiences of the child may have become attached, through conditioning, to unpleasant stimuli, and in this way the activities necessary for learning may have been unlearned or *extinguished* (see Chapter 4). Likes and dislikes can be acquired through signal learning, according to other evidence, and this particular possibility, having such a fundamental importance for the future learning of the child, cannot be ignored. Otherwise, as has been mentioned, signal learning may be of positive usefulness in establishing the common "signals" to be used by the teacher in setting the stage for attention, rest periods, or other regularly occurring events.

A large repertoire of well-practiced *stimulus-response connections* is already possessed by the child when he enters school. The young child can, for example, imitate many essential body and limb movements, and also vocal sounds, at a minimum. These connections are important for further learning, but they have typically been learned in earlier childhood. But some vocal sounds may not have been learned, and it is necessary for the child to acquire these early during his school years. Simple $Ss \rightarrow R$'s of hand movements, arm movements, and directional movements of the body may also have to be acquired in the earliest months of school. Beyond these, one must look for rather special situations to find examples of the learning of simple connections. When a foreign language is being learned, the acquiring of a correctly pronounced unfamiliar sound (such as the French *in*) appears to be a reasonable example of $Ss \rightarrow R$ learning.

Examples of *motor chain* and *verbal associate learning* are not difficult to locate in the context of the school. In the elementary grades, printing letters is a good example of the former, learning the names of the numerals 1–9 in order, an example of the latter. Motor chains must be learned at various stages of school learning, for example, when the student must acquire proficiency in operating and adjusting a scientific instrument. Verbal chains may be learned as memorized formulas or as foreign idiomatic expressions of common usage. It may be noted that such forms of learning do occur throughout all grades, and at the same time that their frequency is relatively low compared with other types.

Discriminations are some of the most important capabilities acquired by young children, who need to learn to distinguish the properties of a great variety of objects and living things, so that they can readily tell round from square, blue from green, three from two. At higher levels, one finds discriminations again of particular importance in distinguishing foreign sounds or the sounds of the native language and in various scientific observations.

Concept learning refers to the acquisition of classifications of object properties, objects, and events. Concepts may be concrete or defined. Beginning in the early grades and throughout his school career, the student will be asked to classify many things and events, from numbers to beetles to families to nations and forms of government. This type of learning is obviously a most pervasive one.

Rule learning has an equally frequent, if not greater, occurrence in the school. The operations that the student learns in dealing with objects, numbers, words, and abstract concepts all involve behavior that is rule-governed.

Problem solving should be, and usually is, a highly frequent kind of learning in the school. Whenever the student is encouraged to combine ideas of any sort and independently arrives at the new idea resulting from their combination, he may be said to be solving a problem.

These types of learning are distinguished because each requires somewhat different conditions of instruction for most effective learning. Good instruction is planned so that these different conditions, applicable to what is being learned, are clearly represented. For a child to learn to distinguish a rectangle and a square (type 5), for example, quite different conditions of instruction are required from those needed for him to learn a rule for finding the area of a rectangle (type 7). Additional examples of the implications these types of learning have for instruction are included in later chapters.

GENERAL REFERENCES

Varieties of Learning
Ausubel, D. P. *Educational psychology: A cognitive view.* New York: Holt, Rinehart and Winston, 1968.
Cofer, C. N. (ed.) *Verbal learning and verbal behavior.* New York: McGraw-Hill, 1961.
Melton, A. W. (ed.) *Categories of human learning.* New York: Academic Press, 1964.
Mowrer, O. H. (a) *Learning theory and behavior;* (b) *Learning theory and the symbolic processes.* New York: Wiley, 1960.
Woodworth, R. S. *Dynamics of behavior.* New York: Holt, Rinehart and Winston, 1958. Chaps. 9–12.

Theories of Learning
See General References to Chapter 1.

3 | Events in Learning and Remembering

The various types of learning, as outlined in the previous chapters, take place under different conditions and they produce different learning outcomes in the sense that the learner acquires a different class of capability in each case. Such differences as these are obviously of importance to the management of instruction.

Other, equally valid, ways of describing learning would emphasize the common characteristics of the process. For example, learning is an occurrence that takes place over an interval of time and thus may be analyzed and described in terms of the components of this time sequence. All of the types of learning described in this book have this common time sequence. When each type is described, in subsequent chapters, these events are compressed in meaning into the single term "learning." Before proceeding with such descriptions of types, however, let us at the outset consider what events are included in any learning sequence.

Figure 1 distinguishes the major portions of a total learning occurrence for all types of learning. Following the presentation of the stimulus situation, there is an interval of time during which this stimulation is *apprehended*. This

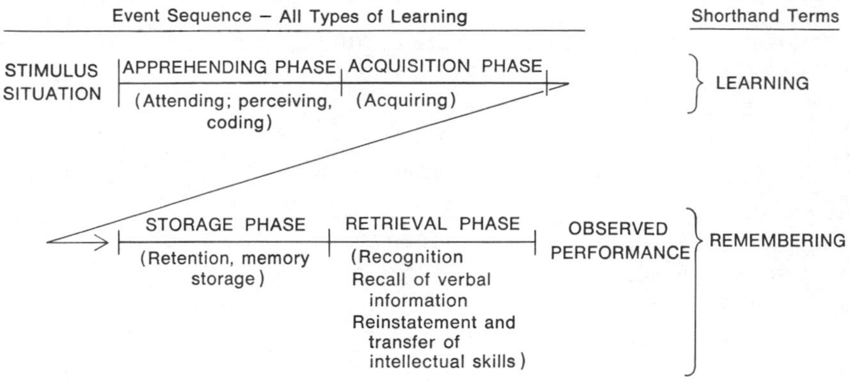

STIMULUS SITUATION | APPREHENDING PHASE | ACQUISITION PHASE

(Attending; perceiving, coding) | (Acquiring)   } LEARNING

STORAGE PHASE | RETRIEVAL PHASE | OBSERVED PERFORMANCE } REMEMBERING

(Retention, memory storage) | (Recognition Recall of verbal information Reinstatement and transfer of intellectual skills)

FIGURE 1. The sequence of events in learning.

is followed by the event denoted as the *acquisition phase,* in which the changes in the central nervous system that underlie the new capability actually take place. It is generally believed that acquisition is then followed by some internal activity that "puts into memory store" the newly learned entity, so that it can be retained over a period of time: this is the *storage* phase. The fourth major phase is *retrieval,* in which the learned capabilities that have been learned and stored are in some manner recovered and exhibited as performances to an external observer. Figure 1 indicates that various more specific terms are used, depending on the purpose, to refer to the events of these four phases. At the same time, there are also two "shorthand terms," somewhat more familiar, which collapse the first two events into *learning,* the second two into remembering.

THE FOUR PHASES OF A LEARNING SEQUENCE

Having laid out the events in the total sequence called learning along a time dimension, we can now proceed to consider them one by one. As will be seen, this further description will require some more detailed definition of the various specific terms given in Figure 1, which are used to distinguish particular processes within each of the four phases.

The Apprehending Phase

It is easy to grasp the idea that a learner who must respond to some stimulation in order to learn must first "register" this stimulation. What exactly is meant by such registration, and what processes are involved in it have continued to be lively subjects for discussion and investigation over many years. Most scholars would agree that an initial event must be that of *attending* to the stimulus, although whether such attending is a process itself containing one, two, or perhaps three stages is a matter still actively debated. For present purposes, though, it will be convenient simply to acknowledge attending as an initial event in learning, which may be thought of as a state that can often be detected by observing what the learner is looking at or listening to.

The event of attending may be considered as leading to the *perceiving* of the stimulus. If one is looking at another person, he may attend in such a way that he perceives his face or his hands or his clothing; or, under other circumstances, his totality as a person. Similarly, one may attend to a window as a part of a wall and perceive it as such, or one may attend in such a way that he perceives eight individual panes of glass. How one attends, and therefore what is perceived, depends upon a temporary (mental) *set* (see Hebb, 1966, pp. 82–101), which the individual may decide to adopt or be stimulated to adopt by means of verbal instructions. It is interesting to note, too, that the act of perceiving implies that the individual is differentiating the stimulus from other stimuli, or its parts from other parts. The limits of what he is able to do in this respect depends largely on discrimination learning that has occurred previously. The prior learning that determines what can be perceived is often called *perceptual learning* (see E. J. Gibson, 1968), and mention will be made of it again in Chapter 6.

Are these two integrally related events, attending and perceiving, all that is meant when we say that stimulation somehow gets "registered"? One finds that with this issue too there is active investigation by experimental psychologists and also active controversy. Some would answer this question in the affirmative. Many, however, would insist on the necessity for still another event, not easy to detect in the learner's overt behavior, but inferred from many sources of evidence. According to this view, a stimulus must not only be perceived but also *coded.* By this is meant that the learner apprehends any given stimulus in an idiosyncratic way, in a way that makes it easy for him to "use" the stimulus. Thus one individual, on perceiving the printed word LUX, may code it as a brand of detergent, while another may think of it as "light," and still another as part of an inscription. Each one may *perceive* the word equally well, but the *coding* they give to it is quite different.

Regarding this initial phase of the learning process, there are obviously questions that cannot be solved merely by rational discussion, and particularly not in this book. Accordingly, it seems most convenient to describe these initial events together as the *apprehending phase* of learning. This phase is concerned with the events that "register" the stimulus situation for the learner and includes attending, perceiving, and coding. For readers who may be interested in undertaking further study and research on this phase of the learning process, it will be evident that the prospect is intricate and fascinating.

The Acquisition Phase

Once the stimuli relevant to learning have been apprehended, the process can proceed. The next phase, which is learning in its narrowest sense, is *acquisition.* Before this specific event occurs, it can be demonstrated that the individual cannot do some particular performance. After the event, even very immediately after it, one can observe that the same individual *can* execute the performance. This is the first indication that a new capability has been *acquired*.

While the phase of acquisition is conceptually quite clear, it is exceedingly difficult to demonstrate in isolated form. To do this, one would have to separate clearly this phase from the apprehending (perceiving, coding) that preceded it; that is, one would have to be able to demonstrate that apprehending can occur under a given set of circumstances *without* learning and under a different set of circumstances *with* learning. Some studies have indeed approached this demonstration, as when it has been shown that animals may perceive a pathway, but not learn to use it. Even more difficult, though, is the demonstration of the difference between the acquisition phase and what follows it, namely, the storage and retrieval phases. In order for the learner to demonstrate that he has learned to do something, he obviously must remember it, even if one asks him to do it "immediately." No truly satisfactory solution to this puzzle currently exists. Most probably, it will be possible some day to distinguish this phase clearly in terms of events within the central nervous system. In the meantime, the distinction is a highly useful and even necessary one.

The Storage Phase

Having been acquired, the new capability must be "stored," if it is to qualify as something that has truly been learned. The change that has been brought about by the event of acquisition now becomes retained, over a period that might be a few minutes or a lifetime.

Some recent evidence suggests that there may be two quite different kinds of storage. One is spoken of as *short-term memory*, which has a limited capacity and a duration of up to thirty seconds. This is the kind of retention operative, for example, when one "holds in mind" a telephone number long enough to dial it. The other, into which the contents of short-term memory may be fed, is the more familiar *long-term memory,* in which retention may persist indefinitely. Some investigators contend, however, that the supposed differences between these two kinds of storage have not yet been established in a convincing manner and that the distinction between the two may eventually turn out to be insupportable. In any case, it is evident that long-term memory is of greatest relevance to instruction in educational settings.

One intriguing possibility, supported by some clinical evidence, is that retention in the long-term sense tends to persist for a lifetime, and in this sense, to be permanent. Penfield (1951) has reported instances of childhood memories in patients whose brains are electrically stimulated under medical treatment, which reproduce in startling detail episodes involving recall of situations, sounds, conversations, and other aspects of events of the past. Such events are in a practical sense forgotten, but traces of them may persist in the brain. If memory traces are in some sense permanent, the reasons for forgetting must be sought in other events, such as interference from other stored memories, or obstacles to retrieval.

Another active field of investigation concerns the *site* of memory in the brain. An early hypothesis, shown to be highly improbable by the work of Lashley (1950), was that some particular portion of the brain was the locus of the storage function. One prominent modern theory considers storage to be a matter of locally organized circuits, or networks, of interacting nervous fibers. And of considerable interest and active exploration is the theory that the site of memory storage is *within* each neural cell, involving alterations in such cell components as RNA and DNA. It seems likely that a fully satisfactory theory of memory will need to take into account both intracellular mechanisms and also those involving interactions among cells (see John, 1967).

All of these facts provide important background knowledge about the storage function of memory. Yet it must be admitted that little is known about this capacity of long-term storage, its persistence over time, or the factors in the learning history of the individual that may interfere with or alter such storage. What is known for sure is that retention does occur, and in a more or less dependable fashion.

The Retrieval Phase

When the individual is called upon to display what he has learned or to put it to use in some way, he must *retrieve* the entity that has been acquired and stored. Retrieval often takes place in a disorganized way, as when the situations described in a novel "remind" the reader of a variety of events originally learned in different contexts. Deliberate retrieval may, however, be undertaken by the individual when he needs the learned items in solving some current problem, or when he is asked such a question as, "What do you remember about X?" With such deliberate retrievals it is usually apparent that certain organizing factors are at work—the individual may recall a variety of specific instances falling into a given category, for example, or he may recall several categories that are meaningfully related to each other (see Ausubel, 1968, pp. 83–123).

It seems likely that the retrieval of verbal information is a process for which the skilled learner has acquired a special set of *strategies* he brings to bear on the retrieval task. How does he decide what to retrieve first? In what order does he go about retrieving items of information? How does he "search" for an item having a particular relevance to his present purpose? Strategies such as these have not been clearly identified or systematically studied, although their existence seems scarcely open to doubt.

While retrieval is often conceived as a matter of remembering verbal information, it seems evident that the term needs to have a broader meaning. Particularly, it is necessary to realize that the individual may be called upon to exhibit a performance that requires him not simply to "tell something" but rather to "do something." Thus there is an important distinction to be made between the *recall of verbal information,* on the one hand, and the *reinstatement of intellectual skills,* on the other. (Included in the latter category are the strategies mentioned in the previous paragraph, which pertain to "how to recall" verbal information.) This distinction is of such importance that it must be discussed more fully in a subsequent section of this chapter.

When retrieval is exhibited as the reinstatement of an intellectual skill, what is observed is a performance in a new situation. The elements of the stimulus situation in which the skill was first acquired are altered, and the learner is required to perform in a novel context. Reinstatement in this sense, then, is one manifestation of the phenomenon of *learning transfer.* For example, when a child has learned to make a plural of words like "radius," one may give him the new task of constructing a plural of a word entirely new to him (say, "gladiolus"). Such transfer of learned and retained capabilities is, it goes without saying, a matter of primary importance to the design and practice of instruction in the schools.

Learned capabilities that can be transferred must, of course, be stored. But they are not "recalled" in the sense that items of verbal information are. Instead, they are applied or used in a new situation. One may suppose, therefore, that the learner may need strategies for learning transfer that are different from those he uses in verbal recall. Evidences for such strategies will be considered in later discussions of transfer and its relevance to school learning.

Here, then, are some common properties of the learning process that apply, whether the learner is engaged in acquiring a new $Ss \rightarrow R$ connection, a new discrimination, a new rule, or any other type of capability mentioned in the previous chapter. Learning as a total process begins with a phase of apprehending the stimulus situation, proceeds to the phase of acquisition, then to storage, and finally to retrieval. All of these events are involved in the sequence of an act of learning. The first two of these phases may occur within seconds. The storage phase may extend over very long periods of time, and retrieval may not occur until there is a reason for it.

This book follows a practice common to many writings on the learning process. A kind of shorthand is used, in which the first two phases are compressed into *learning*, under the assumption that acquisition must naturally be preceded by the phase of apprehending. At the same time, the second two phases are contracted to *remembering*, with the implicit understanding that both storage and retrieval are involved. In subsequent chapters, we may have occasion to discuss the events of learning in any of its four phases. Mainly, however, we shall deal with these two major distinctions of learning and remembering.

REMEMBERING AS THE OUTCOME OF LEARNING

Learning is known by its outcome—that is, the performance exhibited by the learner as the endpoint of a sequence of events. Several different kinds of performances may be required by the researcher or teacher who is making the observation. Naturally enough, these different performances lead to different sorts of inferences about what has been learned. In view of this fact, it seems desirable here to undertake some additional discussion of the phases of learning that make up remembering.

To demonstrate that the change called learning has occurred, one must include the events of remembering. Suppose a child who knows the words asks the question about a strange object, "What is this?" and is told it is a "window fastener." How is it then determined whether there has been any learning? Obviously, the child must now be asked the question when the object is shown to him again, to see if he will be able to identify it as a window fastener. When this happens, even if only a short time has elapsed, it is evident that he not only has acquired this labeling association but has also *remembered* it. The occurrence of learning, in other words, cannot be observed without the occurrence of remembering also.

During relatively short periods of time, under circumstances in which no extreme distractions have been introduced, virtually perfect remembering of single learning events is to be expected. But such conditions for remembering are by no means always present, and perhaps not even usually so. Remembering is highly subject to reduction by a number of factors, including particularly (1) the number of learning events that occur in a given time interval; (2) the presence of distracting (or "interfering") activities following learning; and (3) the passage of time (which may also include interfering activities). In later chapters we shall see how interferences from other events can critically affect particular types of learning, because they are inherent to the process of learning itself.

For purposes of learning relevant to the school, a most important set of questions concerning remembering centers about the effects of the passage of time. The teacher is concerned that what has been learned about a topic on Friday will be remembered until Monday in order that further instruction on the topic may be given. Over the summer holiday students need to remember how to subtract in order to be able to use this skill in learning to multiply and divide in the fall. It is expected that adults will remember many things that they initially learned in elementary grades for a great many years, and even thoughout their lifetimes.

What Is Remembered?

In considering remembering as a set of events that follow learning and that extend over various intervals of time, it is necessary to make certain distinctions about *what* is remembered. For example, it may be said that a person "remembers a picture he has seen before." Or one may say that a fifth-grader "remembers the new words he learned in the fourth grade." Another possibility is that a person "remembers how to ride a bicycle" or "how to compute compound interest." Are all of these examples the same kind of remembering, in the sense that the same class of entity is stored and retrieved in each case? The answer is that they are not the same. We must therefore be concerned with making distinctions among them. The first kind of remembering is usually called *recognition;* the second is remembering *verbal information;* the third is remembering skills, of which a distinctly important category is *intellectual skills.*

Recognition   A learner may retain in and retrieve from his memory a place, a thing, a melody, or an odor that he has encountered and apprehended at some previous time. His performance, in showing recognition, is one of distinguishing an "old" stimulus (one he has previously encountered) from any number of "new" ones that may also be present. Remembering, in this sense of recognition, is often remarkably good, and the individual may be able to recognize a scene, a face, or a tune he has encountered after many years with no intervening experience with the object in question. Furthermore, if one undertakes to assess remembering simply by asking the learner to recognize what he has previously apprehended, his *recognition* score will ordinarily be very high when compared with the amount he can remember by actually *recalling* a performance, which indicates his prior learning of some capability. In other words, it is usually much easier to distinguish an old from a new stimulus than to generate anew (recall or reinstate) a performance that may have been learned in connection with that stimulus.

One interpretation of the usual large advantage of recognition over recall is that whereas each method is sampling the same stored entity, recognition is simply an easier task, and therefore is more "sensitive" and yields higher remembering scores. However, the interpretation of recognition and recall as simply two different measures of the same remembered entity is not the only possible one. Adams (1967, pp. 245–275) summarizes some of the reasons favoring the hypothesis that recognition memory is of a different sort, subject to different laws, than is remembering as measured by a performance, which requires the generation of an organized set of responses, as in recall or reinstatement.

Recall of Verbal Information   One of the most frequent types of remembering consists in the recall of verbal information. In the young child, one may expect much remembering to include words that are labels for objects, actions, object qualities, and events. Adults can recall not only simple labels such as the names for numerals, letters, and objcts but a remarkably large and often highly organized set of "facts" about many subjects. In any case, it is of some importance to note that the kind of performance indicating the remembering is one that requires the individual to *state*, or otherwise *identify verbally* something he has remembered. One asks the learner, "What do you recall about X?" expecting a verbal reply. Or perhaps, "Which of the following (verbal) statements describes the character of George Washington?" Or, "What was the Gettysburg Address all about?" The exact form of the questioning may vary, but in essence what is being required is recall of verbalizable information.

The remembering of verbal information follows a set of laws that have been intensively investigated over many years and that are still only partially understood. The most basic principle is that of *association*, which, as we saw in Chapter 1, was a matter of great interest to the British philosopher-psychologists of the last century. Two ideas (represented by labels or verbal propositions) that have happened to occur together in time form an association such that one idea, when it recurs, tends to bring about the remembering of the other; this is the *contiguity* principle. There are undoubtedly many other principles governing the storage and retrieval of verbal information. Ausubel (1968), for example, emphasizes the principle of *subsumption*, whereby a newly presented piece of information is integrated in a meaningful sense with a previously learned structure of ideas. The new information may be subordinate to the more inclusive structure, in which case the subsumption is "derivative," or the new proposition may be coordinate with the pre-existing structure, and the subsumption is called "correlative." Remembering of an item of verbal information is affected, according to this view, by the degree of stability the organized structure has and the ease with which the newly acquired item can be dissociated from it.

It seems a well-established fact that many words, facts, and propositions are recalled simply because they have been associated, not necessarily meaningfully, with other verbal items. When one asks for "free associations" to words, the resulting verbal responses are often most readily accounted for on the grounds that they have frequently occurred together in the past, for example, the pairs Adam and Eve, sun and moon, rain and snow. In addition, there are frequent idiosyncratic responses, which are usually attributed to the adventitious pairing of the two words or phrases in the past history of the individual. But simple association will surely not, by itself, account for the remembering of verbal information. Such information, we know from a great deal of evidence (see Deese, 1962; Adams, 1967, pp. 153–177), becomes *organized* in memory and is retrieved in an organized manner. Having begun to remember a set of previously memorized words, for example, the individual tends to retrieve them in "clusters" belonging to common superordinate categories (Bousfield, 1953). If he begins with a word like "horse," his recall tends to continue with words for other animals.

Perhaps the most important thing to be noted about the remembering of verbal information, however, is that it is distinguishable from the remembering of intellectual skills, which are to be described next. It seems improbable that one can account for the retention and retrieval of intellectual skills by means of the same laws as apply to the recall of verbal information. Although some procedures of remembering may be commonly shared, the capabilities called intellectual skills appear to be highly resistant to forgetting (as is also true of motor skills) and to storing and retrieving in a manner that suggests they are influenced by quite a different set of factors in the individual's experience.

Reinstatement of Intellectual Skills   The varieties of learning outlined in the previous chapter, and described in subsequent ones, apply to the learning and remembering of *intellectual skills.* Such skills fall into the categories discriminating, chaining, classifying, rule using, and problem solving. They are called "intellectual" skills (as distinguished from motor skills) because they involve symbolic activities, often called intellectual operations, on the part of the individual. Their learning seems strongly affected by a hierarchical ordering that makes one skill dependent on the prior learning of another skill that has a lower location in the hierarchy. The remembering of such skills is similarly affected by their hierarchical arrangement; it is nearly inconceivable for a higher-order skill to be remembered without the remembering of a relevant lower-order skill at the same time. It seems highly unlikely, to take a simple example, that the skill of adding columns of two-place numbers could be remembered without the skill of adding columns of one-place numbers or that the latter skill in turn could be remembered without the skill of adding zero to a single number.

Whereas the remembering of verbal information is usually called recall, we here use the term "reinstatement" to refer to the process of remembering intellectual skills. Both kinds of remembering are important, but it is particularly significant to distinguish them. The organizational principles that govern the recall of verbal entities are not the same as those that apply to the reinstatement of an intellectual skill.

Let us suppose an individual has learned the verbalizable information in a page of a history book. If one asks him to remember what the page said, a number of principles of organization will be apparent in his recall. He may retrieve items that fall into certain categories, others that reflect a temporal sequence, and a few perhaps that appear to be somewhat random "associations." But nothing will require that any given item is recalled because it depends on the recall of another item that is subordinate to it in the sense of actually being involved in the recall itself. Organization will be present, but not this particular kind of organization.

When given a physics problem to solve, it may similarly be true that a student must, as a first step, recall some verbal information. For example, suppose the student were given the following problem: "An oxygen tank whose volume is 2 cu. ft. is filled to a pressure of 3000 lb/in²; what was the original volume of the oxygen when it was at a pressure of 1 atmosphere (assume no temperature change)?" Evidently one of the first things the student needs to do is to *recall* that he must use Boyle's law, that the law states that $PV = P'V'$ (mass and temperature constant), that 1 atmosphere is 15 lb/in²

Notice, however, that while such verbal information is essential, it does not enable the student to solve the problem. To accomplish this, he must be able to *reinstate* some identifiable intellectual skills. Among these are rules about the manipulation of terms in an equation, the substituting of one set of values for an equivalent set, the identification of similar units, and the transposition of terms to obtain a value for V'. Any one of these rules may depend upon one or more subordinate rule-governed skills, in the sense that transposing terms in an equation depends upon the simpler rule of $a \cdot 1/b$ and $a/b \cdot 1$ and upon the even more basic rules of multiplying, dividing, and setting things equal, which are also part of the equation. Each of these rule-governed skills in turn depends upon certain concepts (classifying skills), such as those of number and those that define pressure and volume, pounds and inches. While the student can undoubtedly recall the names of such entities verbally, or verbal statements of their definitions, reinstating them as intellectual skills means being able to demonstrate their use. In other words, reinstating a concept means "demonstrating its referential meaning" rather than simply "making a verbal statement." If one wishes to pursue the matter further, he will see that such concepts in turn depend upon even simpler skills called discriminations. However, it will be best to leave further discussion of this point until it is taken up in Chapter 6.

When a total set of intellectual skills is reinstated for the purpose of demonstrating problem-solving performance, there appears to be a predictable organization of these skills, in the sense that the more complex ones involve the less complex ones as subordinate skills. The "facts" of history may be recalled in a variety of organizations. In contrast, the intellectual skills that must be reinstated to solve a given problem carry with them their own inherent organization. This organization has implications relating to the design of learning for the entire set of skills, as will be seen in Chapter 9.

Thus it may be seen that intellectual skills are *reinstated* when they are remembered. They are put to use in some manner. The important kind of remembering is reinstatement (not "recall"), so far as intellectual skills are concerned. Reinstatement of an intellectual skill occurs when the individual is required to exhibit some particular performance requiring the use of that skill in a "new" situation.

THE FUNCTIONS OF REMEMBERING

It is necessary, then, to distinguish some kinds of remembering in terms of *what* is remembered, whether recognized things and places, recalled verbal information, or reinstated intellectual skills. There is still another way of looking at the process of remembering, and that is in terms of the *functions* it serves in the life of the individual. Viewing remembering from the standpoint of its functions is unlikely to increase one's theoretical understanding of the remembering process. What it may do, however, is provide a way of gauging the importance of the various kinds of remembering for education.

There appear to be three main functions served by remembering in the human being. These three functions, it should be noted, do not correspond to the *types* of remembering just distinguished. Instead, these purposes cut across the content of what is remembered. The question is not *what* (whether recognized object, recalled verbalization, or reinstated intellectual skill), but *what for*? The functions may be described as follows:

1. Temporary Holding. Simply stated, one wishes to "hold something in mind" in order to complete some action. The example of the telephone number held in storage only until dialing is completed is a most familiar instance. The short-order cook "holds in mind" several orders at once, but only until he completes the actions necessary to begin the preparation of the food in each case. Once he has started these orders, he is ready to store additional ones, in a temporary holding manner. Typically, he cannot remember what orders he started a few minutes ago—when the short-order system works properly, there is no need to do this. In such instances, remembering is functioning only as a temporary holding mechanism.

2. Mediational Use. A large proportion of remembering

is for the purpose of mediational use. One remembers something in order to put it to use in learning verbalizable information or, more important, in learning intellectual skills. Whatever is remembered for this purpose *may* be retained for a longer time (that is, after the new learning has been completed) or it *may not* be.

Perhaps the clearest instances of the mediational use of remembered entities are to be seen in the recall of verbal information. If a child is undertaking concept learning, for example, he may be presented with a lesson on varieties of trees. During the course of such a lesson, he may learn that the two major categories of trees are deciduous and evergreen, and that these in turn may contain a number of subcategories such as broad-leaved and needle-bearing. Proceeding farther with verbal information, he may also learn the names, members, and characteristic appearances of several subordinate categories, such as oak, pine, and fir. Such information is included in the lesson primarily to serve the purpose of the child's *learning to classify* trees. The lesson may be followed, for example, by an assessment exercise which asks the child to classify a set of particular trees, not all of which have been specifically mentioned in the lesson itself. By this means it is clearly revealed that the function of most of the specific information given in the lesson has been to *mediate the learning* of a classifying skill (that is, of concepts).

To many curriculum designers, and to many teachers, it is a puzzling question as to just how much of the detailed verbal information contained in lessons of this sort one should expect the student to recall over a long time period. The usual answer to this question is that the student should surely remember *some* of the categories he has learned about, perhaps the major ones, but to expect that he will remember all of these facts is perhaps asking too much. He does not need to remember them all, because if he is later confronted with a practical problem involving the classification of trees, he can resolve his question with the use of reference books. On the other hand, he needs to remember some, because he needs clues as to how to look the information up.

These answers derived from practical teaching experience are undoubtedly correct in their general outlines. It may be noted that they do not provide a clear answer to exactly *what* or *how much* of the factual content of a lesson needs to be remembered for a long time, a question that is raised again in the next section. But they serve to emphasize this highly important point: much of the remembering that is necessary within a lesson has *only* the function of mediating the learning of something else. The variety of detail learned by the student during the lesson pertaining to specific trees like maple, locust, elm, dogwood, white pine, cedar, and linden trees is serving the function of mediating the learning of (1) the intellectual skill of classifying and (2) major categories of verbalizable information pertaining to trees.

An educated adult, when faced with a problem to solve, typically remembers two kinds of entities to mediate his problem-solving behavior. If the problem is not within his specialized field (as many problems are not), he *recalls* enough verbalized information to enable him to look up, in encyclopedias or other reference works, the detailed information he needs. This newly acquired (partly relearned) detailed information is itself stored and recalled as the problem solving proceeds, but only for this mediational purpose. The other major components remembered for problem-solving purposes are intellectual skills, of which the problem-relevant ones are *reinstated*. These skills, it should be noted, can often not be so easily learned (or even relearned) by being "looked up"; the problem solver who can reinstate them readily from his memory has a distinct advantage.

3. Lifetime Retention. The third function of remembering has already been suggested. There are some things one needs to remember all one's life. Of primary importance among these are intellectual skills. The many years of learning engaged in by all of us would lose their major purpose if we could not retain and reinstate a great variety of relatively specific, as well as relatively general, intellectual skills that enable us to discriminate, classify, utilize rules, and solve problems. For one to have to learn anew the intellectual skills needed for the taking of every new practical action or decision is unthinkable. The human being must have a store of intellectual skills that can readily be reinstated. In adults, differences in intellectual capability and functioning would seem to be largely determined by differences among individuals with respect to the variety and complexity of their retained intellectual skills.

The other important category of lifetime remembering consists of verbalizable information. The adult remembers the names of the letters, the names of the numerals, many longer phrases and passages, the names of a great many objects and observable actions in his environment. Beyond these, he recalls a great many "higher-order" categories such as those that classify trees into deciduous and evergreen; modes of transportation into trains, buses, airplanes, boats, and autos; works of literature into prose and poetry; and so on. Again, there are obvious differences among people as to how many detailed facts within any category, as well as how many categories of information, they recall. In solving a particular problem, the individual who recalls many relevant details (learned years ago) may turn out to have a slight advantage—but surely it is very slight, so long as another person can recall the major categories that enable him to look up these same details. It is likely that both these individuals, if they are concerned with accuracy, will probably have to resort to "looking up" the details; thus the practical difference in their problem-solving efficiency may turn out to be very little, so far as recalled verbal information is concerned.

At this point, it is possible to consider together what has been said about *what* is remembered, and what has been said about the *functions* of remembering. Some examples are given in Table 1.

TABLE 1

EXAMPLES OF TYPES OF REMEMBERING HAVING
DIFFERENT FUNCTIONS

TYPES OF REMEMBERING	FUNCTIONS		
	TEMPORARY HOLDING	MEDIATIONAL USE	LIFETIME RETENTION
Recognition of Stimuli	In checking a list of names, recognizing one that is encountered a second time.	In forming categories from a list of symbols, recognizing a symbol previously seen in the list.	In listening to music, recognizing a previously heard melody.
Recall of Verbal Information	In dialing a telephone number, recalling a sequence of digits.	In approaching a problem in genetics, recalling that each human somatic cell contains 23 pairs of chromosomes.	In solving many practical problems, recalling the names of the letters of the alphabet in order.
Reinstatement of Intellectual Skills	(Of questionable applicability.)	In learning to add similar fractions, reinstating rules about the factoring of numbers in denominators.	In solving a problem of comparing and contrasting economic production of different nations, reinstating rules of categorizing.

Educational Implications

As we return to a consideration of types of learning in subsequent chapters, there will be many occasions to bear in mind this view of the common features of learning as a temporal sequence of events. The phases of apprehending, acquisition, storage, and retrieval represent what currently appear to be reasonable inferences about the processes of learning when considered from this time-oriented point of view. All of the types of learning may be viewed in terms of these four phases, and research of the future may be able to identify differences in phases among learning types that are not currently known. In the meantime, some characteristics of learning outcomes, associated with the phases collectively called *remembering*, have been given additional attention in this chapter.

Everyone uses remembering in its temporary holding function—to remember telephone numbers, directions about how to reach a destination, a sequence of actions needed to open a strange container, and many other performances of this sort. Primarily involved in these actions is *short-term memory*, which some theorists (but not all) believe depends on a kind of neural functioning distinct from the rest of memory. In any case, it is not a kind of remembering that accumulates; one remembers the necessary thing or sequence for a moment, uses it, and then forgets it. This is, then, a rather special kind of remembering, and its importance for education seems to be distinctly limited.

Remembering that mediates learning, and that may take place over times varying from a few minutes to several weeks, depending on the length of the "lesson," "topic," or "problem," is evidently of great importance to education. As an estimate, one may say that remembering for mediation defines the largest portion of what is remembered of the learning that takes place in schools. In other words, the major reason for learning most of the facts and generalizations taught in school is for the purpose of *mediating further learning*. As to what this further learning is, which is mediated, it is composed of (1) intellectual skills (discriminating, classifying, rule using, strategies of information processing, and so on) and (2) categories of verbalizable information.

Remembering for mediation itself consists in the retrieval of exactly these two kinds of entities: intellectual skills and categories of verbalizable information. The former must be reinstated, whereas the latter may be only partly recalled and partly looked up. The problem of curriculum planning, as well as lesson planning, then, becomes one of identifying what intellectual skills are needed to mediate the learning, and also what verbalizable information is needed to mediate the learning. The latter category poses an intriguing problem—which of this verbal information is mainly useful for the lesson only (that is, to mediate the learning) and which needs to be remembered for a time longer than the lesson?

Many components of lifetime retention are rather easy to identify. First, the adult individual needs to recall many kinds of verbal information. Primarily, he needs ready access to a store of meaningful words, phrases, and other verbal passages that enable him to communicate his thoughts to other people and to organize them for his own continuing learning. Beyond this "working" vocabulary, there are some interesting questions about how much "specialized" information he needs to be able to recall. Naturally enough, the requirements will be greater in his "areas of specialization." If he is a cook, he will need to recall recipes; if he is a carpenter, varieties and grades of lumber and nails; if he is a chemist, the properties of many chemical compounds. Outside of such areas, however, it would seem that the recall of a large amount of detailed information is not highly important to the individual in pursuing his life goals as an educated adult. Instead, he needs to recall those broad categories of information that will organize many details most efficiently and that will serve as clues for "how to look it up."

The other major category of lifetime retention appears to be freer of any ambiguity: a great variety of intellectual skills must be learned, retained, and reinstated for continuing learning and problem solving. It is true that some specialized skills of this sort may be learned and forgotten; for example, many adults forget how to find a square root using pencil and paper. But the vast majority of them are likely to be continuously useful for many, many years and for many, many purposes. Accordingly, one hesitates to identify intellectual skills that are only temporarily useful (that is, for the mediation of particular learning). One is more likely to think that intellectual skills may be useful at any time during the lifetime of an individual.

Given these two categories of what is remembered for lifetime retention, how can a balance be achieved between them? Obviously, both are important. Intellectual skills are likely to be useful at any time. Verbalizable information is also likely to be useful at any time, but only some of it, since the rest can be looked up and retained for a short period. Is it harmful to require an individual to retain, in the lifetime sense, more factual information than he needs? A definite answer cannot presently be given to this question. But it is clear at the outset that asking him to retain more verbal information than he needs may waste valuable "learning time." Such learning time could more profitably be devoted to the learning, storing, and retrieval of intellectual skills.

GENERAL REFERENCES

Stages of Learning

Gibson, E. J. *Principles of perceptual learning and development.* New York: Appleton-Century-Crofts, 1969.

Hebb, D. O. *A textbook of psychology,* 2d ed. Philadelphia: Saunders, 1966.

John, E. R. *Mechanisms of memory.* New York: Academic Press, 1967.

Varieties of Remembering

Adams, J. A. *Human memory.* New York: McGraw-Hill, 1967.

Ausubel, D. P. *Educational psychology: A cognitive view.* New York: Holt, Rinehart and Winston, 1968.

Deese, J., and Hulse, S. H. *The psychology of learning.* New York: McGraw-Hill, 1967.

4 | Basic Forms of Learning

The previous chapter considered some of the characteristics of learning and remembering that are *general* and *common* to all kinds of learning. In this chapter, we return to the different varieties of learning to describe the first two of the eight types mentioned in Chapter 2.

Some forms of learning are more basic than others. They are basic in two senses. First, the conditions that control their occurrence are relatively simple to establish. Second, the prerequisite states of the learning organism are more largely a matter of innate neural organization than is the case with other forms of learning. These characteristics apply to signal learning and to stimulus-response learning, the two varieties to be described in this chapter. For each of these types, the intention is to discuss the conditions that lead to their occurrence, the nature of the changes that take place in learning, and some of the other characteristics they possess. A number of kinds of life situations in which such learning may naturally occur will also be pointed out.

SIGNAL LEARNING (TYPE 1)

There is a wide acquaintance with signal learning, whether in common domestic animals or in other human beings. Most people have observed one or more instances of signal learning in household pets; for example, the cat or dog may run to the kitchen when he hears his food dish placed on the floor. The cat may run from the driveway when he hears a car approaching. George Bernard Shaw (1959) thought that these things were completely obvious and could not see why Pavlov had to "discover" them. Of course, in a real sense, Pavlov did not discover them; but like the true scientist that he was, he attempted to measure them under carefully controlled conditions. In so doing, he gave us an account of these conditions and characteristics of signal learning that is as valuable today as it ever was.

The Phenomenon of Signal Learning

The learning of Pavlov's dog to salivate in response to a signaling buzzer is, in basic outline, a familiar example to most educated adults. Although it is a good example, it will not be used here. Instead, a signal learning situation is chosen that has been extensively studied in human beings, namely, the eyeblink. There are many precise data on the learning of this sort of connection, and these results are particularly instructive concerning the question of what is learned.

When a small puff of air is delivered to the cornea of a person's eye, the eye blinks rapidly. This is the connection Pavlov called the *unconditioned reflex*, meaning that it is there to begin with, not conditional on any previous learning. Now if a click is sounded about a half second before the puff of air reaches the cornea, we have one of the important conditions for the establishment of a learned connection. The click (or other "neutral" stimulus) is called the *conditioned stimulus* (the "signal"). When this sequence of events—click-puff of air—is repeated a few times, it is usually possible to demonstrate the existence of a newly learned connection, namely,

$$S \underset{\text{click}}{\rule{2cm}{0.4pt}} R_{\text{blink}}$$

This is done by presenting the click by itself, without the puff of air, and noting that the blink response occurs.

It is generally thought to be of considerable significance that the conditioned blink is *not* the same as the unconditioned blink. These two blink responses have many times been shown to be different in carefully controlled experiments. The unconditioned blink is a more rapid response; it occurs in 0.05 to 0.10 second, whereas the signaled blink takes 0.25 to 0.50 second. With suitable methods of measurement, the two are clearly distinguishable as responses. Thus it appears that what is learned is what may be called an *anticipatory blink* to a signal. Such a blink does not avoid the puff of air; if it did, this would be an instance of type 2 learning, which we shall discuss next. But the learned blink anticipates the puff of air; it signals puff-of-air-to-come.

How often does the pairing of signal and unconditioned stimulus have to be repeated in order for a conditioned response to be established? Although there is no single answer to this question, the evidence suggests that a number of repetitions must be used in order to establish a stable response, at least for the eyeblink. Figure 2 shows the form of curves of learning obtained for three groups of subjects differing with respect to "ease of conditioning." These graphs show the frequency of occurrence of the learned response following various numbers of trials in which the pairing of stimuli was made to occur. Other instances have been reported, however, of signal learning taking place much more rapidly than this, depending particularly on the strength of the unconditioned stimulus. Signal-response connections have been shown to occur in a single trial when

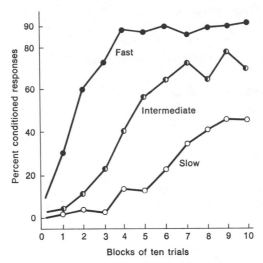

FIGURE 2. Learning curves showing the increase in frequency of conditioned eyeblinks in successive blocks of trials, for groups of subjects whose rate of conditioning was found to be slow, intermediate, and fast. (Data of K. W. Spence, *Behavior theory and conditioning.* New Haven, Conn.: Yale University Press, 1956.)

the signal accompanies a stimulus arousing a strong emotion. This was the case, for example, when the child Albert learned to fear a rabbit when a sudden loud sound (produced by striking a metal bar) was made behind his head at the time he was reaching toward the rabbit (Watson and Rayner, 1920). Following this single event, the child showed fear whenever the rabbit was brought near to him.

Conditions of Learning

With the help of these examples, it should not be difficult to state the conditions necessary for signal learning to occur. Evidently, one must deal with conditions that need to be present *within the learner,* as well as with those conditions that can be manipulated *in the learning situation.*

Conditions within the Learner   In order for signal learning
to occur, there must be a natural reflex, typically a reflexive
emotional response (startle, fear, anger, pleasure), on the
part of the learner. It must be clear that an *unconditioned
stimulus* can evoke such an *unconditioned response*. Further
than this, there is much evidence to indicate that there are
marked individual differences in the rapidity with which
people acquire signal-response connections. Such differences
are not markedly related to intelligence (or facility for
academic learning). But they *are* significantly related to
the level of *anxiety* with which the individual typically faces
life's problems and decisions. Many studies have shown
that people who tend to be anxious acquire conditioned
responses more rapidly than do nonanxious people (Taylor,
1951).

Conditions in the Learning Situation   The conditions for
signal learning that can be externally controlled are those
of *contiguity* and *repetition*.

1. The signaling stimulus and the unconditioned stimulus must be presented in close proximity to each other, in
the order named. These necessary time relationships have
been tested in a variety of situations involving many kinds
of signals and responses. Variations have been found to be
very small ones, so that it is reasonable to think that they
reflect some stable characteristic of nervous system functioning. Learning occurs dependably when the conditioned
stimulus precedes the unconditioned by an interval between
0 and 1.5 seconds, and most readily when the interval is
about 0.5 second. Although conditioning has occurred with
other timings, such instances may not be true examples of
signal learning.

2. As Figure 2 shows, repetition of the paired stimuli is
also necessary. The amount required, however, may vary
considerably depending on the response involved, and on
the intensity with which it is evoked (that is, the intensity

of the unconditioned stimulus). But it seems quite unreasonable to suppose from present evidence that signal learning is an all-or-nothing occurrence. Rather, the connection appears to increase in strength (or dependability of occurrence) as the repetitions of paired stimuli increase in number.

Thus the conditions of signal learning are relatively simple to describe and rather readily controlled. Besides the eyeblink used in our example, conditioned responses have been established for many varieties of behavior in the human being, including salivation, changes in skin resistance, respiration changes, nausea, hand withdrawal, and others. Early investigators attempted to establish signal learning with the use of certain simple reflexes like the knee jerk and the pupillary reflex, but these have generally been found to be extremely difficult to condition. Diffuse emotional responses, or components of them, are, in contrast, rather easy to condition. A response falling in this category, for example, is the "galvanic skin reflex," which has been used frequently for the study of signal learning. When an electric shock is applied, say, to the individual's hand, physiological processes are set in motion that alter the resistance of the skin to the passage of a weak electric current. This change in resistance can be easily and rather precisely measured by means of simple electrodes attached to the skin and connected with a circuit including a galvanometer. Thus a means is provided for measuring the acquisition of a signal connection. In practice, the subject is seated in a chair and the electrodes are attached. Then the skin resistance (galvanic skin reflex, or GSR) is noted on the galvanometer until a fairly steady base reading is obtained. Signal learning then begins by the presentation of, say, a tone signal followed about half a second later by the shock, evoking the change in skin resistance. These events are repeated at suitable intervals, and the presence of the newly acquired signal connection is detected by a "trial" of the signal tone not paired with shock. The conditioned response can usually be established in such circumstances after only a few repetitions.

Some Other Phenomena of Signal Learning

There are some other events that occur in signal learning situations which have great importance for an understanding of this form of behavior modification, as well as of other more complex forms which depend upon it. For one thing, there is the phenomenon of *extinction*, a kind of unlearning, that results in the disappearance of the previously learned connection. There is also *stimulus generalization*, the occurrence of responses to stimuli that are similar to the signal used to bring about learning. Generalization itself may be reduced in breadth so that a much narrower range of stimuli will evoke the response, and this set of events is given the name of *discrimination*.

Extinction   Suppose that a signal response of blinking the eye to the sound of a bell has been reliably established. How may it be eliminated? The most dependable way to bring this about is by repeated presentation, at suitable intervals, of the signal (the bell) *without* the unconditioned stimulus (the puff of air). When these conditions are put into effect, the signal connection undergoes a progressive weakening; in other words, it appears less and less dependably until it fails to occur at all. The rate at which extinction occurs is illustrated in Figure 3. After an initial period of extinction, upon presentation of the signal, the conditioned response may appear again after an interval. Pavlov called this *spontaneous recovery*. However, the connection is obviously weaker, and may be re-extinguished in a few trials in which the signal is presented alone. Ultimately, under the extinction procedure the newly learned connection does disappear completely.

Although the conditions for bringing about extinction are

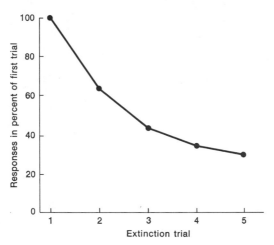

FIGURE 3. A typical curve of extinction for the conditioned galvanic skin response (GSR) showing the decrease in percent of response in five extinction trials that followed immediately after the signal learning. (Data of C. I. Hovland, "Inhibition of reinforcement" and phenomena of experimental extinction. *Proc. Nat. Acad. Sci.*, 1936, **22**, 430–433.)

quite straightforward, it is nevertheless a puzzling phenomenon to explain. There are many different theories of extinction (Kimble, 1961, pp. 281–327). Perhaps the best known are, briefly, (1) that an active process of *inhibition,* generated by the act of responding, depresses the strength of the learned response; and (2) that extinction is mainly a matter of learning other connections that *interfere* with the initially learned one. Despite the theoretical differences that these and other theories imply, there is general agreement concerning the conditions under which extinction of signal learning occurs, as well as on its importance as a basic behavioral event.

Stimulus Generalization   The conditioned response, once established, may be elicited by signals other than the one used to establish it. The closer the physical resemblance between these other signals and the original one, the stronger the response obtained. Suppose that a galvanic skin response

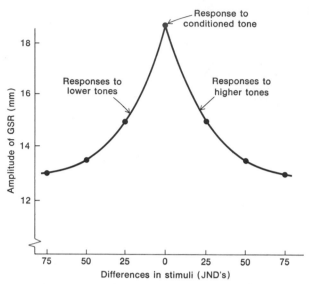

FIGURE 4. The stimulus generalization gradient obtained for a conditioned GSR to a tone of 1000 cycles. Decreasing amplitude of response was found as the stimulus tones used to "test" the responses were made decreasingly similar to the original tone. (Data of C. I. Hovland, The generalization of conditioned responses. I. The sensory generalization of conditioned responses with varying frequencies of tone. *J. gen. Psychol.*, 1937, **17,** 125–148.)

has been conditioned to a tone signal of 1000 cycles per second. It may then also be shown to occur, in somewhat reduced strength, to a tone of 1025 cycles or to a tone of 975 cycles. The signal connection, in other words, is not a highly precise one. *Generalization* may be shown to other stimuli that resemble the original stimulus, as measured along some physical dimension. Hovland (1937) obtained the results shown in Figure 4 when he measured the strength of the GSR to stimulus tones differing from the original signal by increasing amounts of "just noticeable difference" (JND). Evidently, the *gradient of generalization,* as curves like this are called, drops off sharply at first and then more gradually as the amount of resemblance between the original stimulus and the "test" stimulus grows less.

Discrimination   If the connection acquired to a signaling stimulus is somewhat imprecise, as the phenomenon of stimulus generalization implies, its precision may nevertheless be increased. One simply has to make use of the two sets of conditions for learning and for extinction, applied differentially in the presence of the two signals, in order to bring about such an increased precision. Suppose that a response has been conditioned to a tone of 1000 cycles, and exhibits generalization to a tone of 950 cycles. Now, on alternate occasions, the 1000-cycle stimulus is paired with the unconditioned stimulus, whereas the 950-cycle stimulus is presented alone. The latter connection will, of course, undergo extinction, whereas the former will increase its strength as a conditioned response. When this happens, it is said that a *discrimination* has been established. Obviously, this means that the new stimulus generalization gradient surrounding the 1000-cycle tone falls away more sharply than was originally the case.

Naturally, there is a limit to the fineness of discrimination that may be established by means of the contrasting-extinction procedure. This limit is determined by the sensory discrimination capacity of the organism doing the learning. The technique of conditioning and extinction has often been used to determine the discrimination capacity of animals— the limits of color discrimination in the rabbit or the pigeon, for example—since verbal responses are unavailable.

Forgetting   Another important characteristic of signal learning is its great resistance to forgetting. There appear to be few systematic data tracing the course of forgetting of conditioned responses over an extended interval. Most studies have shown some decrement in the learned connection following an interval of disuse. However, there are several observations that indicate remarkable retention over periods of months and years. For example, Hilgard and Humphreys (1938) found that a conditioned eyeblink could be readily elicited after a period of nineteen months.

The procedure for measuring forgetting, of course, should

be carefully distinguished from that used for extinction. In the former case, the learned connection is not tested over the interval concerned, that is, the signal is not presented. In the latter, presentation of the signal alone during a number of trials brings about a disappearance of the learned connection. It is this particular contrast between the two phenomena that emphasizes the active nature of the process of extinction.

STIMULUS-RESPONSE LEARNING (TYPE 2)

Another fundamental kind of learning, simple to observe and widespread in its occurrence, is here called *stimulus-response learning*. Thorndike called it *trial-and-error learning,* but this is probably not a good descriptive name. It is also called *operant learning,* notably by Skinner (1938). Many writers call it *instrumental learning* (Kimble, 1961), and this name has two advantages: (1) it emphasizes the precise skilled nature of the responses involved, as in "using instruments" and (2) it implies that the learned connection is instrumental in satisfying some motive. The phrase "stimulus-response learning" is chosen to emphasize two other characteristics: (1) such learning concerns a *single* connection between a stimulus and a response, not multiple or chained connections, which will be dealt with later; and (2) the stimulus and the response appear to become integrally bound together in such learning, in a way that does not happen with signal learning. A bell really never has anything to do with eyeblinking, except as a signal for it. But because of the occurrence of stimulus-response learning, a colored block may become for a child a thing-to-be-picked-up.

It is difficult indeed to find an example of human learning that might represent stimulus-response learning in relatively pure form. Many instances that seem at first glance to be suitable examples of this class turn out on closer inspection to represent the somewhat more complex forms of chaining or verbal association. The reason for this is not far to seek: it is simply that human beings rapidly acquire a background of prerequisite learning which enters into the subsequent acquisition of these more complex varieties. No doubt this is the primary reason why animals such as white rats and pigeons have been so extensively used to study the characteristics of stimulus-response learning. One can assume a less extensive repertoire of previous learning for these animals than is the case with human beings.

This difficulty makes it necessary to turn for an example to the behavior of the very young human infant. Although the amount of systematic experimental evidence is very limited for infant learning, it can nevertheless be assumed with some degree of safety that not much previous learning has occurred. Accordingly, the example to be considered here is the infant's learned response of holding the nursing bottle in the proper position for feeding. Under what conditions does a child learn to perform this act?

At first, of course, there is the stage at which this behavior has not been learned at all. The parent must hold the bottle tilted at the proper angle in order for feeding to be possible. During the course of feeding, however, the infant will often grasp the bottle in his hands, somewhat unsystematically to be sure. Now suppose the parent begins to release his own hold on the bottle, so that greater pressure is exerted against the child's own hands. So long as the child's hands exert a sufficiently firm grasp in a sufficiently raised position, the feeding continues. Should this muscular tension be relaxed somewhat, a point will be reached in the tilt angle of the bottle where no formula reaches the mouth. Then perhaps the parent pushes the bottle upward into position again, and feeding is restored. By gradually "helping" the child hold the bottle properly, and gradually removing the help so that the child's own responses are appropriate, the stimulus-response connection becomes established. Eventually the child, once given the bottle, can reinstate the necessary response. He has then "learned to hold his bottle."

This learning event appears to be not so much a "trial-

and-error" procedure as it does a "successive approximation" procedure. The learning that occurs here, as Skinner says, is a matter of *shaping.* A set of stimuli, including the sight and feel of the bottle as well as the proprioceptive stimuli from the child's arm and hand muscles, becomes connected with a correct response of holding the bottle in a position from which the formula can be sucked into the mouth. At the same time, a slightly different set of stimuli, involving a slightly different "feel" (when the bottle is lower), results in no food in the mouth. Thus the learning is really a matter of *discrimination* of correct and incorrect stimulation; of that set of stimuli which produces reward (reinforcement) and that set of stimuli which does not. It is equally true to say that the response of holding the bottle correctly becomes progressively *differentiated,* since the muscles involved in making this response actually provide part of the stimulation which is "correct" or "incorrect."

This form of learning is therefore viewed as a gradual process of discrimination of correct from incorrect stimuli. Because some of the important stimuli are internal (proprioceptive, from the muscles), we represent this form of learning as follows:

$$Ss \rightarrow R$$

The small *s* is understood in this paradigm to stand for internal stimuli arising from kinesthesis. The arrow is used to imply the discriminative nature of what is taking place, in contrast to signal learning.

In Skinner's view, the learning we have described is an *operant.* A *discriminated operant,* in contrast, might be established if we had the infant learn to hold the bottle correctly when an additional stimulus (say, a bright light) was presented, but not to hold it correctly when this light was *not* presented. But there appears to be no formal difference between this situation and the one already described, except that *an additional external stimulus becomes a part of the total stimulation.* Any such stimulus may, of course, be made a part of the discriminative task, if one wishes, or alternatively, a stimulus (such as the sight of the bottle) might be removed from the situation. But these changes do not affect the nature of the learning that takes place in any fundamental sense. Thus stimulus-response ($Ss \rightarrow R$) learning, as the term is employed here, is equivalent to "discriminated operant learning."

How rapidly does $Ss \rightarrow R$ learning take place? Is it really a gradual process? The answer depends on how "easy" the required discrimination is. For Thorndike's animals, some forms of responses required to get out of the "puzzle box" were relatively easy, whereas others were relatively difficult. What is meant by "easy" and "difficult" in this case probably has something to do with the animal's natural exploratory behavior, that is, the kind of behavior it exhibits that is not learned. Figure 5, for example, compares the behavior of one of Thorndike's cats in problem box D, which could be

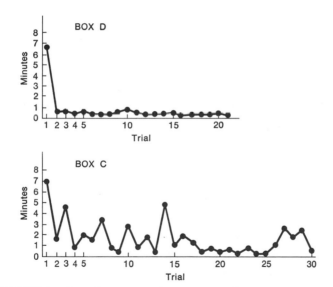

FIGURE 5. Learning curves from one of Thorndike's cats escaping from two different problem boxes. Box D was opened by pulling a string; box C, by turning a button. (E. L. Thorndike, Animal intelligence: An experimental study of the associative processes in animals. *Psychol. Rev. Monogr. Suppl.,* 1898, **2,** No. 4 [Whole No. 81].)

opened by pulling on a string hanging to the right of the door, and in box C, which could be opened by turning a "button" from vertical to horizontal position. Obviously, the discrimination required for D was an easier one, and consequently the learning is very rapid. In the case of C, in contrast, the $Ss \rightarrow R$ appears to be gradually established (or "shaped").

Conditions of Stimulus-Response Learning

It is time now to consider more systematically the nature of the conditions necessary for $Ss \rightarrow R$ learning. As before, it is necessary to take into account those conditions within the learner and those in the learning situation.

Conditions within the Learner   First of all, it is evident that there must be a terminating (or consummatory) act which provides satisfaction (or *reinforcement*). In the example given here, it is necessary that the infant suck on the nipple and thereby fill his mouth with food. This produces what Thorndike called a "satisfying state of affairs." (Presumably, some aspects of this particular sucking behavior may themselves have been previously learned, but this is not important for the illustration. Sucking occurs immediately after birth, and for present purposes may be assumed to be innately determined.)

However, it seems clear that a single $Ss \rightarrow R$ may be established when the terminal reinforcing act does not immediately follow the response, as in the sucking example, but instead is more remote. This is the more usual case when one is dealing with human behavior. For example, a correctly performed $Ss \rightarrow R$ may be followed by a word of praise, "Good!" which is in turn connected with a response that ultimately provides a physical satisfaction. Thus, in order for this condition to be met it is not necessary that the terminating act be an innate one. It is simply necessary for it to be a reinforcing one, to provide satisfaction. For learning to occur, one needs to ensure that there is such a response, terminating in reinforcement, which can be performed by the learner.

Conditions of the Learning Situation　　Turning to the conditions outside the learner, we see that the terminating response must actually result in *reinforcement*. That is, the terminal act must be a satisfying one to the learner. Some theorists hold that "satisfying" simply means something that the learner already does vigorously, whereas others maintain that the act must lead to a reward (such as food, praise, or relief of pain). It is not possible here to consider this matter of the essential nature of reinforcement, as discussed, for example, by Kimble (1961) and Hilgard and Bower (1966). But the fact of reinforcement, which makes the learning of any new $Ss \rightarrow R$ connection dependent upon the directly following occurrence of a "satisfying" act, is widely accepted. In the example of the infant and his bottle, the $Ss \rightarrow R$ learning will not occur if the bottle is empty, and the sucking and swallowing of liquid does not occur (unless, of course, some other source of satisfaction is provided). Modern learning theorists call this condition the empirical law of effect, and its validity is supported by a vast amount of experimental evidence.

Contiguity has an important part to play in the establishment of an $Ss \rightarrow R$ connection. The shorter the time elapsing between the occurrence of the learned response and the occurrence of reinforcement, the more rapidly will learning take place. If the infant had to wait, say, five seconds between the time he tilted the bottle correctly and the time food arrived in his mouth, it would be more difficult for him to learn than is the case when this interval is only a second. This relationship between *ease of learning* and *delay of reinforcement* is well established in laboratory studies of $Ss \rightarrow R$ learning (Kimble, 1961, pp. 140–156).

Repetition of the stimulus situation is also a necessary condition for the occurrence of stimulus-response learning. As Thorndike's findings show (Figure 5), the amount of repetition needed may vary from a single trial to many, depending on the difficulty of the discriminations involved, and the degree to which they conform with responding that is either innately determined or previously learned. The function served by repetition, therefore, appears to be one of *selection* of stimuli to be discriminated, as a number of learning theorists, notably Estes (1959), assume. In successive repetitions of the learning situation, particular samples of the total stimulus situation (including, of course, its kinesthetic components) are associated with particular responses. Some of these are more successful than others in producing reinforcement; the successful ones therefore become selected and the unsuccessful ones drop out of the picture. The correct behavior is gradually *shaped* by means of this selective process. According to this conception, a total learned connection is really composed of a number of individual $Ss \rightarrow R$'s, and learning is a matter of gradual recruitment of the "bundle" of individual connections that lead to reinforcement, rather than to a strengthening of each individual one. This view of $Ss \rightarrow R$ learning is similar to that originally enunciated by Guthrie (1935).

In general, then, if suitable conditions for reinforcement are present both within and outside the learner, the establishment of stimulus-response learning becomes primarily a matter of arranging conditions for the desired *stimulus discrimination* to occur most readily. Anything that is done to make the selection of a correct stimulus sample easier than it would otherwise be will speed up the learning, and thereby decrease the number of repetitions required. If one is interested in *learning efficiency* for $Ss \rightarrow R$ learning, he will seek to arrange the stimulus situation so as to reduce the amount of repetition required for learning. When a dog is learning to raise his paw to the stimulus "Shake hands!" the discrimination of stimuli (particularly those from his muscles) is made easier when his paw is held in position at the time the command is given. Similarly, the infant's learning to hold the bottle correctly is speeded by "help" from his parent in positioning his arms and hands. The connection *can* be learned without such help, but it will require more repetitions of the situation in order for the correct set of stimuli to be selected.

If a learning task puts its emphasis on external stimuli, rather than on proprioceptive ones, the same principle of ease of discrimination applies. Should the external stimuli be faint, or indistinguishable from background stimulation, the acquiring of an *Ss* → *R* connection will be accordingly difficult and require many repetitions. If the stimuli are vivid and distinct, learning will be rapid. A dog whistle that emits a high-frequency tone may not even be heard by human beings; but to the dog, this tone constitutes an easily discriminated stimulus, which sets off the response that begins his return to home and supper.

Stimulus-response learning has been extensively studied in animals like white rats, pigeons, monkeys, and others. Qnantities of objective data have been published concerning the detailed effects of variations in the basic conditions of type 2 learning on the rapidity of the learning event. For example, Ferster and Skinner (1957) have collected a large amount of evidencc about the effects of variations in "schedules of reinforcement" on the learning and execution of *Ss* → *R* connections. The kinds of responses that have been studied by various investigators are of great variety; some of the best known are the traversing of mazes and runways, the pressing of levers, and (in pigeons and other birds) the pecking of keys or discs. Such a vast amount of work on animal learning should not blind us to the fact that *Ss* → *R* learning can also generate essential capabilities in human beings.

Other Phenomena of Stimulus-Response Learning

Extinction   Just as there is a phenomcnon of "unlearning" for signal learning, there is a comparable event in *Ss* → *R* learning, also called *extinction*. In both cases, these events result in the disappearance of a previously learned connection, and it is understandable on these grounds that the two forms of unlearning should be given the same name. But the conditions under which they occur are *not* the same, and this sometimes leads to confusion. It can be argued, of course, that the existence of unlearning in both types 1 and 2 learning increases the likelihood that these forms are really a single one, but this argument does not seem a valid one in view of the important differences between them.

Extinction of a learned $Ss \rightarrow R$ occurs when the reinforcement that follows the learned response is omitted. Under these circumstances, the connection gradually decreases its likelihood of occurrence when the stimulus situation is presented, until it dies away altogether. It may be noted that extinction is not a matter of omitting an unconditioned stimulus (like a puff of air to the cornea, in type 1 learning), but is rather the removal of the reinforcing state of affairs. The latter can be done in various ways. For example, extinction of the infant's $Ss \rightarrow R$ connection of holding the bottle may be brought about, as has been said, by omitting the milk. It may also be accomplished by making sure that the infant is not hungry when the bottle is presented to him (as might happen, for example, if he were fed by the parent before being allowed to hold the bottle). Under such circumstances, little or no reinforcement would follow the learned response of bottle holding, and it would undergo extinction.

Presumably, extinction is itself directly involved in the establishment of a total stimulus-response connection, if one assumes that this is really a matter of selecting a correct "bundle" of individual $Ss \rightarrow R$'s from those that are incorrect. In such circumstances, the incorrect $Ss \rightarrow R$'s drop out, after having occurred once, because of extinction. They disappear because they have in fact been unsuccessful in bringing about reinforcement. Those that are reinforced, on the other hand, become selected and remain to appear on the next repetition of the situation.

Generalization   The generalization of the learned connection to stimuli that resemble the set used in learning is another characteristic that type 2 learning holds in common with type 1. In this case, however, the phenomenon is probably exactly the same one, and not merely an analogous event. Guttman and Kalish (1956) established $Ss \rightarrow R$ learning in which pigeons pecked at a transparent plate transmitting light of a given color. Then the birds were tested with this same color and a range of other colors differing in wavelength from the original color by varying amounts. As expected, the frequency with which pecking occurred to a color decreased regularly as the physical resemblance between it and the original hue decreased. The results showing the gradient of generalization obtained are illustrated in Figure 6.

The connection that is learned, then, has a range of precision relative to the stimulus that is reflected in the gradient of stimulus generalization. How precise it is, and how narrow this gradient is, will depend on the task set for the learner. If one wants an $Ss \rightarrow R$ to be very precise (to either

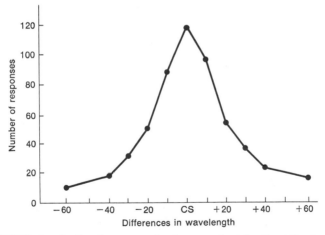

FIGURE 6. A stimulus generalization gradient for the stimulus-response connection of pigeons pecking at a plate transmitting colored light. As the color of the test stimulus was altered in wavelength, the frequency of responding decreased. (Data of N. Guttman and H. I. Kalish, Discriminability and stimulus generalization. *J. exp. Psychol.,* 1956, **51,** 79–88.)

internal or external stimuli, or both), reinforcement must be given accordingly, and considerable repetition may be needed. If the precision desired is not very great, the gradient of generalization will be broader, but the connection may be more rapidly established.

Discrimination   As the previous discussion has indicated, stimulus-response learning involves the establishment of discrimination. The occurrence of learning is conceived to be the selection of stimuli that are successful in bringing about reinforcement, and the rejection (through extinction) of those that are not.

It can readily be shown that differential reinforcement is necessary for establishing the discrimination of stimuli in $Ss \rightarrow R$ learning. This was the result of an experiment by Jenkins and Harrison (1960), who trained pigeons to peck at a key in the presence of a tone of 1000 cycles. Under one set of conditions, this tone was continuously present during learning trials, and the pigeons learned to peck at the key with approximately equal frequency when tested with various tones in the range from 300 to 3500 cycles, and also when the tone was entirely absent. In other words, the discrimination learned under these conditions did not include the tone. In another set of conditions, however, the 1000-cycle tone was made a to-be-discriminated stimulus; that is, reinforcement was given for pecking the key when the tone was present but not when it was absent. The pigeons soon acquired the $Ss \rightarrow R$ demanded of them: they learned to peck when the tone was present, but not when it was absent. A typical gradient of generalization appeared, decreasing in amount as the testing tone departed increasingly from 1000 cycles. Differential reinforcment for the 1000-cycle tone vs. no tone brought about the result that this particular tone became an essential part of the stimulus situation controlling the key-pecking response. A similar result could have been obtained, presumably, with almost any other stimulus, whether tone, light, or whatever. Thus it may be seen that discrimination is the basic event in $Ss \rightarrow R$ learning. It occurs whether one deliberately arranges for it or not, and its precision depends on which particular stimuli are differentially reinforced.

Retention Type 2 learning appears to be quite resistant to forgetting. Skinner (1950) reports the retention of a pecking response in pigeons after four years. It is a common experience that "tricks" taught to animals, such as shaking hands or "playing dead" are remembered for many years, sometimes without opportunity for practice. Similarly, the pronunciation of words in a foreign language, if learned correctly in the beginning, tends to be retained for many year without appreciable loss. Some writers have suggested that the retention of such connections, like the retention of more complex motor skills, is as good as it is because they are relatively isolated acts having few activities to exhibit *interference* with them, in contrast with verbal associations, which have many. However, it is true that when single $Ss \rightarrow R$'s are put together with a larger set that *may* interfere with them, considerable forgetting may occur (Leavitt and Schlosberg, 1944).

The Basic Forms of Learning
in Everyday Life

The relatively widespread occurrence of types 1 and 2 learning makes these varieties important to a general understanding of human behavior. However, responding to signals and executing simple motor acts are obviously no more than a small portion of the capabilities that human beings can and do learn. To be examined next are some examples of the variety taken by these forms of learning in everyday life and in the school.

Some Examples of Signal Learning

Type 1 learning occurs in the lives of all of us. Oftentimes it happens because of environmental accidents rather than as a result of planning by parents or teachers. We learn to respond to many kinds of signals, like automobile horns, the bells of alarm clocks, and certain ejaculatory utterances of other people. Generally speaking, we acquire a connection exhibiting a diffuse, imprecise, "emotional" kind of response to such signals, because they are repeated together with other stimuli (unconditioned stimuli) that generate these responses initially and innately.

A number of kinds of children's specific fears are doubtless acquired by means of signal learning. Children may avoid certain locations, animals, or even people, because there has been a pairing (whether adventitious or otherwise) of the stimuli they present with some unconditioned stimulus like a frightening noise. It seems likely that pleasant emotions can also be aroused in essentially the same way, because of previous pairings with particular persons or situations. Possibly the favorite teddy bear or blanket may become a signal for pleasant feelings for the young child, just as may particular scenes or melodies at a somewhat later stage of the individual's development.

Signal learning is sometimes used by teachers to establish a state of alertness on the part of their pupils. A teacher may deliberately use a clap of the hands, for example, as a signal for "paying attention." Such learning might be accomplished initially by making the hand clap a fairly loud and startling stimulus. After a few repetitions, the teacher finds it possible to generate a similar state of alertness by means of a much gentler hand clap. This, of course, is an example of stimulus generalization.

Some Examples of Stimulus-Response Learning

Type 2 learning has considerable usefulness. It is a kind of learning that characterizes many of the activities displayed by young children, including such things as reaching and grasping for toys or other objects, smiling at the proper people, positioning the body and limbs, and vocalizing particular utterances. As the child acquires a larger and larger repertory of these somewhat isolated $Ss \rightarrow R$'s, they begin to form themselves into longer *chains,* and accordingly it becomes increasingly difficult to isolate "pure" examples of this kind of learning. With adults, finding examples of this kind of learning by itself is a practically impossible task.

Stimulus-response learning is undoubtedly the main variety involved in the initial learning of words by children. An initial utterance like "nha-nha," overheard by a parent, may be "shaped" into a connection that yields the response "ma-ma" by suitable use of the procedure of differential reinforcement. A part of this procedure involves getting the child to respond to the proper external stimulus, which may be "ma-ma" spoken by the parent. Another part requires the discrimination of kinesthetic responses from the child's own vocal and facial muscles. Naturally, deaf children have a difficult time making the required discriminations and so learning the desired $Ss \rightarrow R$. As is well known, language training for deaf children typically takes the form of providing stimuli that such children *can* discriminate. The teacher may, for example, position the child's mouth and tongue so that something approaching the proper articulation will emerge. In addition, the auditory cues available to normal children may be replaced by visual ones, displayed on an oscilloscope. Under such circumstances, it becomes possible for a deaf child to acquire the $Ss \rightarrow R$'s, based on suitably precise discriminations, which produce understandable speech.

Although not a completely pure example, adult learning of the pronunciation of unfamiliar foreign words can also be considered an instance of stimulus-response learning. A German word like *grüss* (as in *grüss Gott*), for example, may be quite unfamiliar to an English-speaking adult because of the pronunciation of the umlaut. In order for him to acquire an $Ss \rightarrow R$ that permits correct pronunciation, discrimination must take place of both aspects of stimulation, external and internal (kinesthetic). The former is provided by discriminating the sound of the word from similar-sounding words, like "groos" and "grease." The latter requires that he imitate the sound of the word, that is, practice saying it, and thus discriminate the "feel" of the word from that of other, incorrect utterances. Several repetitions may be required, involving differential reinforcement, in order for the correct pronunciation of the word to be properly "shaped."

The proper holding of a pencil by a young child is an example of one kind of educational application exhibited by stimulus-response learning. Initially, the pencil may be placed in a correct position in the child's hand by the teacher or parent. This procedure will do for the first two trials or so. But the child must have additional trials in which he himself tries to hold the pencil correctly in writing. Again, the reason for these "trials" is that the proper tactual and kinesthetic stimuli will be selected to be connected with holding the pencil correctly, while others that are incorrect will suffer extinction. With a number of reinforced repetitions, the correct response becomes more and more likely, which is to say that a suitable set of stimuli has been discriminated more and more precisely.

If one were to attempt a generalization, one might reasonably conclude that $Ss \rightarrow R$ learning is almost always involved in the learning of *voluntary motor acts,* including speech utterances. Simple learned acts of the motor sort may be readily identified in young children, and perhaps come as close as any human behavior does to being pure cases of stimulus-response learning.

Reinforcement and the Learning of Receptive Behaviors

Since much of school learning requires verbal communication directed toward the learner, one of the important events in instruction is the adoption by the learner of a *receptivity set* toward such communications. While adult learners normally adopt a set for receptivity as a matter of course, this cannot be said to be true of many children. Accordingly, a good deal of the efforts of a kindergarten or prekindergarten teacher may well be devoted to guiding the learning of receptive behaviors in children. The child must learn to attend to verbal stimuli, to respond to verbal requests, to follow verbal directions. It is of considerable importance that the learning of various receptive behaviors may be usefully conceived as one class of $Ss \rightarrow R$ learning, to which the principle of reinforcement may be applied with particular effectiveness. A receptive set may be considered a unitary capability learned under the same conditions as a much more specific act, even though the effects of such learning are quite general, since they bring about a kind of behavior that precedes the learning of many other things.

The conditions that pertain to the learning of receptive behaviors are those of $Ss \rightarrow R$ learning. In particular, they involve a proper selection of the conditions of reinforcement. According to Skinner (1968, pp. 145–168), they require suitable arrangement of the *contingencies of reinforcement*, in such a way that the reinforcement is made *contingent upon* the occurrence of the behavior to be learned. In oversimplified terms, this means that learning conditions must be so arranged that some satisfying activity follows closely upon the occurrence of the desired receptive behavior. Many specific techniques may be designed to conform to this general pattern, and thus to bring about changes in the direction of increased receptivity. These techniques are often called, as a class, *contingency management*, and their effects are spoken of as *behavior modification*. Some examples of the application of the reinforcement principle to the learning of receptive behaviors follow.

Increasing the "Span of Attention"   The young child may be highly inattentive and may follow the verbal directions of the teacher for only a few minutes at a time. The suggested conditions for learning are to follow each period of attention by reinforcement (perhaps initially a tangible reward), making sure that such reinforcement is given only for instances of attention which gradually become longer and that it is omitted when the "span" lapses to shorter intervals.

Involvement in Learning Tasks   Children are sometimes unwilling to become involved in learning tasks; that is, they are unreceptive to the verbal communications that are an essential part of the learning situation. Receptive behavior may be established, according to reinforcement principles, by first choosing a task the child likes to do and insuring that appropriate verbal directions precede it. As the application of reinforcement is continued, the teacher may then expand the preferred activity to include another that is not originally a part of what the child likes to do. For example, if the child likes to paste circles on construction paper, when preceded by a suitable communication, this activity may be expanded to include identifying particular sizes or colors before pasting.

Following Directions   The preschool or kindergarten child may not follow directions well or consistently. Again, the idea of reinforcement can provide an important clue for the arrangement of learning conditions. One must begin with a task that is short and requires short directions. Preferably, such a task has a specific starting and ending point. It is a task, in other words, for which the child *can* successfully follow directions. Working from this base, the teacher gradually expands the length of the task and the variety of directions required, making sure at each step that there are definite "checkpoints" along the way and that the terminal part of the task is such that the child experiences both success and satisfaction in its completion.

From these few examples it is obvious that working with reinforcement contingencies to establish receptive behaviors is something that requires a great deal of patience. But even more important, it requires careful attention to the *sequence* of events that reflects the correct contingencies. The reinforcing state of affairs must *follow* the to-be-learned behavior, not precede it. The reinforcement must also have a great deal of *consistency* to it; that is, it must occur when the desired behavior appears and be omitted when the desired behavior does not appear.

Behavior modification using the principle of reinforcement contingency is a powerful tool for the management of learning. Of course, it is not at all confined in its applicability to young children. Liking to read good books, being receptive to music and art, acquiring effective study habits, all may pose problems for students of any age and represent behavior modifications potentially attainable by proper application of reinforcement techniques (see Skinner, 1968, pp. 145–168). It is also notable that such techniques have been of particular help in changing the behavior of "emotionally disturbed" children in classrooms in which routines of reinforcement are carefully planned and executed (Hewett, 1968). Still another important field of application is in the training of mentally retarded children (Orlando and Bijou, 1960).

The Importance of Basic Forms
of Learning

These examples of types 1 and 2 learning make it clear that the conditions that bring them about are neither difficult to recognize nor difficult to arrange. These forms of learning have genuine identities; they can be made to happen at will. At the same time, it is evident that they have great limitations insofar as the capabilities they can establish are concerned. If these were the only forms of learning, human beings would certainly not get very far. It would be possible, perhaps, to teach children to tend themselves in various life-supporting functions, to make a variety of simple utterances, to use simple tools. But this would be a far cry from the learning required to make it possible for the individual to read, write, and figure.

As we consider other varieties of learning, there will be many reminders of the importance of this basic learning type.

GENERAL REFERENCES

Signal Learning (Type 1)

Kimble, G. A. *Hilgard and Marquis' "Conditioning and learning."* New York: Appleton-Century-Crofts, 1961.

Mowrer, O. H. *Learning theory and behavior.* New York: Wiley, 1960.

Pavlov, I. P. *Conditioned reflexes.* (Transl. by G. V. Anrep.) London: Oxford University Press, 1927. (Also in paperback; New York: Dover, 1960).

Stimulus-Response Learning (Type 2)

Keller, F. S., and Schoenfeld, W. N. *Principles of psychology.* New York: Appleton-Century-Crofts, 1950.

Kimble, G. A. See above.

Mowrer, O. H. See above.

Skinner, B. F. *The technology of teaching.* New York: Appleton-Century-Crofts, 1968.

Thorndike, E. L. *Animal intelligence.* New York: Macmillan, 1911.

General

Hill, W. F. *Learning: a survey of psychological interpretations.* San Francisco: Chandler, 1963.

Skinner, B. F. *Walden Two.* New York: Macmillan, 1948.

Skinner, B. F. *Science and human behavior.* New York: Macmillan, 1963.

Staats, A. W. *Human learning.* New York: Holt, Rinehart and Winston, 1964.

5 | Chaining: Motor and Verbal

The chaining of behavior is a frequent and widely occurring event within the sphere of learning. The acquiring of chains typically takes place with some rapidity, and often seems a very simple occurrence. But chains are of varying length; they may be as short as the act involved in pushing a light button, or as long as the recitation of "The Rime of the Ancient Mariner." And so naturally they vary in the rapidity with which they are learned.

By chaining is meant the connection of a set of individual $Ss \rightarrow R$'s in a sequence. There are sequences that are made up of motor responses, like that of turning on a television set or a washing machine. There are also sequences that are entirely verbal, like the greeting, "How have you been?" or the pledge of allegiance to the flag. This chapter will deal with both these varieties of chaining, which have much in common with each other. As before, the main emphasis will be one of describing chaining as a phenomenon, and identifying the conditions under which it occurs. For the acquisition of sequences that are nonverbal, the word *chaining* will be used, whereas the subvariety involving verbal behavior will be referred to as the acquiring of *verbal chains* or *verbal associates*.

123

CHAINING (TYPE 3)

When one says to a novice driver, "Now start the engine," one is asking for the execution of a learned chain of $Ss \to R$ connections. If the training has been successful, what will take place is the reinstatement of a sequence something like this: S ("Start the engine") $\to R$ (looking forward and to the rear) . . . S (sight of clear road) $\to R$ (testing for gear in neutral) . . . S (gear in neutral) $\to R$ (turning key to activate starter) . . . S (sound of motor catching) $\to R$ (release of key) . . . S (key released) $\to R$ (depressing accelerator). Each of the individual acts in the chain is something that the learner knows how to do. The trick is to get them done in the proper order.

Guthrie (1935) tells the story of a young girl who had acquired the habit of dropping her coat on the floor when she entered the house. Being annoyed with this practice, her mother had many times scolded her daughter and required her to go back and pick up the coat. But this was quite ineffective in overcoming the unwanted behavior. The mother, however, discovered an effective procedure: she made the girl go out of the house again with her coat on, then come in and hang it up properly. This illustration shows the importance of correct sequencing of the events in a chain. The original chain that was troubling the mother was: enter house $\to$ drop coat $\to$ see mother $\to$ mother says, "Pick up coat" $\to$ pick up coat $\to$ hang up coat. But what had to be established was a shorter chain with quite a different sequence, namely: enter house $\to$ keep coat on $\to$ approach closet $\to$ hang up coat. The mother displayed some most useful wisdom when she realized that the second chain could not be learned by simply adding links to the first one. What was necessary was the institution of the desired chain with correct links from start to finish.

The Phenomenon of Chaining

Unlocking a door with a key provides another simple example of a learned chain that can be used here for analysis.

Of course, the assumption needs to be made that such a chain has not yet been learned, as may be true for a child. Descriptively, what must be learned is a sequence like the following: having the key in his hand, and facing the lock, the child first checks to see that the key is right side up. Then he inserts it into the lock until the stop is reached, turns it until another stop is reached, and pushes the door open. Obviously, each of the individual acts ($Ss \to R$'s) of this sequence must be performed correctly, and in the proper order, or the performance of opening the door will be unsuccessful. If the key is not right side up, it cannot be inserted; if the insertion is not complete, it cannot be turned; and so on. The point is, the chain as a chain *cannot be learned unless the individual is capable of performing the individual links.*

Assuming that the individual $Ss \to R$'s that make up the chain have been previously mastered, it would appear a fairly simple matter to learn the chain. In this example, what is acquired may be represented as follows:

$$Ss \xrightarrow[\text{key}]{} R_{\text{positioning}} \sim Ss \xrightarrow[\text{key up}]{} R \sim_{\substack{\text{inserting} \\ \text{key}}}$$

$$Ss \xrightarrow[\text{key in}]{} R \sim_{\substack{\text{turning} \\ \text{key}}} Ss \xrightarrow[\substack{\text{key} \\ \text{turned}}]{} R_{\text{push door}}$$

The opening of the door constitutes a consummatory act, providing reinforcement for the final link and also for the entire chain.

If one were to undertake to set up conditions in which this chain were to be acquired by a human adult who did not know how to do it, it is of interest to note that *verbal instructions* would be used to guide the sequencing. Most probably, one would say something like this: "First hold the key so that the serrated edge points upward, with the point facing the lock. Then push the key into the lock as far as it will go. Now turn the key in the clockwise direction as far as it will go. Now push the door."

What is the function of such instructions? Evidently their

most important purpose is to provide *external cues* for the
selection of exactly the right links for the chain. Since the
learner is capable of inserting the key into the lock in
several different ways, an additional external cue may increase the probability that he reinstates the correct response
and rejects others. In order to begin the learning, therefore,
there must be a situation like this:

$$
\begin{array}{cccc}
Ss \searrow \text{"serrated edge up"} & & Ss \searrow \text{"push key all the way"} \\
Ss \xrightarrow{\hspace{1cm}} R & \sim & Ss \xrightarrow{\hspace{1cm}} R & \sim \\
\text{key} \qquad \text{positioning} & & \text{key up} \quad \text{inserting} \\
& & \text{key}
\end{array}
$$

The verbal cues provided by the instructions become, for the
verbally competent individual, stimuli that ensure the occurrence of the correct positioning response, or the correct
inserting response, rather than an incorrect one. On the
second trial they may be quite unnecessary.

Verbal instructions may be self-administered. Some
writers have proposed that verbal instructions provided by
the individual himself become a part of the chain being
learned. This was the suggestion made by William James
(1890) in his famous chapter on habit. As James pointed
out, if self-generated verbal cues are an initial part of the
chain that is acquired, they must later *drop out,* since it is
evident that the "reeling off" of a well-established chain
leaves no time for these verbal responses to occur. However,
it is here proposed that verbal instructions, whatever their
origin, are simply accompaniments to the initial establishment of a chain, and not a part of the chain at all. They are
provided on an initial trial or two, in order to ensure that
the correct links get reinstated. After that they may simply
become unnecessary, because the stimuli from one link of
the chain provide a suitable stimulus for the occurrence
of the next link. One does not have to account for the "dropping out" of self-instructions; it is sufficient to realize that
they are not necessary to successful execution of the chain.
They are part of the conditions of learning but not a part of
what is learned.

But what about learners who may not be able to respond to verbal cues, like animals or very young children? The essential problem is the same: a means must be found of providing external cues during the initial learning trial so that the correct links will be reinstated. If an animal has acquired a set of $Ss \rightarrow R$'s that are to be linked together, this can be done by introducing the external stimuli that have been connected with each link at exactly the proper time in the sequence. Later on, it is possible to eliminate these additional external cues and still have the chain performed satisfactorily. And so too with a very young child. One can imagine "guiding" the production of correct links by suitable cues, even when the individual may not be able to respond properly to such an instruction as "serrated edge." The additional stimuli used for this purpose might include pictures (for example, of a key in the proper position), and gestures (for example, a pushing motion of the instructor's hand). Again, these additional cues would no longer be needed once the chain had been learned.

There are many varieties of chains, and sometimes more than a single trial is required to learn them. This is particularly true when the stimuli of one link are difficult to distinguish from the stimuli of another. Under such circumstances, the learner may tend to reinstate a link out of sequence, and thus be unsuccessful with the chain as a whole. This tends to be the situation in a *maze,* whether one is dealing with animals or with men (using a finger maze). When the learner arrives at a certain point in a maze, it may feel and look almost like some other point, and yet require a different response. Yet when the stimuli controlling each link are made distinctive, such a sequence is not at all difficult to learn. Animals can learn fairly long chains quite rapidly, so long as the stimuli for each new link are readily distinguishable (that is, so long as they have been previously discriminated). Gilbert (1962, p. 16), for example, describes an easily learnable chain for a rat composed of the following acts: pull light cord . . . turn light on → press lever . . . buzzer sounds → approach pan . . . obtain food pellet. Human beings learning a finger maze typically make use of additional external cues, such as self-generated verbal instructions ("First right, then left, then left again," and so on), to increase the distinctiveness of the links.

Much experimental study has been devoted to maze learning in animals. Originally, the maze was chosen because it was "hard enough"; in other words, because it contained difficult link discriminations, and therefore required a number of repetitions for its mastery. The study of maze learning tended to obscure the fact that chains, under optimal conditions, are easy to learn. The learning of mazes appeared to be a gradual process primarily because animals were spending their time learning to discriminate the links that composed them (type 2 learning). Maze learning provides an excellent illustration of the fact that one can, if one wishes, get the learner to undertake two kinds of learning at once, in this case, $Ss \rightarrow R$ learning and chaining. But the results of such a mixture are not easy to interpret.

The Conditions for Chaining

The conditions necessary to bring about the variety of learning called chaining can now be described more formally. There are, as usual, some conditions that exist within the learner, and others that may be externally determined.

Conditions within the Learner   Of utmost importance to the acquiring of chains is the requirement that each individual stimulus-response connection be *previously learned*. One cannot expect a chain like opening a door with a key to be learned in an optimal way unless the learner is already able to carry out the $Ss \rightarrow R$'s that constitute the links. He must be able to (1) identify the key's upright position; (2) insert it into the lock fully; (3) turn it clockwise fully; and (4) push the door open. If a novice (a child, perhaps) complains that he cannot do it after being shown how, one immediately suspects that he has not fully mastered one of these links. Similarly, the chain learned in starting the motor of a car requires the previous learning of the individual links. Failure to learn on a single occasion usually indicates that one or more links have not been previously learned (pressing the accelerator as soon as the motor "takes hold" is an example).

If one could make sure that each individual link were fully learned, the additional external cues required could be reduced to an absolute minimum. But to be *fully* learned each link must have as portion of its discriminated stimulus some kinesthetic feedback from the just-preceding response. For example, the key is not only seen to be inserted fully, it also "feels" right, and this "feel" becomes a part of the stimulus for the next link in the chain. Because it is difficult to ensure that all the stimulation for each link has been fully discriminated, additional external cues are added. But the fastest learning of chains occurs when the necessity for these additional cues is at a minimum; and this happens when the individual links have been individually well learned.

Conditions in the Situation   Several conditions in the situation are important to chain learning.

1. Assuming that the links are known, the main condition for the establishment of a chain is getting the learner to *reinstate them* one after the other *in the proper order*. Two different approaches to this sequencing are possible:

   a. One can begin with the terminal act and work backward, as Gilbert (1962) suggests. This ensures that the link one is trying to connect at any given point in the chain will always be introduced in the correct order. Beginning with link 4, one first connects link 3 by waiting for the occurrence of this link and then immediately following it with link 4 (the act leading to reinforcement); then one observes the occurrence of link 2, and follows it with links 3 and 4; and so on. This "progressive part" method, it may be noted, follows the procedure for type 2 learning *for each successive link.*

   b. A *prompting* method may be used, in which additional
external cues are employed to ensure the reinstatement of the links in the proper order, beginning from
the start of the chain. This is the method illustrated by
the example previously given, using verbal instructions
as "prompts."

It is evident that both these methods work. Whether or
not one is more effective than the other, in some or all circumstances, is a question on which insufficient evidence is
currently available.

   2. A second condition is the familiar one of *contiguity*.
The individual links in the chain must be executed in
close time succession if the chain is to be established. The
smoothly executed chain pertaining to unlocking a door,
for example, requires that the insertion of the key be followed by turning it to the right. Some of the stimuli for
the second of these links arise out of the responses made
in the first. Should there be a delay between these two links,
the stimuli for the second connection will not be like those
of the performance aimed for, and under these circumstances the chain may be learned with difficulty. This does
not mean, of course, that it is not possible to learn chains
that have delays deliberately built into them. Such instances
may certainly be acquired; for example, one learns to delay
until the coin has dropped fully into a slot machine before
operating the lever.

   3. A third condition relates to the *repetition* variable.
Presumably, if all other conditions were fully met, repetition
would be unnecessary. The chain would tend to form itself
on the first occasion. Practically speaking, however, it is
difficult to ensure that all the conditions are fully met. The
individual links may be only partially learned, or the prompting may be not fully effective, or some delays may creep
into the execution of the chain. Given these practical circumstances, repetition of the sequence has the function of
"smoothing out" the rough spots, and some practice is almost always desirable for this reason.

Another function of repetition is the prevention of forgetting. Since errors do tend to occur, and are more likely the longer the chain, a means must be provided for practicing each link in its proper order. This effect of repetition becomes much more evident in the recall of verbal chains, which are typically subject to greater interference than are motor ones, as will be discussed in a later section of this chapter. To the extent that the links have been forged accurately and are connected precisely in the proper order, the need for practice will be reduced. Practice is used to permit the extinction of residual incorrect connections, rather than to establish new ones.

4. Finally, there is the condition of *reinforcement* present in the learning of chains. The terminal link must lead to a satisfying state of affairs—the food pellet is obtained, the engine starts, the door opens. The occurrence of some terminal satisfaction appears to be essential to the establishment of chains. If the reinforcement is omitted, extinction of the final link occurs, and the chain as a whole then disappears. It has been found that the reinforcement needs to be immediate in order for chain learning to occur most readily. The introduction of a delay in reinforcement markedly increases the difficulty of learning.

Other Phenomena of Chaining

Since chains are made up of stimulus-response connections, it is natural that one can see various phenomena of these $Ss \rightarrow R$'s exhibiting themselves in chain learning.

Extinction   The unlearning of a chain may be brought about in the same manner as that of a stimulus-response connection, namely, by omitting the reinforcement. When this is done, the terminal connection first disappears, followed in short order by the rest of the chain. This method is sometimes employed to remove undesirable habits. For example, the rather elaborate chain connected with smoking cigarettes (removing the pack from pocket, taking out a cigarette, tapping it, inserting in the mouth, striking a match, and so on) may presumably be destroyed if the terminal act of inhaling smoke becomes nonreinforcing, as when a substance generating an unpleasant taste is placed in the tobacco. It has been suggested that such nonreinforcement might be brought about simply by removing from the smoke its resins, tars, nicotine, and its heat; but this procedure awaits verification.

Generalization   Any or all of the $Ss \rightarrow R$ links of a chain may exhibit stimulus generalization. The opening of a particular lock with a particular key naturally may be expected to generalize to a stimulus situation that includes a lock and key of somewhat different but similar appearance. Of course, should the second lock look the same but work differently, as in requiring a counterclockwise rather than a clockwise turn, the learner will clearly be in trouble. In order to solve the problem, he will at the very least need to learn two different chains containing two comparable $Ss \rightarrow R$ links that are discriminated from each other, perhaps on the basis of the appearance of the keys. A still higher level of generalizing may be provided by the learning of a concept, in accordance with conditions to be described in a later chapter.

Discrimination   As has been emphasized throughout this section, the individual $Ss \rightarrow R$'s in a chain are discriminated entities. The more precise this discrimination is, the better they are for the purpose of chaining. Frequently for practical reasons, pains must be taken to establish special discriminations in one or more links, in order that some recurring confusion may be overcome. Such might be the case, for example, with the two different locks just described. The sequence required to start the engine of one automobile is usually different in some respects from that of another automobile. Here again, the individual who operates both cars may need to undertake special discrimination learning for some particular $Ss \rightarrow R$ in the chain (for example, the one that includes the response for releasing the starter switch).

Forgetting   Motor sequences of the sort described tend to be retained well for long periods of time. Presumably, individual links in chains are subject to differential forgetting. Not a great deal of systematic evidence is available regarding this phenomenon, however. The forgetting of a link in the middle of a chain may, of course, disrupt the entire chain in such a manner that the individual has the impression of having lost the whole. But it is also known that motor chains like those involved in swimming, skating, or bicycling can be recovered in a short time. Once a forgotten link is restored, the entire chain may reappear in its totality. This kind of experience is often reported by instrumentalists who try to reinstate the lengthy chains that make up a long-unpracticed musical exercise.

The Uses of Chains

Although of widespread occurrence among the human being's activities, chains are of essentially humble nature. In the early grades of school, a number of important chain-like skills must be learned. Buttoning, fastening, tying, using a pencil, erasing, using scissors, and many others fall into this category. At a slightly more complex level are the chains involved in printing and writing, which are of considerable importance as components of more elaborate activities to be acquired in the school. Throwing balls, catching balls, kicking balls, and many other fundamental sorts of athletic skills are also acquired as chains in the early years of the individual's life.

In later years of school, there are varieties of additional chains to be learned. Sometimes, these take the form of *procedures*, complex and lengthy chains that often incorporate simpler chains as components. The student may learn in science courses to carry out weighing procedures, liquid-pouring procedures, and many kinds of measurement procedures. Later still, he may learn to adjust and use a variety of scientific instruments, like microscopes, voltmeters, centrifuges—each of them requiring the learning of procedural chains. The vocational student is likely to have to learn a large number of procedures as basic tasks of the occupation he plans to enter. The student of art may learn procedures such as "brush techniques"; the student of music the complex procedures of playing an instrument.

In accordance with the definition used here, chains are nonverbal, although, to be sure, their learning may be facilitated by verbal cues. They cannot therefore be considered to constitute a central part of the school curriculum. But it would obviously be a mistake to call them unimportant as educational objectives. Certain motor skills and procedures are basic to competence as a scholar and even to wholeness as an adjustable adult person. Motor skills, common or uncommon, are an essential part of the process of self-fulfillment, whether they be a part of the activities of golfing, musicianship, artistic creation, or some other human activity.

VERBAL ASSOCIATION (TYPE 4)

If it is true that man is capable of a tremendous variety of performances with the use of his legs, arms, and hands, it is also even more strikingly true that his vocalizations show an enormous versatility. Although the individual sounds he can make are limited in number, the patterns that can be constructed from these sounds are of virtually limitless variety. Such patterns, at least the simplest ones, are learned as chains. But the tremendous variety of these chains as well as the subtlety of resemblances and differences among them make verbal behavior a subject of rather special interest from a learning standpoint. This chapter will deal with only the most elementary kind of verbal behavior, the learning of verbal associations. In later chapters, the roles played by these associations in more complex forms of learning, such as the acquisition of concepts and principles, will be described.

Probably the simplest verbal chains are illustrated in the activity of *naming*. A youngster is told while being shown a three-dimensional object, "This shape is called a tetrahedron." If conditions are otherwise right, the next time he sees this particular object, he will be able to say that it is a tetrahedron. But these other conditions are important. It is fairly easy to identify some conditions which would ensure that the learner would *not* be able to say tetrahedron. To mention two of the most obvious: first, he may not have discriminated the object as a stimulus; and second, he may not have learned its name.

It seems likely that the act of naming a specific object like a tetrahedron is a chain of at least two links. The first of these links is an observing response, an $Ss \to R$ that connects the appearance of the object with some responses involved in observing the triangular character of its sides, and that at the same time serves to distinguish it from other three-dimensional objects of roughly the same size and color. The second link is the $Ss \to R$ connection that enables the individual to stimulate himself to say "tetrahedron" (that is, to say it as a voluntary response, in the manner of stimulus-response learning). As a diagram, a simple act of naming is represented by this kind of chain:

$$Ss \xrightarrow{\hspace{1cm}} R \quad \sim \quad s \xrightarrow{\hspace{2cm}} R$$
$$\text{object} \quad \text{observing} \quad \text{tetrahedron} \quad \text{"tetrahedron"}$$

The small s in the diagram represents a complex of internal stimulation composed principally of (1) those kinesthetic stimuli that have become discriminated by previous responding with this utterance, coupled with (2) the kinesthetic (or other internal) stimuli arising from the observing response. It is this contiguity of two forms of internal stimulation, presumably, that welds the two links into a chain.

Verbal chains with three links are also of common occurrence. A young child learns not only to name an object "ball" but also to say "that ball" or "my ball."

Paired-Associate Learning

When one learns to read a foreign language, it is not uncommon to acquire a large number of "translation responses," in the manner of give-donner, or buy-acheter. The traditional prototype for such learning is the *paired associate*, sometimes used in nonsense form, as RIV-GEX. A great deal is known about paired-associate learning, but a great deal more remains to be studied (Underwood and Schulz, 1960; Cofer, 1961). In terms of conditions for acquiring verbal associates, and the immediate inferences that seem justified from the evidence about them, these appear to be the most important:

1. Nonsense syllables do not perform the function that Ebbinghaus intended for them, that is, of being equivalently meaningless and unfamiliar. The learning of an association between two verbal elements, whether syllables or words, is markedly affected by *previous* discrimination learning of both the first member and the second (Goss, 1963).

2. Most investigators agree that the efficient learning of a two-element verbal association requires the use of an *intervening link,* having the function of *mediation* or coding. The increased ease of learning resulting from the deliberate use of well-chosen mediation links is striking (Jenkins, 1963). Such links are usually implicit ones; that is, they occur inside the learner and do not appear as overt behavior. In the case of an association like "give-*donner,* an effective coding might be "give" → "donate" → *donner.* Many other mediating links are possible.

3. It is difficult to separate the phenomena of learning *single* associates from those of *multiple* associates. The typical paired-associate learning study, after all, uses ten or twelve pairs like RIV-GEX, not just one. This makes such learning an example of *multiple discrimination,* to be described in the next chapter. But in the present discussion, the attempt must be made to select those conditions that affect only the single verbal association.

The typical three-link chain that constitutes a verbal association, then, is one that involves a previously discriminated verbal element (HAT) which functions as the initial stimulus for the chain. Second, it contains another previously learned connection (FIX) that includes the spoken or written response "fix." Third, it contains a mediating (or coding) connection that may be supplied either by the learner or by the instructor, and that puts together the other two links. This coding link may be of almost any sort. For ease of learning, the most effective one will be an "association" or "image" that is most highly familiar to the learner. One learner might supply a link taken from a previously learned chain about "Dick's hatband," and so construct the chain: HAT-Dick's-FIX; this is neat because the response "Dick's" rhymes with the response "fix," and thus may make an easily learnable chain. Another may think of a battered hat that needs *fix*ing, by calling up a visual image to serve as a mediating link.

The effectiveness of visual images as mediating links for verbal associates has long been known, and forms a part of some "memory systems." A previously learned chain of words, having some logical order that makes it easy to remember, may be used to form links with a set of words having no easily memorable sequence. Thus, the previously learned word "altar" may be connected with the to-be-remembered word "wolf" by means of a visual image of a "wolf at the altar." But the same set of events may readily occur without the necessity of a formal memory system. For example, a familiar link for the translation connection *le soleil*—"sun" may be provided by a visual image of a rising "ol' Sol."

Other examples of coding links for certain French words are shown in Figure 7. Verbal links may be formed by choosing English words, already well known to the learner, that bear some similarity to the French word, and some previously learned association with the English associate. On the whole, though, a pictorial link of the sort indicated in the second column of the figure works even better for most

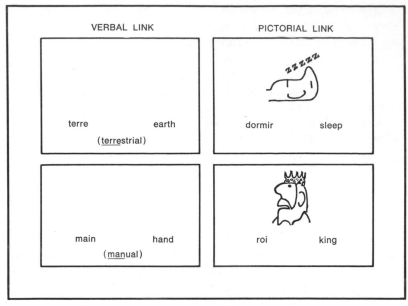

FIGURE 7. Some examples of verbal and pictorial links that can become part of verbal chains for French-English associates.

people. Still another instructional method, at least equally effective, is to require the learner to generate his own coding link—a word, an image, or anything he thinks of that will link the stimulus word with the response word.

Longer Verbal Sequences   Chains of verbal associates may be longer than three links. Relatively brief verbal sequences of previously discriminated words can readily be learned as chains in a single presentation, provided the individual links have been previously well learned. However, even this statement must be made with some reservations, because of the occurrence of *interference* among the links of a chain, which will be discussed more extensively later on in connection with the phenomenon of forgetting.

Obviously, verbal chains may be very long indeed, if we think of the memorization of digits twenty-eight places beyond the decimal point, or, for that matter, of the verbatim learning of verses of poetry or books of the Bible. Are there some limitations on how long a chain can be to be "taken in" or learned as a single event? So far as the evidence from experiments goes (Miller, 1956; Jensen, 1962), it appears that a chain of about seven links (plus or minus two) represents the limit of what can be learned as a single event. This figure describes the *immediate memory span*. Chains longer than this must be broken up into parts in order for learning to occur most efficiently. However, it may be noted also that the length of the span of immediate memory increases when the material is familiar, and has been organized by previous learning.

If presented with an entire verse of poetry to learn, the learner may "break it up" into various pieces, and put the pieces together in various ways. On the whole, the evidence suggests that under many circumstances the most efficient procedure is what is called the *progressive part* method, in which the learner adds a new part (like a line of the poem) as he continues to rehearse the older parts (McGeoch and Irion, 1952). On the first try, the learner may attempt to say line 1; on the next, lines 1 and 2; on the next, lines 1, 2, and 3; and so on. Such a procedure not only ensures that parts are chosen which are within the span of immediate memory, but also allows for the continued practice of earlier learned parts that are subject to forgetting through interference.

Figure 8 shows the rates at which verbal sequences of nonsense syllables were learned, when these were composed of 5, 15, 50, and 100 items. Since these were nonsense syllables, it may be assumed that they were *not* fully discriminated as individual links. Thus, it is quite probable that a sequence of five syllables like BOY ARE HAT TWO RED would have shown close to 100 percent learning after only a single trial. However, the figure does illustrate well the effect of the factor of length of chain on the difficulty of learning.

In the case of lengthy verbal chains, some aspects of the sequence itself may have been previously learned, as well

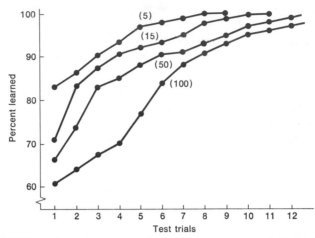

FIGURE 8. Learning curves for verbal sequences of 5, 15, 50, and 100 items. (Data of W. C. F. Krueger, Rate of progress as related to difficulty of assignment. *J. educ. Psychol.,* 1946, **37,** 247–249.)

as the individual links. The English language displays some remarkably predictable sequences, as is illustrated by the completion of such phrases as "Boy meets _____," and "Now is the _____." The predictability of such sequences means that the ordering of English words has in many cases been learned previously (see Miller, 1951). Longer chains may be taken in as a "chunk" under such circumstances. Another implication is that the learning of many prose sequences has already been partially accomplished, not only in terms of the discrimination of links, but also in terms of their order.

Conditions of Learning of Verbal Associates

It should now be possible to state in more formal terms what the important conditions are for the establishment of the capability of reinstating verbal associates and verbal chains.

Conditions within the Learner   The previous discussion leads to the following summary of the conditions for optimal learning:

1. Each link of the chain to be acquired must have been previously learned as an $Ss \rightarrow R$. This means, of course, that the verbal unit must have been discriminated as a stimulus from other units that may resemble it in a physical sense. It also implies that this unit should be discriminated as the response portion of the connection; in other words, it should be readily pronounceable (Underwood and Schulz, 1960).

2. Mediating connections between each verbal unit and the next must have been previously learned. The greater the learner's available supply of these "coding" connections, the more rapidly will the learning take place. Evidence clearly shows (Noble, 1963) that verbal associates are learned more readily the greater the number of verbal "free associates" there are to the syllables or words being chained. But verbal "codes" are not the only kinds of mediators usually available. Visual images or auditory images (as in rhymes) may also serve this function extremely well.

Conditions of the Learning Situation   When conditions within the learner are satisfied, the learning of a verbal chain is a fairly simple matter.

1. The verbal units must be presented in the proper sequence. Various methods may be employed to do this, the two most common being presenting the entire chain to be read from left to right, or presenting the units in the chain one after another. This latter method has been extensively used in laboratory studies of verbal sequence learning.

2. The learner must actively make the responses required by the chain. The importance of this condition, as is true for other kinds of chains, is that the responses generate kinesthetic stimuli which become a part of the next succeeding links in each case.

3. As is true for nonverbal chains, learning is aided by the use of external stimuli that furnish cues for order. This kind of extra cue is provided, for example, by mnemonic devices that may have been previously learned. Students of neuroanatomy sometimes learn the names of the cranial nerves in order by learning a rhyme like "On old Olympus' towering top . . . ," the first letters of which cue the order of the nerves "olfactory, optic, oculomotor," and so on. Pronounced poetic meter serves such a function for chains of medium length, as in "When cur'few tolls' the knell' of par'ting day'." Other kinds of "prompting" stimuli may, of course, be used.

4. For words that have not previously been learned in a sequence, it appears that the limit of verbal chain length that can be apprehended as a single event (for previously unchained material) is seven plus or minus two. In other words, the individual's *span of immediate memory* determines the length of chain that can be learned all at once. There is no limit, apparently, to the length of verbal chain that can be learned part by part, for people have memorized entire books verbatim. For long chains, the *progressive part* method has usually been shown to be a most efficient one.

5. There must be provision for *confirmation of correct responses* in the learning situation. This is often provided by exhibiting to the learner a printed form of the entire verbal chain immediately after he has tried to reproduce it, or of each link of the chain following each response. In the learning of sequences of nonsense syllables, the *anticipation method* is often employed, in which the learner attempts to make each response in the chain within a limited time period (for example, two seconds), and then the printed representation of that response is exposed to him. If he has responded correctly, this exposure enables him to confirm the link by matching what he has just said with what he now sees. Many learning theorists consider such an occasion one of reinforcement; presumably, the satisfaction is obtained from knowing that the response is correct.

The Effects of Interference

One of the most important phenomena that occurs in connection with the learning of verbal associates and sequences is *interference*. Many experimental studies of such learning have led to the inference that the linking of one verbal unit with another (1) tends to reduce the retention of another such linking that has *preceded* it in time, and (2) reduces the probability that a *subsequent* linking will be retained (Underwood, 1964a). In the first case, the interference works "backward" on something previously learned, and so is called *retroactive;* in the second, the interference works forward on something yet to be learned, and is termed *proactive.*

Suppose that one is to learn a verbal chain of six links, such as CAT   RED   SIT   LAM   TIN   ROW, each one of these links having been well learned as an individual word. If one were to require the learning of chains involving two words at a time, such as CAT-RED, or RED-SIT, it is obvious that each such chain could be learned immediately on a single occasion. Yet when the six words are put together as a six-link chain, and exposed one after another, they probably cannot be learned with perfect accuracy on a single occasion. Why is this so? The most probable explanation is that in the process of connecting up a particular link, because of interference, other links (both previous and subsequent ones) become *harder to remember.*

In the chain CAT   RED   SIT   LAM   TIN   ROW, when one has learned CAT   RED   SIT, these links of the chain will be available in memory when one is later trying to recall TIN (as a later part of the chain), and the recall of TIN will to some extent be made less likely. Similarly, having learned TIN, it will be available in memory when CAT, RED, or SIT are being recalled, and this in turn will reduce the likelihood of recall of each of these words in the chain. The longer the verbal chain, the greater will be the effects of interference on any particular link. Most investigators of verbal sequence learning believe, therefore, that interference is the major influence causing the differences in rate of learning shown in Figure 8. Fifteen items in a chain take longer to learn than 5, and 50 take longer than 15, because of the increased amount of interference in each case. In a 15-item chain, each link becomes *harder to remember* because of both proactive and retroactive interference from 14 other links.

If a suitable experimental procedure is used, interference among verbal links can be demonstrated even with chains as short as 3 verbal items. A small amount of interference may be shown under conditions in which a single word is presented for learning, and the learner is instructed to begin immediately counting backword by threes from some given number. This counting activity interferes with retention of the single word to the extent that recall is only 90 percent probable after an interval of 9 seconds. But when a chain of three words is presented, recall following the same interval of counting is only about 30 percent (Murdock, 1961). The difference in retention is apparently due to the increased interference occurring in the 3-word sequence. In other words, even in a short verbal sequence, a large amount of interference occurs among the units of that sequence.

It is evident, then, that there is still another condition of importance to the establishment of verbal sequences. This is a condition designed to *prevent forgetting,* by overcoming interference from the items in a sequence. How can this be done? One general method is to make the positions of the links highly distinctive. For example, it is known that a highly unusual word occurring, say, in the fourth position of a 10-item sequence will be recalled in this position better than most other items in the sequence. An example of an unusual unit in a 5-unit sequence is as follows: PAL BOY CAT 8 SIR. This factor of distinctiveness may also partially account for the better retention of items at the beginning and at the end of a sequence. Rhythm and meter in a verbal sequence may also have the effect of increasing distinctiveness, making poetry generally easier to remember than the same amount of prose.

But by all odds the most important condition for the prevention of forgetting of verbal sequences is *repetition*. Its effects are seen in Figure 8. The longer the sequence, the greater the interference and the more repetition is needed for adequate recall. How does repetition operate in bringing about improved recall of an entire sequence? One good possibility is that repetition is needed to overcome the effects of errors and error tendencies (the latter evidenced by hesitations rather than as overt incorrect responses). As will be mentioned later on, the occurrence of errors implies that *extinction* of a correct link has taken place. If this happens the link may have to be relearned, necessitating an additional repetition. In any case, there can be little doubt that repetition is a most important condition to ensure the retention of verbal chains.

Extinction in Verbal Chains

The importance of interference in the learning of verbal sequences has by now been quite sufficiently emphasized. The nature of the internal events underlying interference is not as yet well understood. However, a most revealing light has been shed on them by an experiment that deliberately arranged for interference to take place in the response links of verbal paired associates (Barnes and Underwood, 1959) and then examined what happened to these links.

First, the learners acquired a set of eight verbal associates of the form GUZ-*level*. Once these were fully learned, they were set the task of learning a new set of associates with the same initial member and a different final member as GUZ-*handsome*. After 1, 5, 10, or 20 repetitions of the second list, different groups of learners were asked to write down *all* the adjectives they could remember as associates for the nonsense syllables. Of course, the learners remembered increasing numbers of the adjectives from the second list, the more repetitions they had. But what happened to the adjectives from the *first* set of chains? The finding was that as the second set became more completely learned, increasing numbers of the first set *could not be recalled*. They suffered what may be called (by analogy with types 1 and 2 learning) *extinction*.

The relationship between interference and extinction found in this study is probably a very important one. It clearly suggests that the important event underlying interference is extinction of previously learned connections. In other words, forgetting, as it occurs in verbal chains, is a matter of interference, and this in turn is more usefully conceived as extinction. When a learner makes an error in attempting to reinstate a link in a verbal chain, by so doing he has to some degree brought about extinction of the correct response. The same process may apply to those occasions when the error is not an overt one, but only an omission or a hesitation. When a correct link suffers extinction new learning must occur all over again if the chain is to be re-established. Hence arises need for repetition to fill in the gaps in a chain that have been occasioned by errors. If it were somehow possible to prevent errors from occurring entirely, perhaps repetition would not be necessary! Unfortunately, the typical verbal chain is so constituted as to make error tendencies highly likely, so that no practical method for eliminating them is apparent.

Generalization and Discrimination in Verbal Chains

Generalization Stimulus generalization of the sort described for type 2 learning can occur within any of the links in a verbal chain. If one first learns a nonsense sequence composed of such units as GEJ, KIV, and HAX, for example, there will be generalizing tendencies to a second list with such units as GEX, KAJ, and HIV. The two sets of units are physically similar both in their appearance and in their sounds, and the response appropriate to a unit in one chain will tend to be connected by generalization to the stimulus of a unit in the other chain. As a consequence, the requirements for discrimination of each link will be severe. The second chain, accordingly, is harder to learn than the first because it tends to give rise to "generalization errors." These in turn have the typical consequences for interference that have already been described, and so make both such chains less likely to be recalled correctly, even when both have been learned fully in the first place. Generalization is shown in such instances to have the effect of making the learning of verbal sequences more difficult by increasing the difficulty of discrimination of the individual links. The same kind of generalization event can also occur among the links of a single chain, with predictable results.

Sometimes, however, generalization seems to work to make a second learning task easier rather than more difficult. The clearest example, perhaps, lies in the generalizing tendencies of *mediating* links. If the learner has initially acquired verbal associates such as BOY-HAPPY, LION-ANGRY, TEACHER-SEVERE, experimental findings show that it is then considerably easier for him to learn the associates BOY-JOYFUL, LION-MAD, TEACHER-HARD. Presumably, the reason is that the coding links for HAPPY and for JOYFUL have considerable similarity, if not identity; and this may likewise be true of a coding link for ANGRY and for MAD, or for SEVERE and for HARD. Although the result is clear, it should perhaps be emphasized here that this reasoning about why it happens involves an extension of meaning of the word "generalization." The original meaning, it will be recalled, pertains to similarity of the physical characteristics of stimuli, and it is a jump from this to speculations about similarities in implicit mediating links. Another possible way of accounting for this latter kind of generalizing will be evident from the discussion of concepts in the next chapter.

Meaningful Verbal Learning

While the learning of verbal sequences, including those containing meaningful words, may be usefully conceived as a process of "chaining," it appears doubtful that this conception is capable of encompassing the whole of what is meant by verbal learning. When a student "learns" a chapter in his history text, for example, one does not expect him to demonstrate this learning by a verbatim oral reproduction of the text. Instead, one may expect him to be able to reproduce the "ideas" that are contained in the text in the proper order. Is such a performance achieved solely by the processes of association and chaining or are some other processes at work? There are several reasons for believing that the learning of meaningful propositions (or verbal information, as we called it in Chapter 3) requires a kind of internal processing that is different from, and may be more complex than, verbal chaining. Some of the major reasons follow.

1. Learning the substance (that is, the "ideas") of meaningful verbal material is accomplished more rapidly than learning the same material as verbal chains to be reproduced verbatim (Jones and English, 1926; Briggs and Reed, 1943).

2. The retention of ideas, as contrasted with the verbatim reproduction of meaningful passages of prose, shows considerable superiority in recall (English, Welborn, and Kilian, 1934).

3. The effects of interference, which are prominently involved in the retention of nonmeaningful material, have in a number of studies failed to appear as influences on the retention of meaningful passages (Newman, 1939; Hall, 1955; Ausubel and Blake, 1958).

Evidences of this sort have led some theorists to hold that the verbal chaining concept is entirely inadequate to account for the meaningful learning of meaningful material. Prominent among these theorists is Ausubel (1968), who proposes that meaningful new ideas are learned by being *subsumed* in an already existing *cognitive structure*, which in turn has been established largely by prior learning. For example, if the learner is to acquire a new set of ideas about the principles of Buddhism, these newly incorporated ideas become organized into an already existing structure. An example of such a structure might be the principles of Christianity, or it could be something even more general such as the principles of comparative religion. In the latter case, one would speak of *derivative subsumption* (Buddhism being a specific example of a more general concept); in the former case, of *correlative subsumption* (Buddhism being in this case an extension or modification of previously learned propositions about Christianity).

In considering retention of newly acquired verbal knowledge, Ausubel theorizes that one must consider, first, the availability in pre-existing cognitive structure of specifically relevant *anchoring ideas.* A second factor that affects retention is the distinguishability or dissociability of the new ideas from the pre-existing cognitive structure. If new propositions of Buddhism, for example, are not sufficiently distinguishable from those of Christianity, they will tend to be lost in retention. Still a third factor influencing retention is the stability and clarity of anchoring ideas, which act to subsume newly learned verbal propositions.

This novel theory implies that the conditions for learning meaningful verbal material are quite different from those previously described for verbal chains. According to Ausubel's theory, learning will take place in an optimal fashion when several additional conditions are present. First, the learning of specific new propositions will be facilitated by the presentation of *organizers,* verbal propositions that indicate the relevance of the to-be-learned knowledge to the pre-existing cognitive structure. Another condition is called *progressive differentiation,* meaning that the most general and inclusive ideas are presented first, followed by increasing detail. (It may be noted that this practice is the opposite of that followed by many textbooks.) Still a third condition is called *integrative reconciliation,* the deliberate and explicit pointing out of similarities and differences between the newly presented ideas and those previously learned. Finally, there is *consolidation,* which means insistence on the mastery of currently presented material before new material is introduced. It can be readily seen that these conditions for learning follow from the basic notion that meaningful verbal learning is a matter of *subsumption* of new propositions into an organized structure that has been previously learned.

Ausubel's cognitive theory of meaningful learning is not the only one that proposes to draw a marked contrast between "meaningful" and "rote" learning of verbally presented ideas. Since it is a highly developed theory, however, it will serve as an outstanding example of a conception of verbal learning requiring inferred processes which are considerably more elaborate than those involved in the notion of verbal chaining. At the same time, it is well to recognize that some theorists continue to hold a kind of faith that the processes described by Ausubel can ultimately be accounted for in terms of the properties of chains of $Ss \rightarrow R$'s, although, to be sure, no one has yet done so. There the matter must rest for the moment.

SOME EDUCATIONAL IMPLICATIONS

It is apparent from our discussion of verbal chaining that representative human performances can easily be found in everyday life, both in and out of school. Children *do* sometimes learn the sequence of letters in the alphabet, whether or not this is considered good pedagogical practice. Students memorize formulas, or key numbers like the square roots of 2 and 3, and occasionally much longer numbers. Children are often expected to learn the Lord's Prayer, the first verse of "The Star Spangled Banner," the Pledge of Allegiance, and a number of other verses, sayings, or quotations. Students often have to memorize the school cheer, and may, of course, learn many lines as amateur actors. But all these seem to lack an essentiality, an urgency, when considered in terms of the larger goals of education. The sequence of the alphabet, after all, is not involved in learning to read. Formulas can easily be looked up. And although

"The Star Spangled Banner" may be of some use in social gatherings, it can gradually "sink in" by being heard many times through mechanical amplifiers. Although few educational scholars would be inclined to say memorization is "bad," it is pretty generally thought to be unimportant. Perhaps it is a matter of priority: students must acquire knowledge and the ability to think, and these goals are heavily emphasized in today's curricula.

It was not always thus in American schools. Half a century ago there was much verbal memorization—the alphabet, the multiplication table, numerical quantities and formulas, poetry, prose writings like the Gettysburg Address, the preamble to the Constitution, and so on. Students practiced reciting the verbal passages they had learned, and declamation contests rewarded oratorical skill in the expression of verbal materials. Verbal memorization is still emphasized today, we are told, in schools in many parts of the world, particularly in Asian countries, and to some extent in Europe.

Is there an educational value to the memorization of verbal sequences? What are the considerations that should enter into a determination of priority for instruction of this sort? The answer to these questions lies in a recognition of the most important usage for recalled verbal phrases, sentences, or passages. This is not to be found in the saving of time realized by recalling a formula rather than looking it up. The major usage of recalled verbal sequences is rather in the area of language itself—specifically, in the construction of verbal utterances that communicate ideas. The question is, What degree of skill is it important for students to have in expressing their ideas in oral form, whether in simple conversation, in informal conference, or in lectures and speeches? To what extent are we interested in providing students with skills of communication and persuasion?

It is no accident that some of the most renowned American orators of previous generations have been men who knew such literature as the Bible and the writings of Shakespeare to the extent that they could repeat whole passages verbatim. These and other literary sources are fundamental to our language. People who are skilled in oral communication are able to recall words, phrases, or entire passages of flowing English, and to weave them into their own vocal utterances in highly effective ways. They are able to do this, not simply because they have *read* these classics of English literature, but because they have *memorized* them. In the terms used in the present chapter, they have learned many varieties of verbal sequences, and can recall them readily. They are able to utilize at will such phrases as "dedicated to the proposition that all men are created equal," or "a tide in the affairs of men," or "seeking the bubble reputation," or "the slings and arrows of outrageous fortune," or "in the course of human events," or "I shall not want," or "with what measure ye mete, it shall be measured unto you," and many, many others.

Naturally, such memorized verbal sequences may also become a source of clichés in both writing and speaking. Phrases such as "stark naked," "utterly exhausted," "starry-eyed wonder," "justifiable wrath," "global diplomacy," and many others, since they have been encountered so frequently in reading material and in everyday speech, become memorized portions of the individual's language repertoire. An orator may sometimes deliberately use such clichés to exploit the appeal they have for his audience. But a skillful speaker is one who has also learned to "play the changes" on such familiar material, so that the completely familiar is avoided. And it is even more important for the writer to seek to avoid excessive use of such phrases, even though they form an important part of his background.

In sum, then, the most direct and obvious employment for memorized verbal sequences is in the construction of created language, particularly in oral speech. The construction of effective original speech does not depend simply on an understanding of rules for grammatical expression. It requires the ready recall of a large fund of verbal sequences that can be woven into novel passages of spoken English in a countless variety of patterns.

Meaningful Learning   What about the educational uses of meaningful verbal learning—learning that is not "rote" or "verbatim"? First, it should be evident that verbal information does get organized in quite definite ways, perhaps in much the ways described by Ausubel (1968, pp. 330–342). Individuals learn and retain inclusive categories, generalizations, and summarizing propositions, which in turn aid their learning and remembering of specific facts. Even the verbatim learning of verbal chains is markedly affected by the presence of organizing principles which are themselves remembered from prior learning (Mandler, 1968).

Organized, meaningful verbal information is essential for virtually all kinds of learning except the simplest varieties. Verbal mediation is surely involved in an intimate manner with the learning of many kinds of concepts, in the learning of rules, and in problem solving. These relations will be described in later chapters. Meanwhile, returning for a moment to the ideas of Chapter 3, the distinction between intellectual skills (with which this book mainly deals) and verbal information is important to bear in mind in estimating the relevance of meaningful verbal learning to the school. The student must have verbal information (names, facts, propositions) readily available in his memory at the time he undertakes the learning of new knowledge or new intellectual skills. He needs verbal information for the learning of *both* these categories.

The question of what verbal information he needs to remember in a lifetime sense is, however, quite a different matter. To learn the intellectual skill of finding the normality of a chemical solution, the student needs to have available (most conveniently, in memory) verbal information about molecular weights of the elements involved. But it is unlikely that these "facts" are themselves what we expect him to remember for a long time. Thus the problem of determining the "content" of verbal information in a course in chemistry is not an easy one. At the very least, it is one that must consider carefully the distinction between items of verbal information which are essential for learning specific intellectual skills and items that are going to be useful for the student to be able to recall verbally many years hence.

GENERAL REFERENCES

Chaining Motor Responses

Gilbert, T. F. Mathetics: The technology of education. *J. Mathetics*, 1962, **1,** 7–74.

Keller, F. S., and Schoenfeld, W. N. *Principles of psychology.* New York: Appleton-Century-Crofts, 1950. Chap. 7.

Chaining Verbal Associates

Cofer, C. N. (ed.). *Verbal learning and verbal behavior.* New York: McGraw-Hill, 1961.

Deese, J., and Hulse, S. H. *The psychology of learning,* 3d ed. New York: McGraw-Hill, 1967. Chaps. 8, 9.

McGeoch, J. A., and Irion, A. L. *The psychology of human learning,* 2d ed. New York: McKay, 1952.

Skinner, B. F. *Verbal behavior.* New York: Appleton-Century-Crofts, 1957.

Underwood, B. J., and Schulz, R. W. *Meaningfulness and verbal learning.* Philadelphia: Lippincott, 1960.

Verbal Learning, Rote and Meaningful

Ausubel, D. P. *Educational psychology: A cognitive view.* New York: Holt, Rinehart and Winston, 1968. Chaps. 2, 3, 4, 8, 9.

Cofer, C. N., and Musgrave, B. S. (eds.). *Verbal behavior and learning: Problems and processes.* New York: McGraw-Hill, 1963.

Dixon, T. R., and Horton, D. L. *Verbal behavior and general behavior theory.* Englewood Cliffs, N.J.: Prentice-Hall, 1968.

Underwood, B. J., and Schulz, R. W. *Meaningfulness and verbal learning.* Philadelphia: Lippincott, 1960.

6

Discrimination; Concrete Concept Learning

Once basic stimulus-response connections have been learned, they may be put together in a sequential fashion (that is, as chains) to generate capabilities of greatly increased complexity. These connections, and the chains built of them, may also be the objects of further learning, as we shall see in the present chapter. First, it may be noted that *sets* of connections (or chains) may become increasingly differentiated, in the sense that the individual members become more readily distinguishable from one another. An initially undifferentiated stimulus object may, through learning, come to be responded to in ways that distinguish its parts, its dimensions, its characteristics. Further, once these fundamental distinctions have been made, still a further learning possibility becomes available to the learner: he may acquire the capability of responding to a group of stimulus objects as a class.

Suppose an individual has learned a simple $Ss \rightarrow R$ to the stimulus provided by a door key. We have already seen that this connection may be combined with others to form a chain that results in the performance of opening a door. But there are other ways of responding to a key, and particularly to collections of keys. To be considered here are the learning of capabilities that may be briefly described as follows:

1. The individual is given a set of three keys, one for each of three different doors in his office. Initially the keys all look alike. Soon the individual can distinguish them by the number of notches and the depth of the first notch.

2. The individual responds to a specific collection of keys as door keys and to another collection as padlock keys and is able to identify an entirely new key as belonging to one or the other of these categories.

Both of these occurrences begin with stimulation provided by collections of stimulus objects or events. However, these are two rather different kinds of capabilities, and it will be seen that the conditions for their establishment also differ. In the kind of learning first mentioned, the individual becomes capable of making different responses to the different members of a particular collection. This is called *discrimination* (or sometimes, *multiple discrimination*). In the second type, the learner becomes able to respond in a single way to a collection of objects as a class, which then extends beyond the particular members that were originally present. This second kind of learning is called *concept learning*. Both these forms of learning are of considerable importance in a practical sense. As will be seen, the second kind is really dependent on the first; and there is a marked contrast in the versatility of behavior produced by learning of the second kind as opposed to the first.

This chapter, then, deals with two different kinds of learning that may be accomplished when an individual is confronted with a set of stimulus objects. In some circumstances, it may be necessary for the learner to learn to respond to each member of the set in a different manner, distinguishing them from each other by name or otherwise, in discrimination learning. Having previously made these distinctions, what may be required is for the learner to acquire the capability of responding to the set of stimuli as a class, which is what is meant by "learning a concept." Of course, the learner may be required to respond to a stimulus set in *both* these ways on different occasions, and this is perfectly possible for him to do.

DISCRIMINATION LEARNING (TYPE 5)

Acquiring discriminations is obviously an undertaking of great importance in everyday life and in school learning. The young child must learn at a very early age to distinguish among the parts of his environment: colors, brightness, shapes, sizes, textures, distances. Adults, too, are constantly being called upon to acquire new discriminations of stimulus objects, such as the locations of doors or streets, the distinctions among newly encountered faces, the taste of wines. As for learning in the school, the student is confronted early with the necessity for learning discriminations among printed colors, shapes, letters, and numerals. Considerably later on, he learns distinctions, perhaps, among the kinds of body tissue, or among the apparent brightness and sizes of stars, or among the patterns of molecular structures. Gibson (1968) describes the relevance of "perceptual learning," which she considers to be a matter of increasing differentiation of parts of the environment, for the learning of the child in his early years. Discrimination learning leads to perceptual differentiation, she points out, within five media: objects, space, events, representations, and symbols. The child's earliest learned perceptions pertain to objects and space, while discrimination learning related to events comes a bit later, as the child becomes able to manipulate objects and to move himself about. Still later, and with much emphasis in early school grades, is the learning of discriminations of representations (pictures) and symbols.

Discrimination learning is often concerned with *distinctive features*. Thus the child learns to respond differentially to those characteristics of objects that serve to distinguish them from one another: shapes, sizes, colors, textures, and so on. Similarly, the child learns to distinguish phonemes, the smallest units of speech, by means of such distinctive features as grave-acute, lax-diffuse, vocalic-nonvocalic, and others. In early school years, he learns to discriminate distinctive features which will enable him to distinguish pictured or drawn representations, and also letters.

The discrimination learning engaged in by the child when learning to differentiate printed letters provides an instructive example of the process. Suppose the child first learns to make the response "oh" to the printed letter o. In its simplest form, this may be an $Ss \rightarrow R$ of the following sort:

$$Ss \xrightarrow{\hspace{2cm}} R$$
$$\text{printed} \qquad \text{oral}$$
$$o \qquad\qquad \text{"oh"}$$

One may proceed from this point to have the child learn other connections, such as:

$$S \xrightarrow{\hspace{2cm}} R$$
$$\text{printed} \qquad \text{oral}$$
$$l \qquad\qquad \text{"el"}$$

Quite possibly, these two different responses to stimuli as different as o and l can be learned quite readily, without the necessity arising for discrimination learning. Obviously, though, we want the child to acquire responses to all of the letters, including such sets as:

$$Ss \xrightarrow{\hspace{3cm}} R_{\text{"pee"}}$$
$$p$$

$$Ss \xrightarrow{\hspace{3cm}} R_{\text{"jee"}}$$
$$g$$

$$Ss \xrightarrow{\hspace{3cm}} R_{\text{"dee"}}$$
$$d$$

$$Ss \xrightarrow{\hspace{3cm}} R_{\text{"bee"}}$$
$$b$$

$$Ss \xrightarrow{\hspace{3cm}} R_{\text{"em"}}$$
$$m$$

$$Ss \xrightarrow{\hspace{3cm}} R_{\text{"en"}}$$
$$n$$

The pupil is asked to learn these names for printed letters so that he can make consistent distinctive responses to them when he encounters them on a page. In some forms of early instruction, children are asked to learn the sounds of letters as responses (*g* as "guh") rather than their names, since these sounds will later be involved in oral reading. There appears to be no clear evidence that this method has an advantage, although it is not unreasonable to suppose that it may. The important thing to be noted, however, is that what is being learned at this stage is *not* the names of the letters (which the child may well have learned previously), but the *discriminations* among their physical appearances.

As noted in the previous chapter, each single one of these performances of letter-naming may be learned as a verbal associate, a chain containing at least three links. Exactly what coding links may be used by the child to acquire such associations is not known, and may vary widely. It is interesting to note, however, that the "alphabet books" often read to children of preschool age attempt to use familiar pictured concrete objects as the source of such coding. For example:

$$Ss \xrightarrow[a]{} r \underset{\text{apple}}{\sim} \quad s \xrightarrow[\text{apple}]{} r \underset{\text{"a"}}{\sim} s \xrightarrow[\text{"a"}]{} R_{\text{"a"}}$$

Thus an entire set of discriminations would be represented as follows:

$$Ss \xrightarrow[p]{} r \sim s \xrightarrow{\quad\quad} r \sim s \xrightarrow{\quad\quad} R_{\text{"pee"}}$$

$$Ss \xrightarrow[g]{} r \sim s \xrightarrow{\quad\quad} r \sim s \xrightarrow{\quad\quad} R_{\text{"gee"}}$$

$$Ss \xrightarrow[d]{} r \sim s \xrightarrow{\quad\quad} r \sim s \xrightarrow{\quad\quad} R_{\text{"dee"}}$$

and so on.

The middle $s \rightarrow r$ in each chain represents the coding link, whereas the others may be thought of as stimulus link and response link, respectively.

Thus the learning of each letter by itself can readily be

understood as a chaining process. But what happens, as far as learning is concerned, when the learner must acquire all the chains at once rather than only one? First, it is apparent that the task of discriminating the stimuli one from the other increases the difficulty of learning. When p is presented alone, the discrimination task is not very demanding, but when p is presented along with g, the chances of confusion owing to lack of discrimination is increased. The chances of confusion in the appearance of p and g, d and b, m and n are well known to teachers of young children. As a set of stimulus associates for multiple discrimination, these letters need to be well discriminated one from the other, preferably so that they can generate very different mediating responses. A technique that is sometimes used is to magnify the differences among the letters when they are initially being learned —for example, by emphasizing the left and right positions of the "tail" on the letters d and b. Another technique, again designed to make stimulus differences more prominent, is to have the children feel cut-out letters, thus providing additional tactual and kinesthetic cues to their differences.

Another site of discrimination difficulty is the final link in the chain—the response link, as it is sometimes called. It may be noted that this is still a matter of stimulus discrimination, this time of the stimuli generated by responses —the small s's of the $Ss \rightarrow R$. If they are not to cause confusion difficulties, the letter sounds themselves must be well discriminated as stimulus-response connections. If learned as letter names, discriminations must be established between t ("tee") and d ("dee"), for example, despite their different appearance. Alternatively, if the sounds of letters are used as responses, there must be discriminations between such responses as "buh" and "puh" as learner-generated sounds.

The second major change in the multiple-discrimination, as opposed to the single-discrimination, situation is that a great potential for *interference* exists, which tends to favor forgetting. No sooner has the learner acquired the proper responses for p and b than he must further learn the names for *d* and *g*. When he attempts to recall any of these, inter-ference occurs and reduces the probability of recall.

Bearing in mind these two sources of difficulty for multi-ple discrimination learning, let us return to the example of the total set of letters that must be learned by the young child. Each of these associates will be most readily learned by itself if the optimal conditions for chaining are in effect. First, the printed letter *p* must be identified distinctively—the learner must be able to match a printed *p* with another printed *p* (appearing with other objects, but not necessarily, at this point, with other letters). Second, the learner must have learned to make a distinctive response to this symbol, let's suppose, "puh." In other words, he must have previously acquired what he is expected to say as a response. And third, a coding response must be available. Of course, this will vary among individuals. *P—pig—puh* would probably serve the purpose, or *p—pie—puh*. Obviously some associates are going to suggest more readily available codes than others; *o—*(rounded mouth)—*oh* may be a particularly easy one.

When all these prerequisite learnings have occurred, the learner faces a task that is not particularly difficult as far as the *individual* chain is concerned. Initially each chain is pro-duced by "prompting," that is, the instructor may expose the letter to be learned, and say its name (or sound), ex-pecting the child to repeat the latter. For each single as-sociate the learner is then able to reinstate the entire chain by himself when the printed letter is presented.

But the task of *retaining* what he has learned is consider-ably more difficult when a multiple set of discriminations is being learned. One solution (a practical one, which may or may not be the best one) is to proceed to learn the associates one by one and then give them more repetitions one by one, in a somewhat different order. (This last condition is used for the purpose of avoiding the uses of cues for sequence, which tend to establish chains that have to be unlearned later.) The question of how many single associates to learn before undertaking recall and repetition is one that has not received a clear answer from laboratory experimentation. It is likely that a kind of "progressive part" learning works as well for this purpose as it does for chain learning (see McGeoch and Irion, 1952). Another approach, however, initially exaggerates the differences among the letters and in successive practice trials gradually reduces these differences to those that are normal. It is possible that the most efficient technique for multiple discrimination of letters may turn out to be one that incorporates both approaches.

The learning of letter names provides a realistic example of multiple discrimination learning as it occurs in school settings. The reader will doubtless be able to think of other instances. For example, the student of a foreign language may be required to learn "translation connections," the foreign equivalents of English words, and the English equivalents of foreign words. Furthermore, the student may be required to learn a *set* of such equivalents at one time in order to perform some subsequent exercise. Many language teachers now believe this is not the best way to learn to read or speak a foreign language, but this problem may be disregarded for purposes of the example. A typical lesson in beginning French might include the following list of equivalents:

cheese	*le fromage*
buy	*acheter*
give	*donner*
face	*le visage*
wood	*le bois*
store	*le magasin*
taste	*le gout*

The student is asked to learn these French words so that he can supply each one to the stimulus of the relevant English word. By so doing, the student is later expected to be able to construct a phrase or sentence indicating, for example, that he wants to buy (*acheter*) cheese (*fromage*) in a French store (*magasin*).

Here again the learning is basically of the same sort. Each individual stimulus must have been previously acquired, and since these are common English words, this may readily be assumed. Each of the French words must have been learned as a response, that is, the learner must already know how to say *fromage*. A coding link is needed, which may be something like "cheese"—"foaming"—*fromage*. Each individual chain may then be readily learned. The difficulty, again, arises in retaining what has been learned, because of the operation of interference. "Buy" must be remembered as *acheter*, but *not* as *donner*, and vice versa for "give." Ease of learning these multiple discriminations will presumably be increased by making them as distinctive as possible, by providing them with distinctive "coding links," or by placing them in different contexts.

Another example of multiple discrimination illustrates the kind of evidence that has been obtained in systematic experimental studies. Gibson (1942) set two different tasks for her experimental subjects, each task requiring the multiple discrimination of thirteen verbal chains. The stimuli for these were nonsense figures, of which six are illustrated for each task in Figure 9. For each of these tasks, the final links were the same monosyllabic words.

Obviously, these two tasks differ considerably in their discrimination requirements, since the stimuli of the first task are much more similar to each other than are the stimuli of the second task. In both cases, the stimuli were first presented together with their associates. On subsequent trials, the stimulus was first presented, and after a brief delay during which the learned attempted to supply the correct associate, the combination stimulus and associate was again exposed. This is a standard experimental method used in studying multiple discrimination learning, called the *anticipation method*.

The results obtained in this study have been often replicated with different materials. The set of multiple discriminations containing highly similar stimuli required, on the average, 19.8 repetitions to learn, whereas the set with stimuli of low similarity needed only 8.9 repetitions. Increasing the similarity of the set of stimulus objects involved in

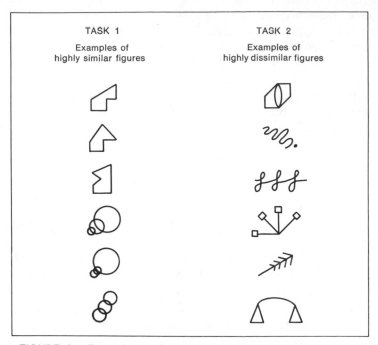

FIGURE 9. Examples of figures used to design sets of verbal chains having highly similar stimuli (task 1) and highly dissimilar stimuli (task 2). (E. J. Gibson, Retroactive inhibition as a function of degree of generalization between tasks. *J. exp. Psychol.,* 1941, **28**, 93–115.)

multiple-discrimination learning, then, has the quite definite effect of increasing the difficulty of learning. The interference that takes place during the learning session is greater when there is more stimulus generalization. The effect is to increase the need for repetition in overcoming the forgetting that occurs when an entire set of chains must be learned at once.

It is of some interest to note that once the multiple discriminations are learned, whether they have been difficult or easy, they then are subsequently remembered just about equally well. This was Gibson's finding when she measured retention of these two different sets of verbal chains after one day, and it has been confirmed in other studies (Underwood,

1953). In other words, once the multiple discriminations have been fully established, retention is no longer affected by interference *within* the set. It may be, of course, and undoubtedly is, affected by interference from other sources, such as the learning of still other verbal chains.

Conditions of Learning
Discriminations

The various examples described should make possible a fairly complete formulation of some propositions regarding the conditions of learning for discriminations.

Conditions within the Learner

1. One way to specify the conditions for optimal learning is to say that the learner must have previously acquired, *in isolation*, each of the chains that make up the set to be learned. Were this to be carried out, it is clear that learning would be a simple matter of exposing these chains to the learner all at once. But this is rather unrealistic, because if the learner has in fact already learned the individual chains, then getting him to reinstate them merely confirms the fact that they are learned.

2. Usually, the learner has not learned all the chains that make up the multiple discrimination, and he may not have learned any of them. In view of this, it may be said that he needs to have accomplished *for each chain*, the same prerequisites that have been previously described for verbal-associate learning (type 4). This means that the initial stimulus links must have been previously discriminated from each other, and that the response links must also have been previously learned as discriminated $Ss \rightarrow R$ connections.

Referring to our previous example of learning letter names, we find that these will occur most readily if we know that the learner (1) can identify each letter by itself, (2) is able to say the names (or sounds) when he hears them, and (3) has available a mediating link. The availability of such links will, of course, vary with the individual. For adults who are acquiring such associates as English-French equivalents, for example, the evidence suggests that those people who have a greater supply of coding links acquire a set of chains more rapidly than those who have fewer available (see Deese, 1961).

Although experimental studies clearly indicate the importance of these prerequisites for acquiring multiple discriminations, it is equally clear that this type of learning has not often been investigated under conditions in which these learning conditions have been present. (In Gibson's study, for example, the learners did not *prediscriminate* either the stimulus figures or the word responses; many other studies can be similarly characterized.)

Conditions in the Learning Situation

1. The entire set of stimuli that are to be associated in different chains must be presented to the learner one by one so that he is able to reinstate the chain for each. On this initial presentation, an external stimulus must be used as a "prompt" to insure the occurrence of the required response in close temporal contiguity with the stimulus. When the child is learning to say "jee" to the letter *g*, the teacher initially uses the sound "jee" as a prompt for his response. It is not apparent that it makes any difference what sort of prompt is used, just so long as it serves to bring forth the required response and thus to establish the chain.

2. If discrimination learning of the links of the various chains has already been accomplished, as previously described, the interference resulting from generalization among similar stimuli will be greatly reduced. Nevertheless, some interference will occur, and this generates the need for *repetition*. Under such circumstances, the amount of repetition required will increase with the number of chains to be discriminated.

3. The arrangement of repetition to accomplish learning of the entire set of discriminations best is a question that has

not yet received a clear experimental answer. Whether one should learn two chains, or three, or four, or ten, before repeating those previously learned is not known. It may not even make much difference.

As was true in the case of chaining, it needs to be emphasized again that repetition in multiple discrimination learning does not appear to have the function of strengthening individual connections. It simply does not make logical sense to think that it does, when it is known that any *single* chain whose component $Ss \rightarrow R$'s have been previously well learned can readily be acquired in one trial (for example, a chain like MAN-THREE by an English-speaking adult). Of course, a chain whose components have *not* been previously learned (as *HOMME-TROIS*, in a person unacquainted with French) may require repetition because its component $Ss \rightarrow R$'s (*HOMME* → *homme* and *TROIS* → *trois*) must be learned. But that is quite another story, as we have already seen in Chapter 5, and should not be confused with multiple-discrimination learning.

The function that repetition clearly does have is that of overcoming the effects of forgetting brought about by interference. Presumably, interference occurs because learned chains undergo some degree of *extinction* when other chains are learned within the same situation In any case, the amount of interference will depend on the number of single chains that constitute the multiple-discrimination task. The more chains there are for the learner to acquire (and differentiate), the greater the amount of repetition needed.

4. Again as in the case of single-chain learning, there must be in multiple-discrimination learning a condition that provides for *confirmation,* the matching of the responses with those that are known to be correct. When the learner reinstates a chain, he must have a way of knowing that it contains a correct terminal response. In practice, this is often done by exposing to him the word that represents a correct outcome, immediately following his response. For example, if he is learning to respond properly to CHEESE-_____, the French word *FROMAGE* may be shown to him (or

said to him) just after he makes his response. Most learning theorists hold that this operation is one of *reinforcement.*

Multiple Discrimination Learning and Verbal Associates

Studies of multiple discrimination learning in the psychological laboratory have to a large extent included investigations of the learning of sets of *verbal paired associates.* Various verbal materials have been used for this purpose, including "lists" of nonsense associates, GIX-REV, WEP-DAK and so on, and meaningful word associates CAUTIOUS-SICKLY, LIQUID-TROUBLED. The generalizations that appear warranted concerning *single* associates of this sort were summarized in the preceding chapter. Here are others applying to *sets* of associates, which are accordingly relevant to multiple discrimination learning:

1. Learning difficulty increases with similarity of the chains. This conclusion applies when the first members of the chains are similar to each other (as in the set DAF-HUF, DAK-ZEP, DAL-POB, and so on), and also when the final members of the chains are similar (as in DAF-HUF, JAL-HUZ, WEP-HUK). As previously mentioned, either of these arrangements implies the need for more precise discrimination of the $Ss \rightarrow R$ links that make up the list. In the typical paired-associate experiment, such discrimination learning has *not* been carried out as a prerequisite to multiple discrimination learning. When such discriminations are pre-established, learning of the set of associates becomes a markedly simpler task (Saltz, 1961).

2. Learning difficulty is also affected by the degree of similarity in *meaning* of word members of the chains (as in a list like ANGRY-GIDDY, ENRAGED-ROYAL, WRATHFUL-PERFECT), but in a somewhat complex manner (Underwood, 1953). In all probability, this kind of relationship needs further investigation if it is to be understood in terms of the mediating links of the words, as suggested in the previous chapter.

3. The most prominent phenomenon in multiple discrimination learning is *interference*. Whenever recall is attempted, whether during the course of learning the entire set or afterward, evidence is obtained of confusion among the links of the chains that make up the set. A response link that has been initially acquired as a part of one chain turns up in recall as part of a second chain, and vice versa. The chains GEX-JOYFUL, DAX-ANGRY, as members of a larger set, have a tendency to be recalled as GEX-ANGRY, DAX-JOYFUL. Such "intralist intrusions" were included as predictions in the theory of interference originally stated by Gibson (1940) and further studied in her investigation of multiple discrimination learning. They appear to be primarily, if not solely, responsible for generation of the need for repetition in such learning.

Perhaps it is worthwhile pointing out, too, that although different responses learned in multiple discrimination are commonly *names* for the objects differentiated, they need not be. The sender of Morse code learns a set of key-tapping patterns to differentiate the individual letters of the message he wants to transmit. The student of the clarinet learns to distinguish a set of printed notes by means of a set of fingering responses, each of which bears a specific relationship to a particular note. The operator of a panel controlling industrial or other machinery may have to learn a large number of different key-pressing responses that distinguish the various signals he receives. In all these instances, multiple discrimination is required of a set of chains that may have been (and preferably are) previously learned as individual entities. And in all these instances there are strong tendencies toward interference among the chains, interference that is overcome by the use of repetition.

Other Phenomena of Multiple Discrimination Learning

It has already been necessary to speak of the phenomena of generalization, discrimination, extinction, and forgetting, because these are directly involved in the conditions of learning for multiple discrimination. It will be worthwhile to review these points briefly.

Generalization   The phenomenon of stimulus generalization occurs among the stimuli being differentiated. It also occurs among the stimuli of the other links in each chain, and this includes the terminal or "response" link. The greater the similarity of the elements of the chains that are to be differentiated, the more difficult is the learning.

Discrimination   Generalization tendencies among the stimuli of each chain create the necessity for discrimination $(Ss \rightarrow R)$ learning of each link of each chain. When such learning is completed as a prerequisite to multiple discrimination learning, the latter occurs most rapidly.

Extinction   Extinction of any particular chain in the set may be accomplished by omitting reinforcement. Accordingly, extinction is important in bringing about the unlearning of *incorrect* response links. When incorrect responses occur, they may be eliminated by omission of reinforcement, or more specifically, by a failure to be confirmed. However, research findings suggest that the occurrence of such errors fosters the extinction of *correct* responses so that they cannot be recalled, and must therefore be relearned. In other words, it seems likely that extinction is the fundamental cause of the interference that is such a prominent feature of multiple discrimination learning.

Forgetting   Forgetting of individual chains is produced by the interference generated by learning other chains that make up the total set. This necessitates frequent review of previously learned chains, by repetition during the learning session. Once the multiple discriminations are all learned, they are still highly subject to forgetting. The curve of forgetting for multiple discriminations is similar to that found by Ebbinghaus for chains: retention falls off rapidly at first, then more and more slowly over a period of days and weeks. Again, properly spaced reviews make it possible to keep retention at a high level.

Some Salient Characteristics

This kind of learning is obviously not a simple sort. It requires a good deal of previous learning of chains, verbal or otherwise, to bring it off with greatest effectiveness. Although in its ideal form it occurs quite rapidly, by its very nature it is highly subject to interference and thus to the occurrence of forgetting. The conditions required for its establishment include as points of major emphasis (1) increasing the precision of discrimination of the stimuli to be differentiated, by means of previous learning and otherwise; and (2) using repetition (review) to overcome the effects of interference among the member chains of the set.

Multiple discriminations are frequently required in the learning that takes place in school. The young child must learn distinguishing features for a great variety of classes of things and events in his environment—rocks, birds, stars, flowers, coins, and many, many others. He must learn to make different responses to many kinds of printed symbols —letters, numerals, words, and other signs. The student acquires a multitude of discriminations during his education—of gases, liquids, solids, parts of the earth and universe, animals, plants, musical notes, works of art. People must learn new discriminations all their lives, of common objects, novel symbols, new faces. But besides the widespread occurrence of this type of learning, it also plays an important role, as we shall see, in other still more complex learning activities which are yet to be described.

CONCEPT LEARNING (TYPE 6)

One way the individual can learn to respond to collections of things is by distinguishing among them. Another way, even more important as a human capability, is by putting things into a class and responding to the class as a whole. In a sense this latter kind of learning seems just the opposite of the first kind. But it is more than that because it incorporates the first kind as one of its preconditions. This latter type of learning, which makes it possible for the individual to respond to things or events as a class, is called *concept learning.*

At this point, it is important to note that the term "concept" has several common meanings. Obviously, it will not be possible to deal with them all at the same time, and it would doubtless be a mistake to try to do so. First, we should consider the most fundamental meaning of the term "concept," which is exhibited in individual behavior by responding to a class of observable objects or object qualities such as those implied by the names "color," "shape," "size," "heaviness," and so on, or by common objects such as "cat," "chair," "tree," and "house." It is customary to refer to these as *concrete* concepts, since they can be denoted by pointing to them; in other words, they are *concepts by observation* (Gagné, 1966a). Later on, it will be possible to describe concepts that are abstract, in the sense that they involve *relations;* these are *concepts by definition.* Examples of the latter are physical concepts like mass and temperature, language concepts like subject and object, mathematical concepts like square root and prime number. Further description of concepts of this definitional sort will need to be undertaken in the next chapter.

Concrete Concepts

The topic introduced here is the learning of concepts that are concrete in the sense that they depend upon direct observation.

Suppose one were to show a seven-year-old child a set of three hollow blocks on a table top. Two of these blocks are for practical purposes identical, but the other is different. The child is told that a small piece of candy is under one of the blocks, but there is no candy under the others. He is to try to "guess" where the candy is, and lift one or more blocks to get it. (We may call the blocks A, A, and B.) Unknown to the child, the experimenter follows the rule of always placing the candy under the *odd* block, the one that is unlike the other two. Initially, of course, the child really does guess, and the connection $Ss \rightarrow R$ is reinforced. Now

$$\begin{array}{cc} & B \quad \text{lift} \end{array}$$

the experimenter places a new set of hollow blocks, of different appearance, C, C, and D, on the table, with the candy under D. (Of course, the spatial placement of the blocks is made unsystematic in all cases.) Now the child, after one or more errors, chooses block D, and the connection is reinforced. Other combinations may be tried, such as BBA, DDC, BBC, FEF, and so on. Eventually, it is found, the child *chooses the odd one*. Once this happens, he is able to perform the task without error for *any* set of blocks, such as XXY, with which he has had no specific previous experience. It may then be said that the child is *using a concept,* or that he is behaving conceptually.

In order for such a statement about the child's behavior to be valid, certain things must be true. First, it must be known that his behavior could not have been learned as a simple $Ss \rightarrow R$ connection, or as a chain of such connections. If one used only a single set of blocks, like AAB, the child could learn to choose the odd one on the basis of its appearance alone (B), as an $Ss \rightarrow R$ connection. Similarly, if one always placed the blocks in the same spatial order, so that the odd one was always on the extreme right, the child could learn a simple stimulus-response connection to a particular location as the stimulus. In order to state that the child is using a concept, one must be able to demonstrate that the performance is impossible on the basis of simpler forms of learning. This can be done, as in the example given, by presenting the child with novel stimulus objects in novel positions. If he responds correctly, it may be justifiably said that he "knows what the *odd one* is," or that he knows the concept *odd.*

The example illustrates a way that individuals have of

responding to collections of things, which is different from multiple discrimination. In this case, there are collections of objects that may vary widely among themselves in appearance. The individual naturally must distinguish among them. But the important thing he does is something else: he responds to them in terms of some *common abstract* property. In a real sense, he *classifies* them.

What the child does in this situation with the blocks may be inferred to be something like the following. He may initially say to himself, "Oh, it's B." Having found that this doesn't work when CC and D are presented, he may say to himself, "It's the one on the right," or "It's the blue one." But none of these verbal chains are successful; they are unreinforced and become extinguished. Eventually, he says to himself, "It's the odd one," and this turns out to work every time. Does he *actually* say these things to himself? It is difficult to obtain evidence that proves this. But so far as the ultimately correct performance is concerned, the child behaves *as if* he could say to himself, "It's the odd one." To be able to state that the child uses a concept, one has only to demonstrate that such an "as if" clause is true.

Returning to our example of concept using in the seven-year-old, it is of considerable interest to ask whether he has to go through this trial-and-error procedure in order to demonstrate his knowledge of the concept *odd*. The answer is, of course, no. It is much easier to bring about the performance required in this situation by saying to the child, "Choose the odd one!" For an average seven-year-old, this instruction should bring about the correct performance immediately. What is shown by the use of this new condition, naturally, is that the seven-year-old hasn't really *learned* the concept in this situation at all. He knew it all the time, and an external verbal cue was sufficient to reinstate the correct behavior.

The trial-and-error exercise is often used by psychologists who study concept using in order to make a detailed analysis of the process. It is not a good example of how concepts are usually learned, but only of how they *may* be learned. But it is nevertheless instructive. Suppose the seven-year-old were a Spanish child who knew no English, and therefore had never learned the word "odd" as an $Ss \rightarrow R$ connection. Naturally, the instruction "choose the odd one" would not enable him to perform the task correctly. In order to find out whether he knew the concept, one would have to put him through such an exercise. Or, the same sort of trial-and-error exercise might be used if one wished to determine whether an animal could use such a concept as *odd*. Harlow (1949) has used similar procedures to demonstrate that monkeys can respond correctly to tasks requiring the concept *odd*.

An Example of Concept Learning

Although the meaning of *concept* may have been illustrated by the previous discussion, the description of the learning of a concept is not yet complete. A concept may be acquired by means of a trial-and-error procedure, but this is not necessarily typical, except perhaps for monkeys. How does a human being learn a concept?

Let it be supposed that a child capable of using language does not know the concept *edge*. Assume it is desired that he exhibit the capability of identifying an edge by name, and more importantly, by identifying any one of a class of things called edges in novel situations. How can such learning come about?

The first step might be for him to acquire the word as a self-generated $Ss \rightarrow R$ connection (type 2 learning), so that when the instructor says "edge" and then asks that the word be repeated, the student says "edge." Next, the student will learn to identify two or three specific edges, by saying "edge" whenever an actual edge is pointed to. By this means he acquires individual verbal associates (type 4 learning). Following this, there need to be several occurrences of multiple discrimination learning (type 5) in which discriminations are established between each edge and a variety of stimulus situations that are not edges. The *side* of a three-dimensional object, the *top,* the *corner*, the *curved surface* —all need to be distinguished from the *edge*. Requiring the student to make these distinctions by means of words is not essential but might readily be done. The important event is the firm and precise attainment of the *edge* discrimination. A similar multiple discrimination may be learned for a flat-surfaced object such as a piece of paper, involving distinctions between *edge* and *surface* and *corner;* still another for a drawn two-dimensional figure, which may show *shading* as well as clear edges.

How many situations need to be used to establish precise discriminations of edge from other stimuli that are not edge? There appears to be no known answer to this question. But it is important to conduct the discrimination learning within stimulus situations that *represent the actual range of the concept being learned;* otherwise, the concept that emerges will be in some sense incomplete. The examples given here seem reasonably appropriate for this purpose. The student needs to know what an edge is in a three-dimensional object, in a flat thin object like a piece of paper, and in a drawn two-dimensional picture.

At this point, all the prerequisite learning has been accomplished. The student can now say "edge" to three different and specific stimulus situations. He is now ready for that particular event called concept learning. The instructor uses a verbal communication, while presenting all three of these stimuli at once (the three-dimensional object, the paper, the drawing). He says, "Each of these is an edge. What is this? (An edge.) And what is this? (An edge.) And what is this? (An edge.)" Finally he takes one more step, and shows the student a new object or drawing with which he has not previously associated the word "edge." The instructor says, "Where is the edge?" The student points to it. A concept has been acquired!

It is not entirely clear whether the use of the final new example is necessary for the learning itself, or whether it is merely a test of what has already been learned. Quite probably, the former is the case. At any rate, the instructor will probably wish to make a more reliable determination that concept learning has really happened, by asking the student to respond to one or two additional examples, each a novel one.

What is the role of the verbal associate—the word "edge" —in this set of events? Obviously, it provides an important shortcut to the learning of a concept. Without it, one would have to engage in rather elaborate means to ensure that $Ss \rightarrow R$'s to each of the specific stimulus situations were all reinstated close together in time. The instructions "This is an edge, and this is an edge, and this is an edge" make it possible for these three common verbal associates to be recalled by the learner in close contiguity. They can be "cued off" by a word, provided only that the student has already learned the chains in which the word occurs. The function of the word is that of an external stimulus to recall, which makes it relatively easy to structure the situation required for learning. When the student knows the word as a common connection for all three examples, instruction becomes a matter of "telling him" what the concept is.

Thus it may be seen that the learning of a concept is not *necessarily* a verbal matter, since concepts can be learned otherwise by animals as well as by human beings. But using verbal cues makes concept learning a relatively *easy* matter for human beings who have already mastered the prerequisites. The kind of verbalization described here, however, needs to be carefully distinguished from the verbalizing that presents a definition. As an example of the latter, an edge might be defined as "a region of abrupt change in intensity of the pattern of light waves reflected to the eye from a surface." It should not be supposed that this kind of verbalizing would be very effective in bringing about the learning of a concept. (Learning of concepts does sometimes occur this way in highly sophisticated adults, but that is another story.) The learner must instead begin with concrete situations, to which he may bring a common verbal associate. When this condition obtains, using the word as an "instruction" is a convenient way of generating the proper conditions for concept learning.

The kind of capability that is established by concept learning may be depicted as follows, using the *edge* example:

(3-dimensional object) $S_{s_1} \longrightarrow r_1 \sim s$

(piece of paper) $S_{s_2} \longrightarrow r_2 \sim s \longrightarrow r$ $\boxed{\text{EDGE}}$ $s \to R$ "edge"

(drawing) $S_{s_3} \longrightarrow r_3 \sim s$

Individual chains to specific edges, established by multiple discrimination learning, are the first components. These come together in a common event in the nervous system that we infer to underlie the concept EDGE. This makes possible the establishment of a common technical connection, which in this case consists in saying the word "edge."

Adults learn new concepts in much the same way. Suppose, for example, an adult who is studying physiology must learn the concept of *striated muscle*. In such a case one assumes that the basic learning of the words has already been accomplished. But the verbal chains must be established that connect several instances of observed tissue samples (actual or pictured) to the response "striated muscle." Furthermore, a number of multiple discriminations must probably also be acquired; the individual must learn to distinguish muscle tissue from other forms, and of course to distinguish striated from smooth and heart muscle. Once these have been mastered, the basic instructional conditions can be carried out for concept learning. That is, various instances of striated muscle are shown at one time (or in quick succession) and identified by the student, who is then ready to classify a new example of striated muscle as a member of the concept class.

Is this all he must learn about a concept in order to be said to "know" it? The answer is yes, so long as the word "know" means nothing more than to use the new entity as a concept.

Of course, an adult will probably go on to learn more about striated muscle in the form of rules (to be discussed in the next chapter). He may learn how striated muscles work, where they occur in the body, their embryological development, and many other things. But these additional learnings will be useless except as sheer verbalizations, unless he first knows the concept by reference to a *class of concrete situations*. It may be noted that this observation about concepts has profound implications for educational practice. It is, for example, the fundamental reason for laboratory work in science instruction. Concepts may be aroused by verbal means, as we have seen. In human beings, their learning is almost always based on verbal chains. But to be accurate tools for thinking about and dealing with the real world, concepts must be referable to actual stimulus situations. These provide them with an "operational" meaning that can come in no other way.

Seven-year-old children show marked differences from four-year-olds in acquiring concepts, presumably because the latter have not yet acquired the verbal chains that make concept learning an easy matter (Kendler and Kendler, 1961). This has been shown by giving children of two age groups a task like that illustrated in Figure 10. In the first task, the children were asked to choose between two exposed squares, one large and one small. Although the relative position of the squares was varied, the *large* one was always correct, and the child received a marble for choosing it. Once this task had been learned, each child was given a second task in which the *small* square was now correct. (Another group of children first responded to *black* as correct, and then were shifted to *white*.) The seven-year-olds took an average of eight trials to make this shift, whereas the four-year-olds required twenty-three. It seems probable that the older children in this study were able to use the concept "opposite" quite readily, whereas the younger children had difficulty with it and tended to continue responding to the situation by means of the simple chain $Ss \xrightarrow{} R$.
$$\text{large} \qquad \text{choose it}$$

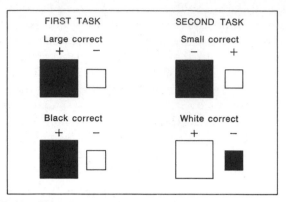

FIGURE 10. Two examples of discrimination reversal problems learned by children of two different age groups (four and seven). After learning the first task, the children were shifted to the second (reversed) task. (H. H. Kendler and T. S. Kendler, Effect of verbalization on reversal shifts in children. *Science,* 1961, **141,** 1619–1620.)

The preavailability of language (verbal chains) has been shown in still other studies to make considerable difference in the acquiring of concepts by children.

The Conditions of Concept Learning

It is now possible to summarize in a more formal way the conditions for the learning of concepts.

Conditions within the Learner   Prerequisites to the learning of concepts are capabilities that have previously been established by multiple discrimination. A set of verbal (or other) chains must have previously been acquired to *representative* stimulus situations that exhibit the characteristics of the class that describes the concept, and that distinguish these stimuli from others not included in the class. Of course, the acquisition of these multiple discriminations is in turn dependent on other prerequisite learnings (the individual chains, and the stimulus-response connections that compose them), as discussed in earlier chapters.

Conditions within the Situation   In human learners, the situational conditions for learning concepts are largely embodied in a set of *verbal instructions*. To have animals learn concepts often requires a somewhat slow and complex procedure that accomplishes the same things as instructions do with human beings (Gagné, 1964a).

1. The specific stimulus objects, to which chains that include a common final link have been previously learned, are presented simultaneously, or in close time succession. Instructions are used to stimulate the learner to recall and reinstate these chains. In terms of the example used here, the instructor asks, "What is this?" in three different stimulus situations and expects the answer "edge" in each case.

2. Instructions go on to elicit the same common link to a stimulus situation belonging to the proper class but to which the learner has not previously responded. Instructions ask, "What is this?" to a new stimulus situation including an edge. Alternatively, the question may be, "Where is the edge?"

3. Once these events have occurred, the new capability may be verified by asking for the identification of several additional instances of the class, again using stimuli to which the learner has not acquired specific verbal chains. If these are successfully done, one may conclude that a new concept has been learned.

4. The condition of *reinforcement* is present in the concept-learning situation. The learner's response of "edge" to the new set of stimuli must be confirmcd more or less immediately if the concept is to be learned. *Contiguity* is also of importance, as emphasized in condition 1. The specific instances need to be presented contiguously, and their names recalled just prior to the presentation of the "new" instance. The absence of contiguity may well be the factor mainly responsible for the slowness of concept learning when it is done in a trial-and-error fashion, as described earlier in this section. When all the specific instances on which the con-

cept depends are "lively" in memory at the same time, concept acquisition is rapid. As for *repetition*, it does not appear to be necessary when other conditions are optimal. Following the step described as condition 2, the provision of new examples (condition 3) may merely serve the purpose of "testing" the presence of the concept. There is no available evidence regarding the question whether these additional instances aid in concept retention, although this may be true.

Generalizing with Concepts

The possession of the capability generated in the learner when a concept is acquired is distinguished from all other forms of learning so far described by the characteristic of *generalizability*. Having acquired the concept *edge*, the individual is able to generalize this concept to other different stimulus situations that have not played a part in the learning itself. He can immediately and without hesitation identify an edge to a roof, a cliff, an automobile fender, a lampshade, or any of a great variety of situations. (Of course, this assumes that the initial situations used to exhibit the concept were sufficiently representative of the total class covered by the concept.) If he has learned the concept *raise*, he will be able to recognize this class of event in such diverse circumstances as the raising of an arm, a flag, or a window. *The effect of concept learning is to free the individual from control by specific stimuli.* This kind of learning, then, is obviously of tremendous importance for most kinds of intellectual activity engaged in by the human individual. He reads in terms of concepts, he communicates with concepts, he thinks with concepts.

It is not surprising, then, that the "test" for the presence of concepts is itself a matter of demonstrating that generalizing can occur. Regardless of what stimuli have been used for learning, the acquisition of the concept *odd* is tested by presenting a stimulus situation that has not been involved in the learning. Similarly for *edge*, or *raise*, or any other concept. There must be a demonstration that the learner can generalize the concept to a variety of specific instances of the class that have not been used in learning. Otherwise, it is not a concept, but merely a collection of specific chains.

The generalizing capabity provided by concept learning goes far beyond the *stimulus generalization* that is a fundamental property of $Ss \rightarrow R$ learning. Of course, this latter property is still present in the links of the chains used to establish the concept, or to arouse it. But it is limited in extent by the physical resemblances of objects or events. Generalizing by means of concepts, in contrast, is not limited by physical resemblances. When using a concept, the individual experiences no difficulty in identifying an *edge* in a large, round swimming pool or in a tiny letter on a printed page. The property held in common by such widely different stimulus situations as these cannot be described in terms of the resemblances of physical stimulation. An *edge,* in other words, is an abstraction from all the specific situations in which it occurs. This is apparently what some writers mean when they refer to concepts as "relationships of stimuli."

The world experienced by the human individual is largely organized by means of concepts. He thinks of his environment, as well as himself, primarily in terms of concepts of objects, places, and events. He communicates with other people, and they communicate with him, to an overwhelming degree by means of concepts. There are concepts of things and places, like chairs and tables and trees and lawns and houses and automobiles; up, down, right, left, between, on top of, next to, and so on. The things in conceptual form are the nouns of sentences, the places are also nouns and sometimes prepositions. Then there are concepts of *events,* which generally are represented by verbs, such as go, stay, take, put, raise, lower, sit, accept, deliver, reject. Children acquire these words as concepts, often in a trial-and-error fashion because of the accidental character of their experiences with them. But a new concept, such as that represented by a technical term, may readily be taught to them in the more systematic manner just described.

An Example—Letter and Phoneme Identification

An interesting example of concept learning of considerable educational importance, and illustrating well many of the characteristics previously discussed, is learning to identify printed letters and syllables as parts of words.

As pointed out in the early portion of this chapter, a prerequisite kind of learning is that of acquiring discriminations such as d—"duh," b—"buh," k—"kuh," and so on. Once such discriminations have been learned, a firm foundation has been laid for the acquiring of letter-sound concepts. The distinction is that letters must now be identified as corresponding to an entire *class* of acoustic stimuli, depending upon their context within a syllable or word. In terms of actual response characteristics, the flat a is pronounced with considerable difference in the words "frantic" and "stagger"; yet as a concept to be acquired for the purpose of reading or listening, it is still a member of the class of letters a. In the word "dumb," the d has a good deal of force behind it, with the tongue far back; in "dirt," however, the d is much closer to a t in sound. But it is a member of the class d, in both cases. For each printed letter there is a class of *phonemes*.

Following the learning of basic discriminations, the child in the course of learning to read must learn to identify phonemes by recognizing a single printed letter for each variety of letter-sound contained in the class. Thus, phonemes constitute one kind of educationally important concept. The acquisition of these concepts takes place under learning conditions comparable to those that obtain for other concepts. The different instances of the class must be presented and each identified (recognized) as belonging to a single class of printed letters. For example, the sound of d in "dirt" must lead to recognition of d, and the sound of d in "dumb" must lead to the same recognition; the sound of b in "book" must be identified as b, as also the sound of b

in "table." The conditions for learning, then, may be described as consisting of the presentation of a sufficient variety of positive and negative instances of the phoneme class, accompanied by suitable provisions for reinforcement and contiguity.

It seems possible that difficulties in learning to pronounce printed words may sometimes result from an unsystematic sequence of learning events. The systematic sequence is, *first,* learn to identify the letters, as *d*—"duh," and so on; *second,* learn to put letters together in longer chains, sometimes called "blending," as in *bat*—"buh"—"a"—"tuh"; *third,* learn to pronounce the entire printed word *bat* as "bat." At this third stage, however, the concepts called phonemes are of particular importance. The child must recognize the printed *t*, for example, as a member of the phoneme class *t* which has a particular sound in this context. By so doing, he is enabled to match the letter combination *at* to a familiar sound in his oral repertoire. Similarly, having also recognized the phoneme *b*, he is enabled to match the entire printed word to the word "bat" in his oral vocabulary. Thus he reads the word. Obviously, in such a sequence, letter discriminations are a necessary prerequisite; but they are not enough. Phoneme concepts also must be learned before word reading can occur successfully.

Some Educational Implications

It would be difficult to overemphasize the importance of concept learning for formal education. The acquisition of concepts is what makes instruction possible. One cannot take the time to present to the student even a small fraction of all the specific situations in which he may encounter an edge, or an "odd one," or a cell, or a striated muscle. But if with the use of a few examples he can acquire these as concepts, one may expect that generalizing will occur to the whole of his experience. He is freed from the control of specific stimuli in his environment and can thereafter learn by means of *verbal instruction,* presented orally or in printed form. He can also communicate his intentions, his actions, and his thoughts to other people, again because the specific words he employs arouse concepts in his hearers that function just as his do.

The young child arrives in kindergarten with many concepts learned, and many not yet learned. He probably has already acquired concepts for a number of common objects in his environment, such as chairs and floors and ceilings and streets and flowers and animals and trees. Most probably he knows such place concepts as *above and below, on top of, underneath, next to, the middle one*. Similarly, he will doubtless respond conceptually to words like "start" and "stop," "go" and "come," "sit" and "stand," and a number of others. But there are many other concepts he still needs to learn that will form the basis of much of his later learning. He may not yet know what "the one before" means, or "the next one," or "double," or "like" and "unlike." As a basis for his reading and writing, he probably has not yet learned to conceptualize word sounds as printed letter combinations. He may not be able to use number names for quantities (whether or not he can recite a verbal chain like "one, two, three," and so on), but he will need to learn these as the foundation of arithmetic. In fact, it is not entirely evident that anyone knows with a high degree of confidence what concepts the typical kindergarten child does not yet have, or what concepts he needs to learn first. The problem is clearly an important one.

As the student progresses in school, he continues to acquire concepts all the time. Once the fundamental skill of reading has been acquired, concepts can often be introduced by means of instructions with accompanying pictures or diagrams. In mathematics this is fairly easy because the stimulus situations that must be responded to with concepts are usually marks on a printed page; adding can be represented by $+$ and substracting by $-$. Languages can also be represented in this way, so that the concepts pertaining to language structure (subject, verb, and so on) are learned in response to printed sentences like "John's hat is on the table."

But with other subjects, there may be greater difficulty in presenting the fundamental situations to be conceptualized, and pictures and diagrams are often employed. Thus, at some stage of science learning, the concept *fulcrum* may be introduced with the presentation of several diagrams depicting levers, or the concept *cell* may be presented by means of an idealized diagram. Most difficult of all are likely to be abstract concepts like *family* and *legislature*, of the type that make up the disciplines of the social sciences.

The great value of concepts as means for thinking and communicating is the fact that they have *concrete references*. The importance of this characteristic cannot be overemphasized. But since concepts are learned by the human being via language, there is often a danger of losing sight of this concreteness. Learning can become oververbalized, which means that the concepts learned are highly inadequate in their references to actual situations. The learner, one may note, "does not really know the meaning of the word," even though he can use it correctly in a sentence. Suppose, for example, a student has merely *read* that striated muscles are made up of bundles of long narrow cells. This verbal information is unlikely to provide him with the kind of concept of striated muscles he needs if he is a student of physiology or anatomy. The danger of verbal superficiality, and the necessity for avoiding it, is recognized in a number of educational doctrines. "Learning by doing" is one of these. Another is the recognition of the importance of the laboratory and the demonstration in science teaching. The concepts of science deal with the real world and therefore must be based on "operations" that are equally concrete.

Besides having concrete references, concepts possess the additional property of freeing thought and expression from the domination of the physical environment. As will be seen in the next chapter, concepts in their generalized form may be linked together in various ways to form principles. "Water boils" is a simple sentence recalling two different concepts to the individual who has already acquired them. But the linking of these concepts results in the conveying of information, of *knowledge*. The tremendous variety of such knowledge that is imparted by means of verbal communication is, of course, a fundamental fact of education. Once concepts have been mastered, the individual is ready to learn an amount of knowledge that is virtually without limit.

GENERAL REFERENCES

Discrimination

Gilbert, T. F. Mathetics: The technology of education. *J. Mathetics*, 1962, **1,** 7–74.

Postman, L. The present status of interference theory. In C. N. Cofer (ed.), *Verbal learning and verbal behavior*. New York: McGraw-Hill, 1961.

Riley, D. A. *Discrimination learning*. Englewood Cliffs, N.J.: Prentice-Hall, 1968.

Underwood, B. J. An evaluation of the Gibson theory of verbal learning. In C. N. Cofer (ed.), *Verbal learning and verbal behavior*. New York: McGraw-Hill, 1961.

Concept Learning

Bourne, L. E., Jr. *Human conceptual behavior*. Boston: Allyn and Bacon, 1966.

Harlow, H. F., and Harlow, M. K. Learning to think. *Scient. Amer.*, 1949, **181,** 36–39.

Woodworth R. S. *Dynamics of behavior*. New York: Holt, Rinehart and Winston, 1958. Chap. 12.

Children's Concepts

Flavell, J. H. *The developmental psychology of Jean Piaget*. Princeton, N.J.: Van Nostrand, 1963.

Lovell, K. *The growth of basic mathematical and scientific concepts in children*. New York: Philosophical Library, 1961.

Piaget, J. *Construction of reality in the child*. New York: Basic Books, 1954. (For other works of Piaget, see references in Flavell.)

Russell, D. H. *Children's thinking*. Boston: Ginn, 1956.

7 | Learning Defined Concepts and Rules

This chapter deals with some kinds of learning that are truly representative of human intellectual capacities. To some readers it may seem, at last, that the types of behavior being described are those with which formal instruction most typically concerns itself, and this is probably the case. It should be emphasized, however, that these forms of learning do not occur within the medium of a *tabula rasa*. On the contrary, they build upon learnings that have preceded them. Although the learning of defined concepts and rules may well represent some frequent goals of a formal schooling process, it would be mistaken to believe that these goals can be reached by simply ignoring all other forms of learning or by pushing the latter into a kind of trash can of unimportant events. The varieties of learning described here are possible only because they have been preceded by the acquisition of a set of prerequisite capabilities that extends down to the simplest stimulus-response connection.

Many concepts cannot be learned in the manner described in the previous chapter, that is, as concrete concepts. Instead, they must be learned *by definition* and, accordingly, may be called *defined concepts*. Sometimes they are called abstract, in order to distinguish them from the concrete

189

variety. More aptly, they may be called *relational concepts*, because they do in fact relate two or more simpler concepts. The concept *diagonal* is a defined concept, not a concrete concept. The statement, "A diagonal is a line connecting opposite corners of a quadrilateral" represents a relation (connect) between the two concepts "line" and "opposite corners of a quadrilateral." An even simpler example is the concept *bottle cap*, which may be defined as the stated relation "closes the top of a bottle." In this instance, it may be seen that the defined concept is actually composed of three separate concrete concepts, "bottle," "top," and "close." This is not always the case, of course; the relation reflected in a defined concept may be composed of one or more concepts which are themselves defined rather than concrete.

The inclusive subject of this chapter is the *learning of rules*. The relational concept is, in a formal sense, one type of rule. The relation expressed by a defined concept may be used, as its name implies, to make it possible for the learner to identify the relation and distinguish it from others: the concept of *uncle* is distinguished from *aunt*, or the concept of *mass* from *weight*. Rules are also used for other purposes, though. They operate to guide the individual's behavior in meeting a host of particular situations and solving a variety of particular problems. The rule that is symbolized in mathematics as $a + b = b + a$ guides the individual's behavior in selecting a combination of seven objects and two objects as being equivalent to a combination of two objects and seven objects; or four objects and five objects as equivalent to five and four. It is not necessary to learn each individual combination of numbers in a rote fashion as verbal chains. Instead, the rule is applied to whatever combination of numbers being dealt with at any moment. The student learns to apply a *rule*, and his behavior may be said to be *rule-governed*.

The ability of human beings to respond to the enormous variety of situations in which they operate effectively, despite almost infinite variety in the stimulation they receive, makes it at once apparent that rules are probably the major organizing factor, and quite possibly the primary one, in intellectual functioning. The $Ss \rightarrow R$ connection, once proposed as the unit of mental organization, has now been virtually replaced by the rule in the theoretical formulations of most psychologists. Even those who still favor the connection as a fundamental entity of neural functioning are forced to concede that the preponderance of observed human behavior occurring in natural situations is rule-governed. When a young child constructs the imperfect sentence, "Daddy, in" to express his intention that his father enter the house, he is applying a rule—perhaps an inadequate one, by adult standards, but a rule nonetheless. One knows this not from observing the single instance of the child calling his father but from additional observations that indicate the child can construct the same kind of sentences applicable to his mother, his dog, or to other people. The stimuli in these other situations are all different and may actually not have occurred previously in the child's life. Yet his sentence-constructing behavior can be seen to be *regular,* or rule-governed.

DEFINITION OF RULE

From the examples already given it is possible to see the outline of a definition of what is meant by the term "rule." It must be an internal state of the individual, which governs his behavior. It must not be the verbal statement that simply represents the rule, like the proposition, "Things equal to the same things are equal to each other." It must be something that accounts for regularity in behavior in the face of virtually infinite variations in specific stimulation. A rule, then, is *an inferred capability that enables the individual to respond to a class of stimulus situations with a class of performances,* the latter being predictably related to the former by a class of relations.

An illustration is as follows: The individual responds to a class of stimulus situations ($2 + 3$, $3 + 4$, $7 + 5$, and so on) with a class of performances ($3 + 2$, $4 + 3$, $5 + 7$, and so on) that are predictably related to the stimuli by a relation that may be expressed as "independence of order." The rule that governs his behavior may be represented by the statement, "adding the class of numbers *a* to the class of numbers *b* is independent of the order in which *a* and *b* are combined." It may be noted that we as external observers may *represent* the rule by this verbal statement. In fact, we *must* represent it in some way if we are going to talk about it. However, we do not know how the individual being observed would represent the rule, and at this point we are not concerned with that question. What *is* observed is that the individual responds regularly to a large class of specific situations; in other words, he *applies* a rule.

Consider another illustration of the definition: pronouncing English words with long *a* or short *a*. The child learns to pronounce printed words like "mate," "dame," "sane," and so on, with a long *a* and words like "mat," "ram," and "fan" with a short *a*. If his behavior is rule-governed, this may be demonstrated by asking him to pronounce a word new to him, such as "concentrate," or even a novel pseudo-word like "jate" or "raf." When he responds to these situations correctly, one may say that he is exhibiting a class of performances (pronouncing the letter *a*) to a class of stimuli (various *a-* and *a-e* combinations of printed letters), these being related to each other by a class of relations, long when *e* follows, short when *e* does not follow.

Typically, it may be seen that a rule is composed of several concepts. In the example just given, there is the concept "long *a*," the concept "*e* at end of syllable," and the relational concept "follows." When the individual possesses the rule as a capability, one observes that he is able to identify these component concepts and also to demonstrate that they relate to one another in the particular manner of the rule. In accordance with the theoretical position taken here, the individual must have learned these component concepts as prerequisites to learning the rule. Assuming he has acquired these concepts, learning a rule becomes a matter of learning a correct *sequence* for them—it is the *e* that follows the *a*, not the other way around. The assembly of such a rule sequence obviously bears some resemblance to what happens in learning a chain. It is possible to suppose that rule learning may actually be a kind of "concept chaining" (as contrasted with the chaining of connections described in Chapter 5).

Rules are obviously of many types, insofar as their content is concerned. They may be defined concepts, serving the purpose of distinguishing among different ideas, and they may be capabilities that enable the individual to respond to specific situations by applying classes of relations. In language learning, the individual acquires rules for pronouncing, for spelling, for punctuating, for constructing ordered sentences. In mathematics, all number operations require the learning of rules. In science, the individual learns many rules having the form of defined concepts, like those for force, mass, density, energy, and so on, and many others that relate these concepts, such as $F = ma$. Evidently, rules may vary in such properties as abstractness and complexity, although the dimensions of these characteristics have not been specified.

RULES AND VERBALIZATIONS

One of the essential distinctions that must be made is that between a rule as *an inferred capability* and the representation of a rule as *a verbal statement* (or *a verbal proposition*). The process of communicating rules, or describing them as learned capabilities, requires that one use words and other symbols to represent the rules. But the term "rule" should not mean the same thing as its representation as a verbal proposition.

When a student is able to state the proposition that represents the rule, one does not usually assume from this evidence that he has, in fact, learned the rule. For example, a student may be able to state the verbal proposition, "A millimeter is four hundredths of an inch," but his statement of this rule is unlikely to be taken as convincing evidence that he "knows the rule." Obviously, he may have learned the proposition as a verbal chain. To determine whether the rule, rather than merely its verbal statement, has been learned, one must find out whether the student can (1) identify the component concepts, namely, *inch* and *four hundredths*, and (2) show the relation between these concepts that constitutes a millimeter. There are various ways of doing this, but all of them appear to reduce to the act of *demonstrating* what a millimeter is. The student might be shown a scale of inches divided into hundredths and asked the question, "If each of these major divisions is an inch, show me how to determine how many millimeters an inch contains." The expected performance would be for the student to identify the "four hundredths," and by counting, obtain the number 25.

While "knowing the verbal statement" does not necessarily mean "understanding the rule," it is, nevertheless, equally important to recognize that verbal statements usually enter into the process of *learning* a new rule in a crucial way. Once a child has learned to use language, from that point on the process of learning is vastly facilitated by the use of verbal statements as *cues* to the learning of new defined concepts and rules. Adult learning, in many spheres, is largely carried on by the use of verbal statements read in textbooks or other written materials. When a student reads for the first time that a *gene* is *an element of the germ plasm that transmits hereditary characters*, he is able to learn a great deal from this verbal statement itself, particularly if he has previously learned its component concepts "germ plasm," "transmits," and so on. Thus the communicative function of such verbal statements and their role in learning need to be affirmed without question, even though the fact that the student can recall them as verbalizations is inadequate evidence that he has learned the rule.

RULE LEARNING (TYPE 7)

The previous discussion has made it plain that the learning of *rules*, to be described here, may be understood to include the learning of *defined concepts*. Although these two entities may serve different purposes for individual performance, they are not distinguishable insofar as their learning properties are concerned.

The simplest kinds of rules are naturally those that the young child learns. He is not able to learn the complex rules of which adults are capable—first, because he has perhaps not yet acquired all the prerequisite concepts, and second, because he has perhaps not yet acquired the subtle discriminations that underlie certain complex rules (or defined concepts). It will be most useful, therefore, to begin our description with very simple rules and later show how they can grow in complexity.

Examples of Rule Learning

A young child may be told, "Round things roll." Such a statement obviously represents two different concepts: (1) *round things* and (2) *roll.* Under what circumstances might it be expected that learning has occurred from the making of such a statement? What are the conditions under which one can be pretty certain that the child has learned the rule that round things roll?

It seems fairly evident that if learning the rule is to be expected, the child must already know the concepts *round things* and *roll.* If he has not already acquired the concept *round,* he may end up learning a more restricted rule, such as *balls roll,* and therefore be unable to show that a half-dollar will roll, or a saucer. Accordingly, if he is to acquire this rule in its fullest sense, he must know the concept *round* in its full sense, as it applies to a variety of objects, including round discs and cylinders as well as spherical objects like balls.

Similarly, he should have previously acquired the concept of the event *roll.* Naturally, this must be distinguished (by multiple discrimination learning) from such events as *sliding* and *tumbling.* Such a concept as this may be considerably more difficult to learn than *round,* in fact, since the stimulus events of rotating about an axis may not be easy to discriminate from other events involving the motion of bodies. But again, if the child faces the task of learning the rule and not just a partial rule, he must have acquired the concept *roll.*

With these prerequisites, the remainder of the situation for learning is provided by a representative set of stimulus objects and by a set of verbal instructions to which the learner responds. The stimulus objects might include a set of unfamiliar blocks, some of which are round, some not, and an inclined plane. The instructions might go like this: "I want you to answer the question, What kinds of things roll? . . . You remember what "roll" means (*demonstrate with one round object*). . . . Some of these objects are *round.* Can you point them out? . . . (*Student responds*). . . . Do all *round* things roll? (*Student answers* 'Yes'). . . . Show me. . . . (*Student responds by rolling two or three round objects*). . . . Good! . . . What kinds of things roll? (*Student responds* 'Round things roll'). . . . Right!" With the completion of this exercise, it is reasonable to conclude that the rule has been learned. However, to test this, a new and different set of blocks may be presented to the student, and he is asked to answer the question, Which of these will roll?

To an adult, this instruction may seem elaborate and detailed, but it surely will not have this appearance to a kindergarten teacher. Why does one not simply say to the child, "Round things roll; remember that"? There are two major reasons. First, the child may not recall the concepts *round* and *roll* at the time they are presented to him in the sentence. Special pains are taken to be sure that these concepts are highly recallable at the moment the rule is stated. The second reason is to ensure that the child does not simply learn as a verbal chain the words "round things roll." This, of course, is very easy for him to do, since the statement is a short chain and he already knows the links. But the purpose of the instruction in this case is not to have him learn a verbal sequence; rather, it is to have him learn a *rule*. Consequently, he must be asked to exhibit terminal responses that are possible only if he can, in fact, put together the concepts *round* and *roll*. Knowing the rule means being able to demonstrate that round things roll, not simply to say the words.

Adults often have to learn principles that are structurally more complex than this. A student of biology, for example, may encounter the rule (which might be equally well termed a defined concept): *Metamorphosis occurs when the larva of an insect turns into a pupa.* It seems quite evident that in this case too, if he is to learn this principle, the adult must not only have learned the relatively well-known concepts *insect* and *turn into* but also the less familiar concepts *larva* and *pupa*. One may suppose that the adult who has the intention to do so can learn the new rule entirely from the verbal statement itself. To do this properly, he might think of an actual example or two of insect larvae turning into pupae, that is, exhibiting metamorphosis. It may be noted, though, that he is more likely to be able to learn this new rule adequately if he has seen metamorphosis in the laboratory or museum, on a field trip, or in a picture. For one cannot be sure that when an adult is confronted with the verbal proposition, "Metamorphosis occurs when the larva of an insect turns into a pupa" he will, in fact, learn it as a rule, although this may well be what he is expected to do. Just as the child can learn this statement as a verbal chain, so too can the adult.

For adults, then, the external conditions of learning rules are often reduced to verbal statements in textbooks or lectures. Provided the component concepts have been previously learned, verbal instruction *can* be sufficient, although it may not be. The way to tell whether it has been, of course, is to give a test that requires the student to *demonstrate.* The test must probe for the rule, not simply for the verbal sequence. A test that says, "Metamorphosis occurs when the _____ of an insect turns into a _____" (or something equivalent) will not do. In contrast, a test that presents pictures of an insect in various stages of development, including the larva and pupa, and requires the student to "show what is meant by metamorphosis" (or something equivalent) will be able to determine whether the rule has been learned.

As these examples indicate, rules having the simplest formal structure are composed of two concepts. One can think of these as being arranged in a chain, since one has precedence over the other, in the sense that it occurs first in a time sequence. "It *A*, then *B*," where *A* and *B* are concepts, may perhaps be considered the simplest form of rule (Gagné, 1964a). The concept *A* describes the class that must be included in the stimulus situation for this chain, whereas *B* refers to the class of objects or events that stimulates the terminal link in the chain. To what extent these "conceptual chains" resemble the more directly observable motor or verbal chains (whose links are $Ss \rightarrow R\text{'s}$) is not known, although some learning theorists postulate that their properties are the same (Kendler, 1964). The need for contiguity, however, in the members of a conceptual chain that is a rule seems to be just as important for rule learning as it is for learning other chains (see Chapter 5).

Although the two-concept rule may be simplest, it is probably not as typical or frequent in occurrence as the three-concept rule, which is the form of many defined concepts. An example is the rule, "A pint doubled is a quart." This statement verbally represents the three concepts *pint, quart,* and *doubled.* It is interesting to note another typical characteristic, namely, that two of these are "thing concepts" while one is a "relational concept." Berlyne (1965, p. 114) refers to rules such as this as transformational chains and distinguishes their components as situational thoughts and transformational thoughts. In any case, one can represent the chainlike nature of such rules, as in the following diagram.

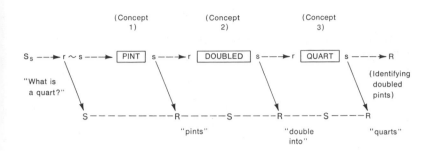

The terminal response, here designated as *identifying doubled pints,* may take many forms as long as it constitutes a demonstration of the rule. Also indicated in the diagram is the possibility of formation of the verbal chain "pints double into quarts," which is the verbal representation of the rule.

Since rules are chains of concepts, they naturally vary in length. A simple rule like *birds fly* can be expanded to *birds fly south in the winter,* containing four concepts rather than two. Defined concepts, which are one variety of rule, can sometimes become quite lengthy, as in the following examples: (1) *forgetting is a decrease in performance from the level exhibited immediately following the learning which has produced that performance, occurring after a time interval during which no practice has occurred;* (2) *mass is that property of an object which determines how much acceleration will be imparted to the object by the action of a given force.* Usually such rules as these are stated at the end of a sequence of instruction rather than at the beginning. To learn them typically requires breaking them up into simpler parts, which are then finally put together as a total rule. Of course, the learner may know them as rules without necessarily being able to state them in an exact verbal form. Knowing them, as has been said, means being able to demonstrate their use in specific situations, whether or not they can be repeated as verbal sequences.

Conditions of Rule Learning

It is time now to make the attempt to draw together in a somewhat formal fashion the conditions of rule learning that derive from these examples.

Conditions within the Learner   The prerequisite for acquiring the chains of concepts that constitute rules is knowing the concepts. *A pint doubled is a quart* is easily learned as a rule when the learner has already learned *all* three concepts involved in it. There is, of course, a kind of "partial" learning of a rule that may result when the individual knows only some of the component concepts. Should a learner know all the concepts except *doubled,* it is apparent that some kind of rule could still be learned, but it would be an inadequate one.

As previously emphasized, knowing the concepts means being able to identify any members of the class by name. It is only when such prerequisite concepts have been mastered that a rule can be learned with full adequacy. Otherwise, there is the danger that the conceptual chain, or some parts of it, will become merely a verbal chain, without the full meaning that inheres in a well-established rule. It is unfortunately true that inadequate rules *can* be learned. It is a challenge for instruction to avoid these, and it is a challenge for measurement techniques to distinguish them from adequate ones.

Conditions in the Learning Situation   The major external conditions of rule learning are embodied in *verbal instructions*. The example of instructions used with round things roll will be useful to recall here.

1. The conditions of rule learning often begin with a statement of the general nature of the *performance to be expected when learning is complete*. In the previous exam-

ple, the instructor says, "I want you to answer the question, What kinds of things roll?" Why does he say this? Isn't he simply stating the rule, giving it away, so to speak? The main reason for making such a statement, which the learner "holds in mind" during learning, appears to be this: it provides the learner with a means for obtaining immediate reinforcement when he has reached the terminal act. Having this statement for a model, he will be able to know when he has *finished learning* and, in many cases, when he has acquired the correct rule. Since rules may be long chains, the learner may need to have a conveniently retained reference to tell him when the end is reached. The instructor, though, cannot be said to be "telling the rule." He does not state the rule itself but only the kind of performance that will demonstrate the attainment of the rule.

2. Verbal instructions continue by *invoking recall of the component concepts*. The instructor says, "You remember what 'roll' means. . . . You remember what 'round' means." In many cases, the recall of these concepts is stimulated entirely by verbal means. In others (as in the example previously given), the class of stimuli that represent the concept may also be shown; the student may be asked to recall the *roll* event by identifying one and the *round* thing by picking one out. Pictures, of course, may be used for this purpose as well.

3. Verbal cues are next given for the rule as a whole. In our simple example, the verbal statement, "Round things roll" accomplishes this purpose. However, it should be noted that these verbal cues to the rule need not be an exact verbalization of the entire rule; they are in this case only because the rule is such a short one. If the rule were one from elementary geometry, for example, "An angle is formed by the intersection of two rays," the verbal cues may be contained in such statements as, "Here are two rays. They intersect. We have an angle." Such statements do not correspond exactly to an acceptable verbal definition. Yet they function as well or better in providing verbal cues to stimulate the learning of the rule.

4. Finally, a verbal question asks the student to demonstrate the rule. The instructor says, "Show me." The exact form is not of great importance as long as it truly requires the student to demonstrate the rule in its full sense. Added to this may be the requirement of asking the student to state the rule verbally, as when the instructor asks, "What kinds of things roll?" But note particularly that such a verbal statement is not essential to the learning of the rule, nor does it prove the student has learned the rule. Then why is it done? Probably for a very practical reason: the instructor wants the student to be able to talk about the rule later on, and so he teaches him the right words to say. This is undoubtedly useful, but it is important to note that this kind of verbal chaining ("learning the definition") is an unessential part of rule learning itself.

5. The presence of some familiar learning conditions may be recognized in rule learning. *Contiguity* appears to be an important condition applicable to the time interval between the recall of component concepts (step 2) and the verbal cuing of the rule with these parts properly sequenced (step 3). *Reinforcement* is provided when the rule is exhibited in its complete form. The instructor may say, "Right!" Even prior to this, the student may receive reinforcement by matching his terminal act with a form remembered from the initial instruction (step 1). *Repetition* has not been shown to be an important condition for this kind of learning, nor for its retention (Gagné and Bassler, 1963). However, the particular finding cited was obtained when the rules learned occupied an isolated position within other varieties of rules. The possible need for repetition in the form of review exercises to overcome the effect of interference should not be discounted. Forgetting, after all, is a highly likely occurrence with any kind of learned capability.

The Instructional Sequence   The conditions for learning rules that are in the situation, then, are largely incorporated in an *instructional sequence*. Perhaps it will be worthwhile here to recapitulate that sequence (see Gagné, 1963a), since

it may be considered to represent the requirements for instruction of rules whether practiced by a teacher, a film, or
a textbook:

Step 1: Inform the learner about the form of the performance to be expected when learning is completed.

Step 2: Question the learner in a way that requires the
reinstatement (recall) of the previously learned concepts
that make up the rule.

Step 3: Use verbal statements (cues) that will lead the
learner to put the rule together, as a chain of concepts, in
the proper order.

Step 4: By means of a question, ask the learner to "demonstrate" one of more concrete instances of the rule.

Step 5: (Optional, but useful for later instruction): By
a suitable question, require the learner to make a verbal
statement of the rule.

Hierarchies of Rules

Although it is useful to discuss the learning of a single
rule, most rules are not learned in isolation, except perhaps
by the young child. Instead, the school student or the adult
typically learns related sets of rules pertaining to a larger
topic. What he learns is an *organized set of intellectual skills*.
The individual rules that compose such a set may have
demonstrable relations to each other in a logical sense. They
are also related to each other in the *psychological* sense that
the learning of some are prerequisite to the learning of
others, just as concepts are prerequisite to the learning of
rules. Here the interest centers on the psychological organization of intellectual skills and not on the logical organization of verbal information which may be involved in their
learning.

The psychological organization of intellectual skills may
be represented as a *learning hierarchy,* often composed
largely of rules. As previously shown, two or more concepts
may be prerequisite to (and in this sense subordinate to)

the learning of a single rule. Similarly, two or more rules may be prerequisite to the learning of a superordinate rule. Once the latter is learned, it may combine with another rule to support the learning of still another higher-order rule, and so on. The entire set of rules, organized in this way, forms a learning hierarchy that describes an *on the average* efficient route to the attainment of an organized set of intellectual skills that represent "understanding" of a topic.

An example of a hierarchy of rules for a topic in elementary nonmetric geometry is shown in Figure 11 (Gagné and Bassler, 1963). The topic as a whole consists of intellectual skills applicable to the identification of points, lines, planes, their intersections and separations. In other words, what is being taught is a hierarchy of rules by means of which the individual student can specify the properties of these well-known geometrical entities. He must learn not simply to recognize points, lines, and planes, but to demonstrate the existence of these entities as dependent on the application of certain rules. (It will be evident that the kinds of rules involved here are mainly *defined concepts.*)

Although it is not possible to describe the entire topic in detail, it will be worthwhile to comment on some of the contents of this hierarchy, to see how it represents the intellectual skills to be learned. At the lowest level, the boxes numbered VI and V represent *concepts* that must be known at the start. VIa is the concept *separation* (*of entities into groups*). VIb is *point.* Va is *set of points,* a new name for what most uninstructed students would simply call a "line." Beginning with these fairly simple concepts, which are typically acquired in the manner described for type 6 learning, the learner is ready to attain a new set of interrelated *rules*.

First he learns to identify and draw a straight *line* (IVa), which is a set of points extending indefinitely in both directions. Later, he learns the rule that defines a *line segment,* namely, that part of a line which consists of two points and the set of points between (IIIa). Then he learns to identify

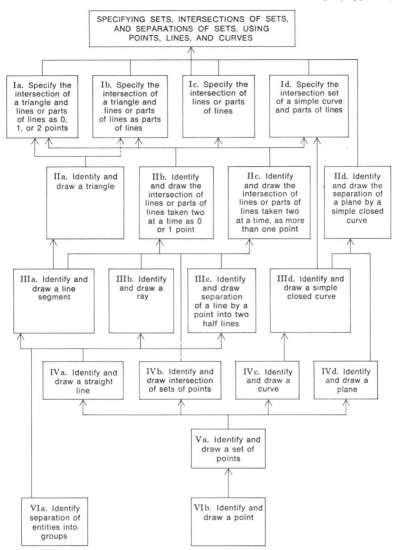

FIGURE 11. A learning hierarchy composed mainly of rules (defined concepts) to be acquired in a topic of elementary non-metric geometry. The topic to be learned is shown in the top-most box. (From R. M. Gagné, and O. C. Bassler, Study of retention of some topics of elementary nonmetric geometry. *J. educ. Psychol.,* 1963, **54,** Figure 1, p. 125. Copyright 1963 by the American Psychological Association and reproduced by permission.)

and draw a *ray*, the set of points formed by a point on a line and one of the half-lines made by this point (IIIb). Later still he learns to define and make a *triangle;* this is made up of three points not on the same straight line and the line segments that join these points (IIa). Picking up another thread of rules that build on each other, the student has also learned about *intersections* of lines and parts of lines (IVb, IIb, IIc). Finally, putting together these ideas of a *triangle* and of *intersections,* he comes to learn rule Ia, which enables him to state that the intersection of a triangle and lines or parts of lines as 0, 1, or 2 points. If he has indeed mastered these rules, one building on the other, he is able at this stage to provide examples of intersections of lines with triangles that form sets of 0, 1, or 2 points and to justify the drawing he makes. Such a drawing must not only "look" right; the learner will be able at this stage to say why it is right.

Evidence of the Hierarchical Nature of Learning What happens when learners actually undertake to acquire a set of rules that appear to have this hierarchical structure? Does the mastery of one set actually affect the learning of the next "higher" set, as would be expected? This expectation was tested in a study with sixth-graders, who were asked to learn these definitions of nonmetric geometry from booklets prepared as a self-instructional program (Gagné *et al*, 1965). These materials had a carefully organized sequence in which the concepts shown at the bottom of the hierarchy (Figure 11) were presented first, then the rules at levels IV, III, II, and I in that order until the final task was given as a terminal exercise. Following the completion of this program, a test was given that measured achievement of the rules at levels III, II, and I and on the final task. The results of this test were analyzed to answer the following kinds of questions concerning the dependence of learning of each rule on the attainment of prerequisite rules: If a student could demonstrate his knowledge of rule Ia, did this mean he also knew IIa, IIb, and IIc; if he could *not* show knowledge of Ia, did this mean he did *not* know one or more of the prerequisites IIa, IIb, or IIc?

The results showed that the learning of "higher-level" rules was dependent on the mastery of prerequisite "lower-level" rules in a highly predictable fashion. For example, of the seventy-two students who performed correctly on rule IIa, only one did not perform rule IIIa correctly on the test. Of the eighteen students who did rule IIa incorrectly, all did rule IIIa incorrectly. The prediction that learning IIa depends on knowing IIIa was borne out, therefore, with a frequency of 99 percent. For all the other possible comparisons, as shown in Figure 11, the frequency of correspondence between predictions and findings ranged from 95 to 100 percent. The learning of organized intellectual skills, according to these results, appears to be predictable from the *pattern of prerequisite rules* that make up the hierarchy of skills to be acquired. This conclusion has been verified in a number of studies of the learning of topics in mathematics (Gagné and Paradise, 1961; Gagné, 1962; Gagné, Mayor, Garstens, and Paradise, 1962; Gagné and Bassler, 1963). There is every reason to suppose that topics with other kinds of content would yield similar results.

Determining the prerequisites for any given rule may be accomplished by asking the question, What would the student have to know how to do in order to be instructed in this rule? For example, if he is to learn rule IIc, "Identify and draw the intersection of lines or parts of lines taken two at a time, as more than one point," he must know the rules that govern the construction of lines (IVa) and intersections of sets of points (IVb) and also the rules pertaining to various parts of lines, including the line segment (IIIa), the ray (IIIb), and the half-line (IIIc). The reason is that the higher-order rule IIc *incorporates* these other rules as a part of it, in the sense that the behavior it demands may involve any or all of these subordinate rules on any given occasion. Knowing rule IIc means being able to deal with intersections of sets of points whether these are line segments, rays, half-lines, or indefinitely extended lines. Rule IIc is truly a higher-order generalization, made up of a class of human performances that are themselves made possible by the acquisition of lower-order rules.

If all the prerequisite rules are known, does this mean that the higher-order rule is immediately known also? No, this is not enough. It has to be learned. If the lower-order rules are known, the conditions within the learner are satisfied, but not the conditions of the learning situation. There must be some *instruction,* which includes the steps of informing the learner about the expected form of the performance expected, encouraging recall, and cuing the proper sequence of acts, as described in a previous section, "The Instructional Sequence."

Another Example of a Rule Hierarchy Many subjects taught in schools, perhaps most, have an organization that can readily be expressed as a hierarchy of rules. Another example of such a knowledge hierarchy, applicable to a topic of restricted scope in physics, is shown in Figure 12. The rule of identifying horizontal and vertical components of forces as vectors is seen to depend on several subordinate rules. In order to perform correctly in accordance with this rule, the student has to be able to (1) identify the forces acting on the body in opposition to each other (keeping it in equilibrium); (2) represent the forces and their directions as parts of triangles; and (3) identify the trigonometric relationships in a triangle (sine, cosine, tangent, and so on). Each of these rules in turn is based on one or more subordinate rules that must also be learned as prerequisites. Still other "lower-order" rules (such as the definition of a triangle) are not shown in the figure, but could surely be identified as underlying those that are illustrated.

Many other topics learned in school have the character of organized sets of intellectual skills and may be represented as hierarchies of rules. The rules of syntax and punctuation in English obviously display these characteristics. All sciences, as well as mathematics, are composed of sets of

VECTOR RESOLUTION OF FORCES

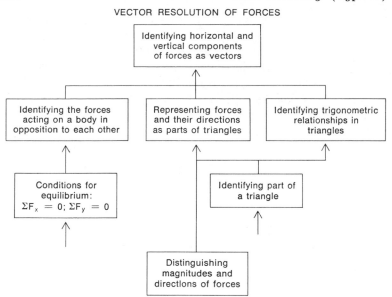

FIGURE 12. A hierarchy of rules comprising the topic "Vector Resolution of Forces."

rules that build on each other. In the social sciences, the total structure is often a looser one, but individual topics— classifying family relationships, comparing and contrasting systems of government, formulating predictions of social trends—can obviously be viewed as examples of intellectual skills having a hierarchical character. A variety of kinds of rule hierarchies can be used to represent the learning of a foreign language: beginning with the elementary concepts of word-sounds and proceeding through the complex rules governing the generation of communicative speech.

Retention of Rules

Usually, the contrast is striking between forgetting the simpler forms of learned capabilities (such as chains and multiple discriminations) and forgetting the more complex forms (concepts, rules). The latter kinds of learning show marked resistance to forgetting and are frequently remembered with little loss over periods of months and years. In a typical study, it was shown that learners who learned simply the verbal statements of rules forgot most of them within a month, whereas those who learned the rules themselves (so that they could demonstrate them) showed almost perfect retention after the same interval (Katona, 1940). Retention of factual details in prose passages has been found to be much less good than retention of ideas, that is, of the rules contained in these passages (Briggs and Reed, 1943). Many studies of rules and organized sets of rules encountered in school learning have demonstrated high degrees of retention over periods of many months (Ausubel, 1968, pp. 111–115).

Presumably, the factor of interference operates to produce forgetting of rules as it does with other forms of learning. But something about the organized nature of rules appears to resist the effects of interference and to maintain retention at high levels. How this works is not known, although it offers a challenging problem for experimental research. The practical implications, however, are quite clear. Learning rules not only produces a capability commonly referred to as "understanding" but at the same time it establishes a capability that is retained well for relatively long periods of time.

SOME EDUCATIONAL IMPLICATIONS

The learning of *rules* is obviously of vast educational importance, if only because of the fact that rules make up the bulk of what is learned in the school. They include as an important component the kinds of learned entities that are tpically referred to as *defined concepts*. While the distinction between rules and defined concepts needs to be maintained, we are concerned here to emphasize that these two entities, considered as human capabilities, are formally alike. In the case of the defined concept, the individual is using a rule in order to *identify* something that itself embodies a relation; in the case of another kind of rule, the individual may be concerned with *demonstrating* the relation itself. But in both cases he is dealing with a sequence of subordinate entities that in the simplest instance of all contain the components concrete concept → relation → concrete concept. An example is *a latch* (concrete concept) *opens* (relational concept) *a window* (concrete concept). The entire range of the category *rule*, then, includes defined concepts, rules that pertain to language (such as pronouncing *ie* as "ee"), rules that have the character of scientific principles (like $F = ma$), and even very complex rules (such as those applicable to the division of fractions), among others. As will be seen in the next chapter, the category also encompasses a very important variety of rule applicable to the learner's own behavior, which is called a *strategy*.

The kind of performance of which the learner is capable when he learns a rule is called *rule-governed behavior*. Such behavior differs from simpler categories like discriminations and chains in that rule-governed behavior exhibits the learner's capability of responding to entire *classes* of stimuli with *classes* of response. For example, the individual is able to respond to *any* red signal light by bringing to a stop by *any* means *any* vehicle he is driving. It would be an entirely inadequate description of such behavior to say that the individual had learned the $Ss \to R$ connection $Ss \xrightarrow[\text{red}]{} R\ _{\text{stop}}$. He may, of course, also have learned such a connection, but his behavior as described here goes far beyond what such a capability would make possible. His behavior in making classes of response to classes of stimuli is, nevertheless, regular and, therefore, is called rule-governed.

Another distinction of great relevance to education, emphasized in this chapter, is that between the *rule* (the inferred capability that makes possible the regular performance) and the *verbal representation* of the rule (often called a *proposition*). The individual may learn a rule without learning the proposition, although the human adult often learns both, in view of the fact that the proposition may be used as a cue to the learning of the rule. The learner may also be able to demonstrate the rule without being able to verbalize the proposition or to recall it as a verbal statement. Many examples of this latter state of affairs may be given: the individual who correctly doubles the consonants in words ending in *ing* can probably not recall the verbal statement of the rule, although he may originally have learned it as a verbal proposition. The rule continues to be present as a capability, but the verbal statement is gone from his memory.

However, the important role of verbal statements in the learning of new rules must be recognized. Much of adult learning is accomplished by reading printed verbal statements in textbooks and other materials. Such verbal statements communicate the to-be-learned rule and often constitute the first step in its learning, particularly when the component concepts have previously been learned. Reading that *hydrogen is a univalent element* may make possible little learning (except that of a verbal chain) if the student has not previously learned the component concepts *univalent* and *element*. If he has learned these, however, such a statement becomes an effective communication for learning a new rule. When followed by an action that, in effect, demonstrates the application of the rule to one or more specific situations, the learning of a new rule can be inferred to have taken place.

Most school learning is a matter of learning rules, including those rules that define. Typically, the learning of a topic, or part of a course of study, can be viewed as a *hierarchy* in which the most complex rules representing "endpoint" objectives require the learning of simpler rules as prerequisites to efficient attainment. These simpler rules in turn imply the learning of still simpler ones, including those that are defined concepts and that in their turn may rest upon previously learned concrete concepts. While such an analysis can theoretically be carried to the point of revealing underlying discriminations, chains, and even simpler connections, it is not often useful to do so, since the students with whom one is dealing may usually be assumed to have already acquired such intellectual skills, perhaps in the earliest grades. Accordingly, learning hierarchies most often represent an ordered set of rules which the student needs to learn in order to achieve an understanding of the topic to be acquired.

GENERAL REFERENCES

Learning Defined Concepts

Ausubel, D. P. *The psychology of meaningful verbal learning.* New York: Grune and Stratton, 1963.

Ausubel, D. P. *Educational psychology: A cognitive view.* New York: Holt, Rinehart and Winston, 1968.

Glaser, R. Concept learning and concept teaching. In R. M. Gagné and W. J. Gephart (eds.), *Learning research and school subjects.* Itasca, Ill.: Peacock, 1968.

Klausmeier, H. J., and Harris, C. W. *Analyses of concept learning.* New York: Academic Press, 1966.

Miller, G. A. *Language and communication.* New York: McGraw-Hill, 1951.

Mowrer, O. H. *Learning theory and the symbolic processes.* New York: Wiley, 1960. Chaps. 4, 5, 6, 7.

Rule Learning

Berlyne, D. E. *Structure and direction in thinking.* New York: Wiley, 1965.

Bruner, J. S., Goodnow, J. J., and Austin, G. A. *A study of thinking.* New York: Wiley, 1956.

8 | Problem Solving

Surely one of the major reasons for learning rules is to use them in solving problems. The activity of problem solving is thus a natural extension of rule learning, in which the most important part of the process takes place *within the learner*. The solving of a problem may be guided by a greater or lesser amount of verbal communication supplied from the outside, but the most essential variables are internal ones. It is particularly significant to note that the components which appear to make problem solving possible are the rules that have previously been learned. Problem solving may be viewed as a process by which the learner discovers a combination of previously learned rules that he can apply to achieve a solution for a novel problem situation.

Problem solving is not simply a matter of application of previously learned rules, however. It is also a process that yields new learning. The learner is placed in a problem situation, or finds himself in one. He recalls previously acquired rules in the attempt to find a "solution." In carrying out such a thinking process, he may try a number of hypotheses and test their applicability. When he finds a particular combination of rules that fit the situation, he has not only "solved the problem" but he has also *learned* something new. The newly learned entity is not formally different from a rule.

It may be more complex, and it is surely new (to the learner), but it is a rule with the same properties of broad applicability as other rules.

The sequence of events involved in problem solving, in broad outline, is generally agreed upon by those who have studied this behavior, and is often referenced to the writings of Dewey (1910). The initial event is the *presentation of the problem,* which may be done by means of a verbal statement or otherwise. The learner then *defines the problem,* that is, he distinguishes the essential features of the situation. As a third step, he *formulates hypotheses* which may be applicable to a solution. Finally, he carries out *verification* of his hypothesis, or of successive ones, until he finds one that achieves the solution he seeks. Relating these steps to our previous discussion, it may be noted that only the first step is an external event; the rest are internal. Furthermore, the entities with which these internal processes deal are *rules.* When the problem is defined, rules have been recalled and selected. The hypotheses that are formed are new rules, the successful one of which will be learned when its application has been tested and confirmed (see Gagné, 1966).

This chapter is concerned with a description of both the external and internal events in problem solving. It will be seen that problem solving depends upon rules, and especially upon a particular type of rule governing the individual's own thinking behavior, called a *strategy.* The phrase "problem solving" is used throughout to refer to the finding of solutions to *novel problems* and should be carefully distinguished from an undesirable use of the term referring to routine substitution of numerical values in mathematical expressions of the same type—a kind of "drill." Sometimes the kind of behavior being described here is called *productive problem solving.*

PROBLEM SOLVING (TYPE 8)

The kinds of events called problem solving are of infinite variety; yet they appear to have several formal characteristics in common. An individual may have the problem of parking his car in a spot that is closest to his work but at the same time free of parking restrictions. A student may have the problem of figuring out why the moon has phases. A scientist may have a problem of accounting for a discrepancy in the predicted and measured velocity of a type of nuclear particle. A fiction writer may have a problem of conveying a representation of slothfulness by describing only the actions of one of his characters. All these situations imply the existence of problems that are to be brought to some successful termination by thinking. All these problems are solved by the use of *rules*, simple or complex. Rules are the stuff of thinking.

One might be tempted to conclude, therefore, that problem solving is a set of events in which human beings *use rules to achieve some goal*. This is quite true; yet it is not the whole story. The results of using rules in problem solving are not confined to achieving a goal, satisfying as that may be to the thinker. When problem solution is achieved, something is also *learned*, in the sense that the individual's capability is more or less permanently changed. What emerges from problem solving is a *higher-order rule*, which thereupon becomes a part of the individual's repertory. The same class of situation, when encountered again, may be responded to with great facility by means of recall, and is no longer looked on as a "problem." Problem solving, then, must definitely be considered a form of learning.

Some Examples of Problem Solving

At some point in the study of modern algebra, the student may be asked to demonstrate that the following statement, in which a and b are rational numbers, is true:

$$(a + b)21 = a \cdot 21 + b \cdot 21$$

If the student has acquired certain rules previously, he is able to do this in the following steps:

(1) $(a+b)21 = 21(a+b)$; by the commutative property of multiplication

(2) $(a+b)21 = 21 \cdot a + 21 \cdot b$; by the distributive property

(3) $(a+b)21 = a \cdot 21 + b \cdot 21$; by the commutative property

Of course, it is possible for the student to be instructed to take these specific steps, thus acquiring a rather lengthy verbal chain. But the intention here is to illustrate the instance in which he is not instructed by display of the steps themselves (either in a text or on a chalkboard). Rather, he is simply given *the problem:* "Show that this statement is true: $(a+b)21 = a \cdot 21 + b \cdot 21$." To him, the problem is one of selecting and using certain number rules, which he has previously learned, in an order that will make it possible for him to arrive at a logically correct solution.

In considering this example of a set of events as problem solving, it should be borne in mind that it is the *first encounter* of the student with this problem that is being discussed here. Once these operations have been performed, of course, they may be repeated many times with any numbers belonging to the class concerned. Most adults naturally carry out these operations very rapidly, and in fact would be inclined to accept the given statement as true by inspection. But a young student who meets this problem for the first time has no such recalled experience to fall back upon. All he knows is that numbers can be manipulated in accordance with certain rules. To him the situation is a brand new one, and he must *supply* the steps in thinking that will achieve a solution. The most notable things about the problem situation, from the standpoint of such a child, are two. First, instructions inform him of what he wants to achieve, namely, a form of statement in which the product of two numbers is equal to the sum of two products. Second, he obviously has to be able to recall from previous learning some particular rules.

As a second example, let us turn to a problem of a fairly

simple and concrete sort, used for the experimental study of problem solving. Here the student is presented with a set of square figures made from arrangements of wooden matches, examples of which are shown in Figure 13. In each case, he is given the problem of transforming one pattern of matches into another in a stated number of moves. The object is for him to be able to make such transformations for a variety of match patterns he has never seen before, not simply to remember the particular patterns on which he practices. In the studies performed with such problems (Katona, 1940), the following results were obtained:

1. The least effective method of establishing the desired capability was showing the learner how to solve several problems by actually moving the matches until the learner could recall the correct moves.

2. Of considerably greater effectiveness was a method in which the learner was instructed in a *verbal proposition.* (Two different propositions were used, one called "arithmetic," which stated that the matches with double functions should be changed to have single functions; the other called "structural," which instructed the learner to proceed by creating holes and loosening the figures. These were about equally effective.)

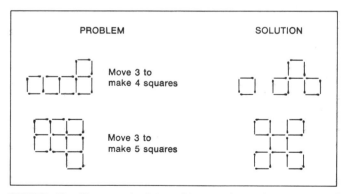

FIGURE 13. Two matchstick problems, with their solutions. (G. Katona, *Organizing and memorizing.* New York: Columbia University Press, 1940.)

3. Best of all for solving new problems was a method that proceeded a step at a time to illustrate the changes that would be brought about by using a rule but without stating the rule verbally. Several examples were used to demonstrate the operation of the rule by shading drawings of the squares so as to create "holes" in the original figure. This was called "learning by help," and could equally well be termed "guided discovery." In other words, the performance of the learners subsequent to the presentation of these examples led to the inference that they had *discovered* the rule required for problem solving.

These conclusions throw considerable light on the events of problem solving. As in the previous example, the learners were instructed about the terminal achievement to be expected, the goal of their activity. Again, these results make clear that a higher-order rule is acquired when problem solution is achieved, which rule may be immediately generalized to other new situations presenting problems of the same class. Presenting the *solutions* of problems to the learner was markedly ineffective for learning. Undoubtedly the reason is that such presentations did not require the acquisition of the higher-order rule; the solutions could be learned as simple chains. Using verbal cues to stimulate learning, by stating the higher-order rule verbally, brought about problem solving in some learners but not in others. The most dependable method of instruction used illustrations to stimulate the learner to discover the rule for himself.

A third example of problem solving is taken from a famous study by Maier (1930). The learner was first brought into a room about 18 by 20 feet in size, containing only a worktable. He was provided with a set of materials, including some poles, lengths of wire, pieces of chalk, and several clamps. The problem, as told to the learner, was to construct two pendulums so designed that each would make a chalk mark at a designated point on the floor when swung over it. As shown in Figure 14, the correct solution to the pendulum construction problem was achieved by clamping two poles together, wedging them vertically against another pole that

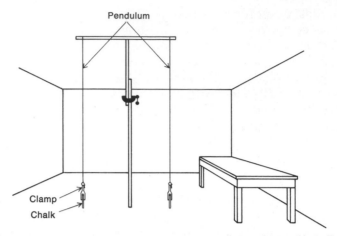

FIGURE 14.   The solution to Maier's pendulum problem. (N. R. F.
Maier, Reasoning in humans: I. On direction. *J. comp. Psychol.,*
1930, **10**, 115–143.)

they pressed horizontally against the ceiling. From the latter
were suspended two wires weighted at their lower ends by
clamps that held the pieces of chalk at the proper height so
that they marked the floor when the pendulum was swung.

With some of the subjects in this experiment, Maier used
an additional set of instructions that seem to have had the
function of recalling certain previously learned rules (see
Gagné, 1964a). These included instruction on (a) how to
make a plumb line by using a clamp, a pencil, and string;
(b) how to make a long pole out of two short ones, using a
clamp; and (c) how to hold up an object against a wall with
two poles, by wedging them tightly. With still another group
of subjects, an additional instruction was added to the
effect that the problem would be simple if he "could just
hang the pendulums from a nail in the ceiling." (Nails were
not among the materials provided.)

The results of this study showed that the added instructions which fostered recall brought about solution in a
greater proportion of learners than did the simpler instructions stating the problem. The final additional set, which
Maier called *direction,* improved the probabilities of solution

still more. The proportions of college students solving the pendulum problem under each of these three conditions were 0 out of 15, 1 out of 18 (with added instructions), and 4 out of 10 (with instructions plus direction).

It is evident that the verbal instructions used in this experimental situation were fulfilling a number of different functions. Briefly stated, these were as follows:

1. They informed the learner about the nature of the performance expected of him. In other words, they defined his goal—two pendulums that could make chalk marks on the floor.

2. They were deliberately used to bring about the recall of certain subordinate rules.

3. They were employed to "channel" or "guide" the learner's thinking. They did this by emphasizing what was *not* a good direction for thought (for example, the table was not to be used in the construction, and no nails were available) as well as what *was* a good direction (hanging pendulums from the ceiling).

Although the pendulum problem seems simple when one knows the solution, this appearance is deceptive, since none of the college students was able to solve this problem when only the "problem-stating" instructions were given. To increase the probability of solution, additional resources were needed. These came from within the learner in the form of recalled rules applicable to the problem. They also came from the external situation in the form of verbal cues employed to guide thinking in the proper "direction."

Conditions for Problem Solving

On the basis of these and other examples, it is possible now to make a summary of the conditions of problem solving, recapitulating a number of the points already made.

Conditions within the Learner   In order to solve a problem, the learner must be able to recall the relevant rules that he has previously learned. In the pendulum problem, rules of weighting a length of wire, clamping a marking tool, wedging poles to hold an object up, and clamping two poles to make a longer one must all be recalled if the problem is to be solved. For matchstick problems, some rules governing the construction of multiple patterns of squares need to be recalled, either in "arithmetical" or "structural" terms. For the mathematical problem, the principles of commutativity and distributivity must be known and recalled. Thus, so far as the individual is concerned, a problem is never solved "in a vacuum." Problem solution always depends upon previous experience of the learner, or more specifically on the recall of previously learned rules.

CONDITIONS IN THE LEARNING SITUATION

1. There is *contiguity* of the rules that are to be "put together" to achieve solution, and the stimulus situation that sets the problem. The component principles, in other words, must in some sense be "held in mind" all at once, or be reactivated at will in close time succession.

2. The required contiguity may be made more highly probable by recent recall of relevant rules. One function of verbal instructions is to ask the questions that stimulate such recall. Thus, in the pendulum problem, the problem solvers were reminded that they knew the rule of weighting a string to make a plumb line and the rule of wedging sticks together to hold up an object, among others. For these learners, these particular rules were "vivid" and readily available for recall when they entered the problem situation.

3. Verbal instructions that are externally provided may "guide" or "channel" thinking in certain directions. (Such guidance may, of course, be provided by the learner himself in self-instructions.) Guidance may vary in amount or completeness, always short of describing the solution itself. At a minimum, guidance of thinking takes the form of informing the learner of the goal of his activity, the general form of the solution; this amount of guidance appears to be

required if learning is to occur at all. Greater amounts function to limit the range of hypotheses to be entertained by
the learner in achieving solution. For example, the emphasis
given in Maier's "direction" instructions limits consideration to the ceiling as a locus for the hanging of a pendulum
while at the same time excluding hypotheses concerning the
use of a nail as a device from which to suspend it.

When these conditions are present, the learner is able
to solve the problem, although the time required for this
solution is likely to vary with the amount of guidance provided as well as with certain abilities of the learner.

What kinds of individual differences may affect the problem-solving process (see Gagné, 1966b)? First, it appears
that a solution is more likely to be achieved rapidly depending on the *store of rules* the individual has available. The
person who has a greater variety of rules on which to draw
—some of which turn out to be relevant to the problem—
will have a greater chance of arriving at a solution. Second,
individuals may vary in the *ease of recall* of relevant rules.
Third, there may be differences in *concept distinctiveness*
among individuals, making it possible for one to distinguish
relevant aspects of the stimulus situation and thus to "define
the problem" more readily than another. Fourth, there is the
important possibility that the *fluency of hypotheses* may
distinguish one individual from another on the basis of the
facility with which rules are combined into hypotheses. Intellectual fluency factors have been emphasized by investigators of "creativity," including Taylor (1958), Getzels and
Jackson (1962), and Guilford (1967), among others. Finally, there may be differences in ability to *match specific
instances to a general class*, an operation performed by the
problem solver in verifying his solution.

Differences in individual abilities such as these are sometimes identified in studies of problem solving that attempt
to differentiate among people with respect to the ease with
which they solve problems. The major emphasis in the
preceding description, however, has been on those factors
that are essential for the act of problem solving, regardless

of how individuals may differ. Contiguity of rules, recall of relevant rules, and guidance provided by verbal instructions are these essential factors. As for repetition, it appears to have no part to play in the process of solving problems except insofar as it may at some previous time have affected the recallability of subordinate rules. Once problem solution is achieved, learning appears to be unaffected by repetition. What is learned is highly resistant to forgetting.

It is also evident that the capability established by problem solving is one that generalizes immediately and without repetition to an entire class of problems. The learner is able to demonstrate the truth of a class of mathematical sentences or to solve a class of match problems or to construct pendulums in a class of problem situations. He has acquired a *higher-order rule* that is capable of being generalized in a wide variety of stimulus situations belonging to a given class.

Problem Solving and Discovery

In a fundamental sense, the capability learned by problem solving (type 8) is no different from that which may be learned by combining subordinate rules in the manner described as rule learning. Both learning types result in the establishment of higher-order rules. The two kinds of learning appear to differ only in the *nature and amount of guidance* provided by verbal instructions. In rule learning, the instructions include a sentence or question that verbally cues the solution, but in problem solving they do not. For example, one group of learners of matchstick problems was told to "remove those matches that serve a double function" while another group was not given this instruction. The first group may be said to have engaged in rule learning, the second in problem solving. A higher percentage of the second group was successful in achieving the higher-order rule (Katona, 1940, pp. 88, 95), and retention of the rule was also superior in this group.

Problem solving as a method of learning requires the

learner to *discover* the higher-order rule without specific help. Presumably, he thus constructs the new rule in his own idiosyncratic manner and may or may not be able to verbalize it once he has done this. A study by Worthen (1968) compared an instructional method emphasizing discovery with one emphasizing expository presentation in sixteen classes of students in the fifth and sixth grades, who were studying mathematical concepts over a six-week period. This investigation found the expository method resulted in superior recall of rules learned when measured immediately following the learning period. The presentation of problems by means of a discovery method, however, led to a greater amount of transfer of the rules acquired. Since the latter is the more important practical outcome, it appears that the encouragement of discovery, under conditions in which problem solving is appropriate to the instructional objectives, can be of great value as a component of teaching technique. This particular study is of considerable significance in view of the uncertainty of interpretation of many studies of "discovery learning" (see Shulman and Keislar, 1966), whose findings are based upon relatively brief topics.

The evidence of experimental studies concerning the use of discovery in problem solving certainly does not demonstrate that higher-order rules *must* be learned by discovery (see Ausubel, 1968, pp. 471–473). In much adult learning, for example, the guidance provided by verbal instructions may be so complete that the rule to be learned is stated verbally during the course of learning. The key to achievement of a higher-order rule does not lie solely in the discovery method. Nevertheless, the evidence strongly suggests that achieving a higher-order rule by means of problem solving produces a highly effective capability that is well retained over considerable periods of time. For example, the hierarchy of rules of nonmetric geometry described in the previous chapter was learned by sixth-graders using a method of instruction that encouraged discovery; that is, the verbal instructions did not state the "solution" until the learners had had a chance to construct it for themselves.

Retention of the final task was found to be very high when measured after nine weeks (Gagné and Bassler, 1963). A study by Guthrie (1968) of problem solving in cryptograms showed a marked advantage of the discovery method of instruction for transfer to a task involving new rules, suggesting that exploratory strategies relevant to such new learning may have been engendered by the discovery method of instruction.

The discovery method is liable to gross misinterpretation in practical learning situations. Some writers and practitioners have treated problem solving as though it could be achieved with a *minimum* of instructions and prerequisite knowledge of rules. This is obviously an incorrect point of view, as the evidence shows. College students who tried to solve matchstick problems *without* prerequisite knowledge of rules and *without* guidance were markedly unsuccessful. Similarly, students who were told only the goal of problem solving for the pendulum problem, without being reminded of subordinate rules and without "direction," were unable to solve the problem. Problem solving, or discovery, is only the final step in a sequence of learning that extends back through the many prerequisite learnings that must have preceded it in time. To be successful, problem solving must be based on the prior attainment and recall of the rules that are combined in the achievement of the solution, the higher-order rule. Of course, the individual learner may be set a problem that is "beyond him" in the sense that he must acquire all the subordinate rules himself before he achieves a solution. Solving a problem under such circumstances may happen on certain occasions and in particular individuals, but to advocate such an approach as a practical learning method makes no sense.

To summarize, discovery or problem solving involves the combining of previously learned rules into a new higher-order rule that "solves" the problem and generalizes to an entire class of stimulus situations embodying other problems of the same type. Problem solving occurs when the instructions provided the learner do not include a verbally stated "solution," but require him to construct such a solution "on his own." When this happens, the individually constructed higher-order rule is effective in generalizing to many situations and is at the same time highly resistant to forgetting. But the capability acquired by this means does not appear to differ in a fundamental sense from that which may be acquired when instructions include the statement of a "solution" (unless, of course, the latter is learned simply as a verbal chain). What is learned in either case is a higher-order rule, which is based upon some previously learned simpler rules.

Problem Solving and Creativity

No one can fail to stand in awed admiration of the great intellectual discoveries of history—Newton's laws of motion, Kepler's principles of planetary movement, Einstein's general theory of relativity. Equally awe-inspiring are artistic creations in painting, sculpture, music, and literature, which have also been generated by individual discovery. What do these remarkable achievements of genius have to do with problem solving as described here?

A great scientific discovery or a great work of art is surely the result of problem-solving activity. The solution to a problem, we are told, often comes to the thinker in a "flash of insight," although he may have been turning the problem over in his mind for some time. As problem-solving behavior, these creative acts are based on a tremendous amount of previously acquired knowledge, whether this be of the "public" sort known to science, or of the "private" sort known to the artist. Many creative thinkers testify that they have previously immersed themselves deeply in the subject matter of the problem, often over considerable periods of time. Indeed, it would be strange if they had not done this. Nothing in such testimony supports the idea that there is anything very different about the problem solving that leads to discoveries of great social import. The act of discovery, even in the relatively predictable sense that it occurs in everyday learning, involves a "sudden insight" which transforms the problem situation into a solution situation. As we have seen, it, too, requires that the learner have previous knowledge of the rules involved in the solution.

But the major discovery, in contrast to the common garden variety, involves a feat of generalizing that goes far beyond what may be expected in the usual learning situation. There is an "inductive leap," a combining of ideas that come from widely separated knowledge systems, a bold use of analogy that transcends what is usually meant by generalizing within a class of problem situations. An excellent example of such inventiveness is provided by the kinetic theory of gases. What was known, on the one hand, was a set of principles concerning the behavior of gases, the relations among the variables of temperature, pressure, and volume. On the other hand, there were the laws of motion, the effects of force in imparting acceleration to objects of specified mass. The stroke of genius in this case was one of hypothesizing that the gas was composed of particles (molecules) that had mass and whose reactions to force could, therefore, be considered to obey the laws of motion. From this single new synthesizing idea, this remarkable higher-order rule, the consequences follow that permit the confirmation of the theory. But the central idea itself was arrived at by putting together subordinate rules from two widely disparate systems of organized knowledge. A problem of this magnitude had to be solved by combining two sets of rules that originally seemed to have only the remotest connection with each other.

What has learning to do with creative discovery? The most obvious and dependable answer is that discoveries of great social importance have been made by men with a great store of intellectual skills. They are men who have acquired many kinds of hierarchies of rules. They have been deeply immersed in the rules of the discipline within which they work and, often, in the rules of other disciplines also. How did they learn these rules? Just as everyone else does—by combining sets of subordinate rules—partly, perhaps, with the aid of verbal instruction and partly by making the "small" discoveries that may be involved in the acquiring of the higher-order rules of any particular topic or system of intellectual skills.

Some scholars are highly dissatisfied with this kind of answer concerning the relation between learning and Discovery with a capital "D." Surely, they say, it is reasonable to suppose that if discovery is used constantly as a method of learning, this will predispose the individual to make the great Discovery? So far as any present evidence is concerned, such a proposition is wishful thinking at best; at worst, it is mere verbal sophistry. The use of discovery as a method of learning rules, as we have seen, may lead to individual capabilities that are highly effective from the standpoint of generalizability, applicability, and retention. In other words, this method of learning may generate a solid basis of intellectual skills in the individual. Furthermore, because it is a method rich in reinforcement value, the solving of problems within structures of intellectual skills to be learned may create a love of learning, a "thirst for knowledge" in the individual learner. But it is a vastly different thing to suppose that this kind of learning will necessarily predispose the individual to become a "creative" thinker, capable of making a great contribution to science or art. To be sure, the variables that produce genius are surely not entirely innate and must prominently include factors in the individual's experience, arising from his environment. But except as a method for acquiring prerequisite intellectual skills, "practicing discovery" seems an unlikely choice of antecedent variable to be involved in the production of genius (see Ausubel, 1968, pp. 473–497).

The Learning of Strategies
in Problem Solving

Turning back again to the conditions governing the type of learning called problem solving, we have emphasized in the present description the importance of verbal instructions in providing guidance to the thinking process. It is clear also that these instructions may be furnished by the individual himself when he is engaged in solving a problem without the aid of tutor or textbook. The formulation and use of such *self-instructions* is naturally an event that is itself dependent on a learning process. Among the other things learned by a person who engages in problem solving is "how to instruct oneself in solving problems." Such a capability is basically composed of higher-order rules, which are usually called *strategies*. The manner of learning this particular variety of higher-order rule is not different in any important respect from the learning of other rules. But whereas the higher-order rules previously discussed deal with intellectual skills relevant to the subject matter being learned, strategies pertain more generally to the behavior of the learner, regardless of what he is studying. In this sense, they are "content free." Strategies may not appear as a part of the goals of learning, but they are nevertheless learned. Considering the range of behaviors to which strategies are pertinent, it would appear that certain kinds of *study skills* may well be included. Rothkopf (1968) defines a class of *mathemagenic behaviors* which are used by the learner as capabilities for learning and remembering. Skinner (1967) emphasizes the importance of *self-management behaviors* which guide the individual in learning. *Strategies* in discovery and problem solving are described by Bruner (1961).

Strategies have not been much studied in connection with the learning of school subjects but they have been explored in laboratory situations. One example is a task in which the individual is asked to predict which of two lights, one on the left and one on the right, will come on in a series of trials. Unknown to the experimental subject is the fact that the lights have been arranged to come on in completely random patterns, but with predetermined frequencies (such as 6 right to 4 left). It has been shown that what the individual tends to do in this situation is to try out, one after the other, a great variety of *strategies*. For example, he may begin by instructing himself, "Alternate right and left" and progress to "Two right then one left" and to considerably more elaborate self-instructions, such as "Single alternate, then double alternate, then one right, then three left, and repeat" (Goodnow, 1955). It seems quite apparent that the strategies used in such a situation are based on simpler rules and concepts.

Rothkopf (1968) has found that questions interspersed at intervals following passages of reading material to be learned have the effect of improving retention of the information in the text, as compared with reading of the same material without questions. Furthermore, this effect was found to pertain not only to portions of the text to which the questions were directly relevant but also to portions to which they were not relevant. On the basis of such evidence as this, Rothkopf hypothesizes that the effect of questions is to establish certain kinds of "inspection behaviors," a class of "mathemagenic behaviors," which facilitate learning and retention of information obtained from the study of printed texts. Although these facilitative effects surely differ in kind from those that may be involved in problem solving, they appear to belong in the general category of *strategies*. These findings serve to emphasize what a considerable variety of strategies need to be taken into account in a general description of the conditions of learning. There must be strategies of attending, strategies of coding, strategies of storage and retrieval, strategies of hypothesis forming— and strategies that are particularly relevant to solving problems. All such strategies constitute a special class of rules and thus may come to be a highly useful portion of the repertoire of intellectual skills available to a sophisticated learner.

The use of strategies in forming concepts has also been studied in the laboratory (Bruner, Goodnow, and Austin, 1956). In this group of studies, learners were asked to identify a concept of classification in sets of cards, each containing two figures that could be categorized in various ways—on the basis of shape of figure, color of figure, number of figures, and number of borders. The concept sought might be the class of cards containing *two yellow rectangles*. It was found that learners adopted several different kinds of strategies, which might be said to characterize their "style" of solving this kind of problem. Some of these strategies were relatively "conservative," in the sense that a wrong choice did not require starting all over again with a new hypothesis, whereas others were relatively "risky" in the sense that they jumped to a hypothesis before the evidence was complete. The study confirms the idea that a variety of strategies is used in solving problems and that particular kinds of strategies tend to be favored by particular people. It also makes clear that a given problem of this type may be solved with more than one strategy.

The implication of these studies is that, when engaged in solving problems, individuals may learn to instruct themselves, to adopt strategies which guide their thinking. Presumably, these "self-instruction rules" are learned much as other rules are. But they do not appear as a part of the problem solution itself; they simply aid the process of problem solving. In a similar manner, it is reasonable to suppose that strategies are learned and used by individuals in solving any kind of problem.

Obviously, strategies are important for problem solving, regardless of the content of the problem. The suggestion from some writings is that they are of overriding importance as a goal of education. After all, should not formal instruction in the school have the aim of teaching the student "how to think"? If strategies were deliberately taught, would not this produce people who could then bring to bear superior problem-solving capabilities to any new situation? Although no one would disagree with the aims expressed, it is exceedingly doubtful that they can be brought about solely by teaching students "strategies" or "styles" of thinking. Even if these can be taught (and it is likely that they can), they do not provide the individual with the basic firmament of thought, which is a set of externally oriented intellectual skills. Strategies, after all, are rules that govern the individual's *approach* to listening, reading, storing information, retrieving information, or solving problems. If it is a mathematical problem the individual is engaged in solving, he may have acquired a strategy of applying relevant subordinate rules in a certain order—but he must also have available the mathematical rules themselves. If it is a problem in genetic inheritance, he may have learned a way of guessing at probabilities, before actually working them out—but he must also bring to bear the substantive rules pertaining to dominant and recessive characteristics. Knowing strategies, then, is not all that is required for thinking; it is not even a substantial part of what is needed. To be an effective problem solver, the individual must somehow have acquired masses of organized intellectual skills.

Learning Hierarchies and Problem Solving

Just as it is true that complex rules depend upon prior learning of simpler rules, so also a final task of problem solving may be shown to derive facilitation from previously learned relevant rules. Actually, the structure of such a hierarchy is not in itself different from those described in the previous chapter—the learning of higher-order rules is contributed to by prior learning of subordinate rules. What may be different is that the final task of such a hierarchy is presented with little verbal guidance and, therefore, has the character of a problem-solving task. An example is shown in Figure 15 (Gagné, 1962).

The final task depicted here was one in which ninth-grade students were asked to develop a general formula for the cumulative sum of n terms in a number series, using as variables in the formula the value of any term in the series (N) and its position in the series (T). The form of the expressions they were to develop may be illustrated by the example $\Sigma = 2N - 1$, applicable to the series 1 2 4 8 16 __ __. (The cumulative sum of this series through the term 16, for example, is $2 \times 16 - 1$, or 31.)

Students first learned those subordinate rules that they

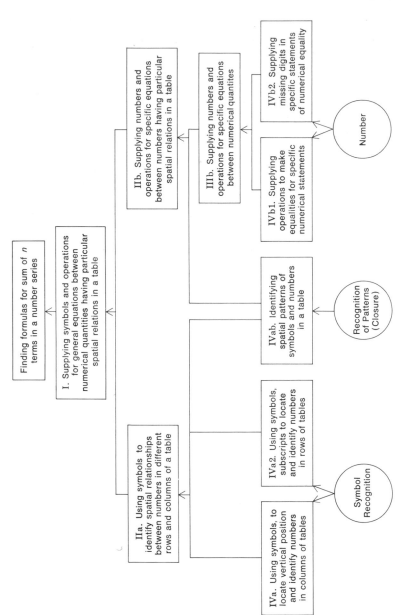

FIGURE 15. A learning hierarchy supporting the problem-solving task of finding formulas for the sum of *n* terms in number series. (From R. M. Gagné, The acquisition of knowledge. *Psychol. Rev.*, **69**, Figure 1, p. 359. Copyright 1962 by the American Psychological Association and reproduced by permission. Figure as adapted by J. M. Scandura [Ed.] in *Research in Mathematics Education*. Washington, D.C.: National Council of Teachers of Mathematics, 1967. Reprinted by permission of the National Council of Teachers of Mathematics.)

The boxes in the figure read:

Finding formulas for sum of *n* terms in a number series

I. Supplying symbols and operations for general equations between numerical quantities having particular spatial relations in a table

IIa. Using symbols to identify spatial relationships between numbers in different rows and columns of a table

IIb. Supplying numbers and operations for specific equations between numbers having particular spatial relations in a table

IIIb. Supplying numbers and operations for specific equations between numerical quantites

IVa. Using symbols, to locate vertical position and identify numbers in columns of tables

IVa2. Using symbols, subscripts to locate and identify numbers in rows of tables

IVab. Identifying spatial patterns of symbols and numbers in a table

IVb1. Supplying operations to make equalities for specific numerical statements

IVb2. Supplying missing digits in specific statements of numerical equality

Symbol Recognition

Recognition of Patterns (Closure)

Number

did not already know. As the figure shows, these ranged
from relatively simple rule-governed behaviors like IVa,
locating the vertical position of numbers in a table when
rows and columns are identified by letters, to the more complex rules involved in a task like IIb, formulating equations
expressing relations between numbers having specific spatial
arrangements in a table. It may be noted that none of these
subordinate tasks has anything to do *directly* with number
series; thus they are not subordinate in a logical sense to the
final task. They are subordinate, and supporting, in the
sense that the final problem-solving task required the
learners to look at the number series and their cumulative
sums as a tabular array (thus the requirement of finding
relations in a table), and also to generate a common relation among specific sets of numbers (hence the subordinate
rules dealing with number equations). The learning hierarchy, in other words, derives its relations not from logic
but from a consideration of learning and its prerequisites.

Initially, some of the students could do only a few of the
tasks in the hierarchy, while others could perform all but
the final task. The next step in the study was to teach all
of the students all of the tasks except the final one. This
was found to be possible and was carried out. Following
such learning, it was found that six out of seven students
were able to solve the final problem, with some additional
small amount of instruction on it, and no additional practice. The final task they were required to achieve had the
characteristics of a problem-solving activity, since it was a
number series with which these learners had had no prior
acquaintance. The students who were successful in solving
the problem can reasonably be said to have *discovered* the
solution.

This study shows the importance of prior learning of
relevant rules for problem solving. No doubt the students
were able to bring to bear different kinds of strategies in
achieving the solution. Undoubtedly, also, they brought to
the final task differences in "brightness" or "aptitude." Yet
what appeared to be a factor of prime importance determin-

ing their capability of solving the novel problem was the availability of relevant rules that they had learned prior to the time they attempted to solve this problem.

GENERAL REFERENCES

Problem Solving

Berlyne, D. E. *Structure and direction in thinking.* New York: Wiley, 1965.

Bruner, J. S., Goodnow, J. J., and Austin, G. A. *A study of thinking.* New York: Wiley, 1956.

Duncan, C. P. (Ed.). *Thinking: Current experimental studies.* Philadelphia: Lippincott, 1967.

Gagné, R. M. Problem solving. In A. W. Melton (ed.), *Categories of human learning.* New York: Academic Press, 1964.

Johnson, D. M. *The psychology of thought and judgment.* New York: Harper & Row, 1955.

Katona, G. *Organizing and memorizing.* New York: Columbia University Press, 1940.

Mandler, J. M., and Mandler, G. *Thinking: From association to Gestalt.* New York: Wiley, 1964.

Wertheimer, M. *Productive thinking.* New York: Harper & Row, 1945.

Woodworth, R. S. *Dynamics of behavior.* New York: Holt, Rinehart and Winston, 1958. Chap. 12.

9 | Learning Hierarchies

Each of the eight varieties of learning conditions, whether it occurs more or less accidentally or is deliberately employed in formal instruction, establishes a different kind of capability in the learner. This capability may be narrowly specific, as in responding to a signal, or it may range in generalizability to the kind of competence attained in rule learning and problem solving. But in all cases, the capability itself embodies an identifiable *intellectual skill,* something that the learner *is able to do* with reference to his environment. People do not learn in a general sense, but always in the sense of a change in behavior that can be described in terms of an observable type of human performance. As previously pointed out, a successful act of learning is inferred from the fact that the individual can now do something he could not do before. The nature of the intellectual skills with which the learner begins, as well as of the capability with which he ends up, are both essential for this inference.

THE LEARNING HIERARCHY

Illustrations have been given in the last two chapters of learning sequences in which the rule or problem-solving task to be learned was analyzed into simpler capabilities that needed to be learned as prerequisites. When such an analysis is continued progressively to the point of delineating an entire set of capabilities having an ordered relation to each other (in the sense that in each case prerequisite capabilities are represented as subordinate in position, indicating that they need to be previously learned), one has a *learning hierarchy.* The analytic process may be carried out, if desired, until the simplest kinds of learnings ($Ss \rightarrow R$'s, chains, discriminations) are reached and identified. In dealing with school subjects, however, carrying the analysis to such a point is rarely useful. Instead, it is usual to stop at the point where one has identified the capabilities that can be assumed to be present in the group of learners to whom the learning hierarchy is applicable. In other words, the lowest "boxes" in a hierarchy represent the kinds of performances all students in the group already know how to do. (If there is doubt concerning this assumption for any particular group, of course, it can be checked.) Accordingly, many learning hierarchies representing topics in school subjects are constructed without carrying the analysis to the point of identifying such previously learned capabilities as chains and discriminations. Many hierarchies turn out to depict, at their "lowest" levels, defined concepts, and to proceed from these to rules and higher-order rules.

Another noteworthy characteristic of learning hierarchies is the kind of statements included in the "boxes," each of which is intended to describe a single capability to be learned. These descriptions represent *what the learner is able to do when learning has been accomplished.* They are, therefore, stated as *performances,* of the general sort exemplified by the statement, "Given a printed sentence with incorrect punctuation, rewrites the sentence with proper use of commas, semicolons, colons, and dashes." Each statement should probably contain the phrase "exhibits the capability of" to be truly complete; such a phrase is omitted only to conserve space. Other contractions of phrasing are also frequently used for the same reason. For example, the previous statement might be stated as "edits sentences for correct punctuation," as long as it could be assumed that the reader were aware that this meant beginning with an incorrectly punctuated sentence, and also that the appropriate punctuation marks were comma, semicolon, colon, and dash. When the communicability of the statements of capability is in doubt, however, it is surely best to employ precise statements, even if they are long.

What is represented by the individual superordinate-subordinate relation that recurs throughout a learning hierarchy? Simply this: the superordinate capability will be more readily learned (on the average, throughout a group of students) if the subordinate capabilities have been previously acquired and are readily available for recall. Each subordinate capability has been identified as such because it is known (or initially, hypothesized) to contribute positive transfer to the learning or the superordinate capability (see Gagné, 1968). It should be possible to demonstrate that for students who learn the designated subordinate capabilities as prerequisites, their learning of the superordinate capability will be markedly facilitated compared with students who have *not* learned the subordinate capabilities. The word "markedly" is used to indicate that the positive transfer should be substantial, otherwise the identification of subordinate capabilities, while perhaps not completely invalid, may not be of practical importance. A learning hierarchy, then, identifies a set of intellectual skills that are ordered in a manner indicating substantial amounts of positive transfer from those skills of lower position to connected ones of higher position.

The basic functional unit of a learning hierarchy consists of a *pair* of intellectual skills, one subordinate to the other. As shown in Figure 16, the theoretically predicted consequence of a subordinate skill that has been previously mastered is that it will facilitate the learning of the higher-level skill to which it is related. In contrast, if the subordinate skill has not been previously mastered, there will be no facilitation of the learning of the higher-level skill. This

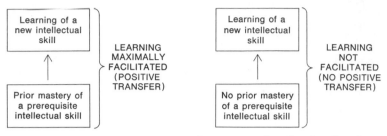

FIGURE 16. Representation of theory regarding the functional unit of a learning hierarchy, relating the learning of an intellectual skill to the prior mastery of a subordinate skill.

latter condition does not mean that the higher-level skill cannot be learned—only that, on the average, in the group of students for whom a topic sequence has been designed, learning will not be accomplished readily. Of course, as previous examples have already demonstrated, the functional unit depicted here may occur in variant forms; there may be two or three subordinate skills that contribute positive transfer to a higher-level skill. Or a single subordinate skill may facilitate the learning of more than one higher-level skill. For purposes of simplifying the discussion, however, it is convenient to consider the operation of these intellectual skills in pairs.

Does a learning hierarchy describe a "route" for the learning of a topic? Yes, in the sense that it represents what is expected to be a general pattern to be followed for *all* the students in the group: make sure that relevant lower-order skills are mastered before the learning of the related higher-order skill is undertaken.

What about the really bright student—will a procedure based upon this principle slow him down? This is definitely not the intention; neither is it necessary. First, the bright student may already know some of the subordinate skills that are not known to the student of lesser ability. The learning hierarchy, however, does not imply that one should set about giving instruction on those subordinate skills that the bright student already knows! Making a determination that they *are* actually known (in other words, testing for their presence) may still be a good procedure to follow, particularly if, out of half a dozen subordinate skills, one turns up that happens to have been "missed." In using the learning hierarchy as a guide to a "learning route," the proper procedure is, first, find out what the student already knows; second, begin instruction at that point.

There is a second reason why the learning hierarchy may not represent a point-to-point learning route for the truly bright student. Such a student, because of previously learned capabilities or innate capacities, may be able to "skip over" a particular subordinate skill and learn the higher-order skill without it. When this happens, the theory would say this particular learner has been able to acquire the higher-order skill by using a problem-solving approach that probably also utilizes some very important (and previously learned) strategies. In a sense, he is able to acquire both the subordinate and the superordinate skill in one intellectual jump. Hopefully, instructional procedures will be such that no obstacles will prevent him from doing this. It must be remembered, however, that the same size of jump is not going to be possible for the rest of the students, who do not have this kind of intellectual virtuosity. The learning hierarchy is supposed to provide a basis for finding a suitable learning route for *every* student.

Relation of Learning Hierarchies to Instruction

In describing the conditions of learning, the distinction between *external* and *internal* conditions has been given frequent emphasis. It will be evident that learning hierarchies pertain only to the *internal conditions*, in other words, to the capabilities that are to be learned and to the capabilities that are prerequisite to these. A hierarchy may identify component capabilities which are rules, others subordinate to these which are concepts, or discriminations, or chains, or even single $Ss \rightarrow R$ connections. These capabilities, however, insofar as learning is concerned, represent only the

internal conditions—those subordinate capabilities that need
to be recalled when a new higher-level skill is about to be
learned.

Representations of learning hierarchies are limited to the
description of and interrelations of intellectual skills. Thus,
a hierarchy does not represent *external* conditions of learning, as they have been described in previous chapters. Accordingly, the learning hierarchy does not picture the
procedures of instruction. The intention is not to depict *how*
an individual may come to learn a particular intellectual
skill—what kind of instruction to give, how much guidance
of learning to introduce, what sequence of communications
to follow, and so on. What is shown is only the internal conditions for learning, the prerequisite capabilities that will
provide the positive transfer to a new learning event. Identifying these capabilities and assuring their availability are
matters of critical importance for instruction.

PLANNING SEQUENCES OF INSTRUCTION

The existence of capabilities within the learner that build
on each other in the manner described provides the possibility of the *planning of sequences of instruction* within
various content areas. If problem solving is to be done with
physical science, then the scientific rules to be applied to the
problem must be previously learned; if these rules in turn
are to be learned, one must be sure there has been previous
acquisition of relevant concepts; and so on. Thus it becomes possible to "work backward" from any given objective
of learning to determine what the prerequisite learnings
must be—if necessary, all the way back to chains and simple
discriminations. When such an analysis is made, the result
is a kind of map of what must be learned. Within this map,
alternate "routes" are available for learning, some of which
may be best for one learner, some for another. But the map
itself must represent all of the essential landmarks; it cannot afford to omit some essential intervening capabilities.

The importance of mapping the sequence of learnings is mainly just this: it enables one to avoid the mistakes that arise from omitting essential steps in the acquisition of knowledge of a content area. Without such a plan, omissions of this sort are unfortunately easy to make. It would be pleasing to everyone, for example, if a learner could progress to the capability of extemporaneously composing sentences in a foreign language without previously learning to use individual words. But in fact such "skipping" is unsuccessful and, if tried, may result in serious "blocking" that may persist for a long time. Attempts to skip essential capabilities in mathematics can lead to similar consequences. The same is true of almost any content subject. Following a pre-planned sequence, then, and thus avoiding the omission of prerequisite capabilities along any route of learning, appears to be a highly important procedure to adopt in achieving effectiveness for instruction. One of the most readily apparent implications of the descriptions of learning conditions contained in previous chapters pertains to the planning of instructional sequences. If one is to take into account the differences in conditions applicable to each type of learning, the feature of *differential starting points* is crucial. Before any act of learning is undertaken, there needs to be a plan for learning in any subject area.

DESCRIPTION OF LEARNING CONTENT

In educational circles, the content of learning is often referred to as large categories of subject matter—English, mathematics, and so on. Although these categories may have a certain usefulness as entities for planning and managing schools and school systems, they nevertheless have some rather unfortunate characteristics as content terms. Chief among these is that the categories are so large that each includes a considerable variety of different kinds of human performances. The existence of such general "subject" categories makes it difficult to determine what human capabilities they do or should include. As a single example out of many possible ones, it is reasonable to think that one kind of capability a child ought to acquire in the primary grades is making an *accurate description of an unfamiliar object.* But is this "English," or "language," or "science"? An even more subtle and at the same time seriously unfortunate consequence of subject-matter categories is that they tend to engender a belief in their reality apart from their component human competencies. Thus there may be a tendency toward the false belief that "English" as a content for learning is something more than being able to read, write, and speak English competently; or that learning "mathematics" is something more than learning to solve problems logically and quantitatively.

These difficulties in identifying the content of learning would be avoided if care were taken to put the emphasis where it belongs, which is on the attainments of learners. When an act of learning occurs, the individual is enabled to accomplish something he could not accomplish previously— whether this be spelling a word or constructing a German sentence or writing a sonnet or performing an experiment. Such newly acquired accomplishments need to be identified in terms that are much more circumscribed than the "subjects" of the current-day curriculum.

When the outcomes of any learning event are described in terms of the performance such learning makes possible, it becomes apparent that the kinds of capabilities inferred deserve to be called *intellectual skills.* They are capabilities that make it possible for the individual to execute not a single specific task but an entire class of tasks. The outcomes of learning for formal school instruction are not primarily specific facts like "six times seven are forty-two," but rather the rules that enable the student to "find the product of whole numbers." An objective to be emphasized is "demonstrating the mechanical advantage of a lever" rather than "recalling the formula $F \cdot l = F' \cdot l'$." The rule learning aimed for in a social studies area, for example, is "predicting the social consequences of an increased rate of personal income tax," not "stating the amounts of rate increases in personal income tax between 1924 and 1968." While various kinds of verbal information ("facts," "propositions," "generalizations") play an important role in the *learning* of new intellectual skills, they do not represent a stable basis for describing what the individual "takes away with him" from his education. Intellectual skills, on the contrary, *do* tend to remain with the individual over long periods of time, partly perhaps because they continue to be used over and over again.

Learning hierarchies are the best way to describe the "structure" of any topic, course, or discipline. They describe the intellectual skills the individual needs to possess in order to perform intellectual operations within that subject—to learn about it, to think about it, to solve problems in it. Verbal information about a subject *can* be looked up (although, of course, a specialist in the subject has a great many facts, propositions, and generalizations stored in his memory). Intellectual skills, however, cannot be looked up; they must be learned. One does not expect the ordinary individual to be able to recall more than a small fraction of the words in a dictionary; one does expect him, however, to be able to exhibit the rule-governed behavior of finding any word in a dictionary. The latter is an intellectual skill he has learned and which is expected to remain with him for a lifetime, assuming at least occasional usage.

In the remainder of this chapter, the attempt will be made to examine the *learning structure* of some topics within various subjects of the curriculum. To do this, it will be necessary to break them down into smaller units representing fairly specific intellectual skills. Since these do not necessarily correspond to the "topics" in which a subject is customarily divided, a certain degree of novelty can be expected. It may be noted that in most cases these structures represent hypotheses about the arrangement of intellectual skills within each subject that have not been verified, although they are capable of verification. Accordingly, they do not represent final answers to questions of subject matter structure, but only an initial suggestion of such an answer. However, they do make it possible to state the relations between the content of instruction and the requirements of internal learning conditions as these latter have been described in previous chapters.

Each of the following sections describes, for mathematics, science, English, and foreign languages, a learning hierarchy pertaining to a component of each of these subjects. It is of importance to note that there is no intention of describing a "maturational sequence" relating the learning of an individual to his stage of growth or chronological age. Simple kinds of learning (types 2, 3, and 4, for example) occur throughout the learning history of the individual, no matter how old he may be. For example, a student of calculus must learn to identify the printed symbol for integration under essentially the same learning conditions that obtain when a student of arithmetic learns the printed symbol for division. In both cases, a learning hierarchy can be identified in which increasingly complex forms of learning build on these simpler forms. It is this kind of sequence of learning, independent of the stage of growth of the individual, that is the focus of interest. At the same time, it is inevitable that some correlation will be present between the sequence of simple-complex learning and the sequence of earlier-later events. The individual learns simpler things first, then more and more complex things; while all this is happening, he is also growing older. The next chapter includes a discussion of the learning hierarchy idea as a general principle of intellectual development.

SOME LEARNING STRUCTURES
Intellectual Skills in Mathematics

Mathematics is a subject that lends itself well to the illustration of learning hierarchies of intellectual skills. The reason is, quite simply, that mathematics is preponderantly composed of intellectual skills and not very much verbal information. Regarding the latter, there are the names of numbers and number operations, certain number sums and products, a few squares and square roots, and similar verbalized knowledge—not a large collection, compared with most school subjects. These are the items that must be "memorized," or stored mainly as verbal chains. But all the rest is a set of intellectual skills, beginning with simple concepts like the small natural numbers, and ranging in complexity to highly elaborate rules used in solving novel problems or in inventing new mathematical systems.

The learning structure of mathematics has been considerably illuminated, particularly in its early phases, by developments in the teaching of the "new mathematics." Some issues of desirable sequencing of topics within this subject have not yet been settled by mathematics scholars interested in pedagogy. Others, though, have been clarified tremendously, and there is reason to hope that many of the inconsistencies which may have tended to make students "block" on the subject have now been removed.

Before proceeding to consider a learning hierarchy for a particular mathematical topic, it will be worthwhile to attempt a general view of the kinds of learning as they relate to the activities involved in mathematics performances. As is true with other subjects, it will be apparent that the simpler kinds of learning are present in mathematics activities, although interest usually centers on the learning of concepts and rules, as well as on the discovery of higher-order rules.

Stimulus-Response Learning   At early ages, before they go to school, children often learn to say the names of common numbers from one to ten, and perhaps beyond that. Later on, they may learn to say many other new technical words, such as "multiply" and "cube root" and "secant" and "hyperbola" and "rhomboid" and a host of others. Acquiring these as self-generated responses is the major portion of what is acquired in mathematics under conditions of simple stimulus-response learning. One other simple connection of some importance is learning to hold and make marks with a pencil.

Chaining   The nonverbal chains that are basic to mathematics learning include primarily the printing of letters and symbols and the drawing of larger figures, such as geometrical forms. Some of these may be learned in preschool years, whereas others are learned in the early grades.

Verbal Sequences   Many kinds of verbal sequences are important and fundamental to mathematics learning. Before a child goes to school, he may have learned to name a sequence of numerals in their proper order, say from one to ten or from one to twenty. Such a child may be said to "know how to count," although the learning of a verbal sequence of this sort is not what is meant by "counting" in mathematics education. More useful sequences are of the verbal associate variety, in which the child learns to name printed numerals, to say "seven" when he sees 7. Later on, and throughout many years of studying mathematics, he will learn to associate names with new printed characters; he will learn the names of an exponent, a radical, an origin, a parabola, a parallelogram, and many, many others.

Discriminations   Some of the fundamental discriminations the child learns permit him to differentiate one specific object (a marble, say) from two, two from three, three from four, and so on up to six or seven. For more objects than this, he must learn to count, as will be seen later. Actually, the only multiple discriminations that are assumed as being essential in formal instruction on numbers are those between nothing and one and between one and two. But more than these are usually informally learned, nevertheless; primitive and uninstructed human beings can readily discriminate four fingers from five without recourse to counting. Another basic set of multiple discriminations that must be acquired early are the distinctions between printed numerals and other symbols. The printed 9 must be distinguished

from the printed 6, + from ✕, and so on. Later on, there are
other discriminations to be learned that will be a source of
difficulty if they are not mastered: the positions of the
coefficient, the exponent, and the subscript; parentheses
and brackets; separations and intersections; the extents of
angles; the directions of lines; adjacent and opposite angles
and sides of triangles and other geometrical figures; and a
variety of symbols, such as Greek letters and the operation
signs of logic. Whenever potentially confusable symbols or
figures are newly introduced in mathematics, discrimination learning must occur. To assume that it has already
happened, or to deliberately skip over it, is to invite later
difficulties with more complex forms of learning.

Concept Learning   *Alike* and *different* are two concepts that
are essential to later learning in mathematics, as they are for
most other subjects of the curriculum. Sometimes these concepts are learned by children in preschool years. Attaining
them as concepts means being able to say about *any* objects,
pictures, or symbols that they are alike or unlike. As indicated in Chapter 6, the conditions for such learning require the use of a variety of concrete examples of representative kinds of objects and pictures. It is worth emphasizing,
too, that if he is to be successful, the child who sets out to
learn these concepts must have previously acquired discriminations of the specific objects introduced as examples.

A fundamental concept of early instruction in numbers is
the *set*. A set is the concept of quantity abstracted from a
variety of groupings of specific objects—marbles, balls,
beans, pieces of chalk, boys and girls, or whatever. One of
the earliest tasks of mathematics instruction, many scholars
believe, should be the acquiring of the concept of set by the
student. At the same time, or perhaps even earlier, the concept of the *member*, the single unit, of a set needs to be
acquired. The point of such instruction, of course, is to free
the notion of quantity from control by specific stimuli. When
the child has learned *set* and *member of set* as concepts, he
is able to generalize them to any and all objects, whether or

not he has seen the objects previously. By combination with previous learning of verbal associates, he is then able to name such sets as one, two, and three and to assign these names to quantities of objects independently of their other stimulus characteristics.

There are other simple concepts involved in early mathematics instruction, which can often (although not always) be assumed to have been previously learned. Some examples are the event concepts of *adding to* and *taking away*. These are important for later learning, when instruction will be concerned with adding something to a set or taking something away from a set. The concepts of *separation* and *combining* are similarly important. A set of objects may be made into two sets of objects by separating some of its members from others, that is, by actually introducing a physical distance between them. Also, two physically disparate sets may be combined into one by eliminating a boundary or spatial separation between them.

Many other concepts are learned as the student proceeds with the study of mathematics, including add, subtract, multiply, divide, fraction, proportion, base, decimal, and so on, to quite a lengthy list. Included, of course, are geometrical concepts like point, line, plane, triangle, rectangle, parallel, and countless others. As mentioned in Chapter 7, it is usually desired at some stage to have the student learn the *definition* of, for example, a triangle. The definition, however, is a rule, and requires that the student has previously learned *triangle* as a concrete concept; knowing the concrete concept *triangle* means only that the student can *identify* triangle as a class, not that he can define it. The stage of learning concrete concepts is an essential one and should not be skipped over in instruction in the desire to have the student formulate "exact" definitions.

Rule Learning　　Returning to the earliest content of mathematics instruction, it is evident that it is the intention of modern mathematics to teach the child to count and to add by acquiring *rules*. Having the concepts *set, member of set, adding to,* and *taking away* makes it possible for the child to acquire rules that, if stated verbally, would run somewhat as follows: "The set called '2' is formed by adding a member to the set '1'; the set called '3' is formed by adding a member to '2'; the set called '4' is formed by adding a member to set '3'; and so on." Once acquired, these rules make it possible for the child to *order numbers,* in other words, to count. Another principle he is able to acquire is how to form zero (not to be confused with the simple discrimination "not any"). Zero is that set which may be formed by taking one member away from the set 1. Progressing from this point, the child learns how to add by applying certain rules of combining (joining) sets. By combining the sets 3 and 2, or the sets 4 and 1, the set 5 is obtained, and the child learns that the statements $3 + 2$, $4 + 1$, and 5, all name the same numbers.

To trace the sequence of learning through even a small number of topics of mathematics is obviously impossible in this space. Needless to say, mathematics is filled with rules, and they build on each other in cumulative fashion. An example of a hierarchy of principles that may be acquired in early geometry instruction is given in Figure 11.

Problem Solving   Rules can also be learned in mathematics by a judicious use of the discovery method of instruction; in other words, by problem solving. For example, having learned counting rules, children can be led to discover the rules governing the placement of numerals as a means of naming sets 10 through 20, and thus begin to learn to use the decimal system. Again, building further on this rule and those previously learned, they can discover how to add two-digit numbers, and so on, until an ever-growing structure of interconnected rules has been mastered.

The Order of Learning Types   These examples from mathematics provide an answer to this kind of question: Is there a sequence of forms of learning, from simple to complex, that should be followed in instruction? The answer is yes, but such a sequence cannot be applied to whole "subjects" like mathematics; it can be made to apply only to individual "topics" of mathematics. It would be incorrect to suppose that the learning of all of mathematics begins with stimulus-response learning and progresses through various other types of learning to problem solving. As we have seen, there is some stimulus-response learning as well as some discrimination learning even in an advanced topic like the integration of area, whereas some problem solving can occur even in the elementary topics of counting and adding. Thus, *within a topic*, it is clear that a progression of learning types from simple to complex may be identified.

An example of a learning hierarchy applicable to a prekindergarten topic in mathematics is shown in Figure 17. The relative simplicity of this task illustrates important characteristics of such a hierarchy. What is to be learned by the child is described in the topmost box. The instructions

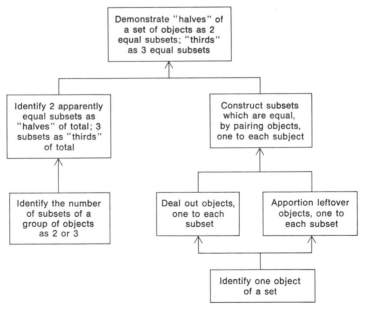

FIGURE 17. A learning hierarchy for a prekindergarten mathematical skill. (Suggested by the work of Resnick, 1967.)

for such a task would be something like: "Here on the table are some objects. Show me how you would divide the whole set into halves." In constructing a hierarchy of subordinate learnings for such a task, one asks, "What would the child have to know how to do, in order to learn this task, given instructions such as these?" In answering such a question, it is necessary to "think through" what the child is actually doing when he is exhibiting such a performance. (Some investigators, particularly Resnick [1967], suggest that one may need to *write out* as sequential steps, rather than simply think out, what the learner must do in performing a task.) Such an analysis leads to the conclusion that the child must be able to (1) identify two apparently equal subsets of a total group as "halves" and three such subsets as "thirds" and (2) construct actually equal subsets by pairing objects one to each set. It may be noted that the first of these capabilities is a defined concept, the second a rule. At any rate, these two capabilities are hypothesized to be prerequisite to the final task, and are so represented in Figure 17.

Further analysis shows that the task of identifying "halves" means that the child must be able to identify "two"; and for "thirds," "three." This capability is accordingly represented as a prerequisite. Similarly, an analysis of the task of constructing equal subsets leads to the identification as prerequisites of the two capabilities "dealing out objects, one to each subset," and "apportioning left-over objects, one to each subset." These in turn may be seen to require as a prerequisite the very simple concept of one (of a set).

The learning hierarchy that results from this analysis depicts the *internal conditions* for learning each capability. It also shows a hypothesized progression for separate learning events within the topic, a progression that represents the most efficient route for learning (on the average, for a group of learners). Not all mathematics educators will necessarily agree that the progression of required learnings must be exactly as shown. This is not a matter of extreme importance at this point, however. What is important is that there must be *a progression something like this*, in which the rule to be learned is put together from prerequisite rules, while these in turn depend on previously learned concrete concepts, which are based upon previously learned discriminations (not shown in the figure). That any one of these prerequisites is essential can readily be determined by empirical studies and by experience in teaching the topic. The most serious errors in instruction are likely to occur when the hierarchy, whatever its detailed structure, remains unrecognized.

A second example of a learning hierarchy in the field of mathematics pertains to the topic of adding integers, as shown in Figure 18. This topic was taught to a group of seventh-graders by means of programmed instruction contained in booklets (Gagné, Mayor, Garstens, and Paradise, 1962). As the hierarchy indicates, two separate final tasks were distinguished, one of simply finding sums of positive and negative numbers (Task 2) and the other of constructing a logical demonstration of the addition of positive and negative numbers (Task 1). The prerequisites of these two tasks were considered to differ somewhat and also to contain capabilities in common, as the figure indicates. The analysis of these tasks was performed in the manner previously described and was carried to the point at which it could be reasonably assumed that all children were able to do the tasks (those designated as Va and Vb). The results of this study confirmed that the hierarchy of prerequisites had been well identified.

The results also made possible an answer to the question, Does the learning of a prerequisite capability transfer positively to a higher-order capability? Results will be summarized here that are *illustrative* of the findings, and the reader is referred to the original monograph for further information. Consider capability IIa. According to the figure, there should be considerable positive transfer to the learning of this capability from the prerequisite learning of IIIa. To examine this evidence, one can begin with a group of 133 students who knew how to do IVa. Of this original group, 108 learned to do IIIa, while 25 did not. Did a higher propor-

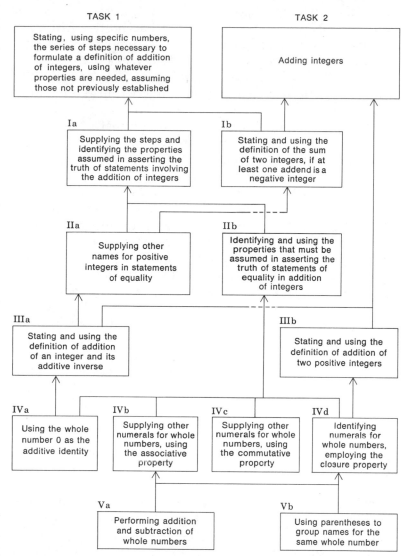

FIGURE 18. A learning hierarchy pertaining to the addition of integers. (From R. M. Gagné, J. R. Mayor, H. L. Garstens, and N. E. Paradise, Factors in acquiring knowledge of a mathematical task. *Psychol. Monogr.*, 1962, **76,** No. 526, Figure, 1, p. 4. Copyright 1962 by the American Psychological Association and reproduced by permission.)

tion of those who had learned IIIa then learn IIa, compared with the proportion learning IIa who had *not* learned IIIa? The answer was quite clear—the first proportion was 83 percent, while the second was only 12 percent. This is a high amount of positive transfer and indicates that the capability identified as IIIa has an important function in the learning of this topic.

Comparably high degrees of positive transfer, measured in this manner, were found to obtain for every one of the prerequisite capabilities identified. This study makes clear, then, that evidence of the importance of each hypothesized capability in a hierarchy can be obtained in a group of students who have had an opportunity to learn them. It is worth emphasizing again that the transfer obtained is (usually) not 100 percent—*some* students are able to learn higher-order skills without first acquiring the prerequisite skills identified. But when results from the total group are considered, the amount of facilitation of learning provided by prerequisite learnings is often very great. Should the amount of transfer be small or zero, of course, the indication is that the skill in question is not necessary as a prerequisite; in other words, the hypothesis is not confirmed. Before using the hierarchy as a guide for the sequencing of instruction, one would under such circumstances eliminate that particular capability and revise the hierarchy accordingly.

Intellectual Skills in Science Instruction

The hierarchy of capabilities that is learned when an individual studies science has several features in common with the learning of mathematics. There appear to be two primary reasons for this. First is the fact that both subjects must start with a consideration of concrete objects in order that the earliest forms of learning will be made possible. And second, the student of science very early begins to use the concepts and principles of mathematics, for example, in counting and measuring natural phenomena or in dealing with proportions and directions and sizes.

The typical student who begins the study of a particular topic in science, say in the seventh grade, has already learned many of the basic prerequisites that he needs in order to acquire the new concepts and principles he will encounter. Some of them may have been acquired in studying mathematics, to be sure.

Basic Types of Learning   It would not be particularly profitable here to try to spell out in detail all the relevant instances of basic learning that are prerequisite to the study of science. Suffice it to say that many $Ss \rightarrow R$ connections, such as orally saying the names of common objects and events, are needed, as well as others pertaining to the use of the hands in using a pencil and the eyes in scanning the environment. Chains related to hand movements must also be learned, and others involved in moving the limbs and the entire body in going forward and backward and in moving the eyes and head in looking up, down, right, and left. Verbal associates are also of fundamental importance to later learning in science. The names of all sorts of common objects and events in the environment must be learned—chairs, tables, houses, floors, ceilings, trees, flowers, cats, dogs, and many, many others, as well as specific events like going, coming, standing, sitting, running, and so on. Most of these basic capabilities are acquired before the child goes to school. When they are not so acquired, early instruction needs to make provision for their learning.

Discrimination Learning   The fundamental content of science is natural objects and events. The very early kind of learning that the child can and must undertake is the *discrimination* of the sensible characteristics of objects and events. Yellow objects need to be distinguished from blue ones and green ones; bright objects from dull ones; rounded objects from angular ones. Loud sounds are to be distinguished from soft ones; high sounds from low ones; brief sounds from extended ones. Heavy objects must be distinguished from light ones; smooth objects from rough ones; sharp objects from dull ones.

It is probably a mistake to suppose that all these discriminations will have been mastered before kindergarten attendance is begun. To an adult they appear painfully elementary. Yet a certain proportion of adults are unable to identify yellow as distinct from orange, or to know whether an object has a rounded edge. It seems probable that such deficiencies can in many instances be traced back to some learning deprivation in their initial school years. Early school instruction, therefore, needs to take pains to avoid gaps in the multiple-discrimination capabilities of the child. The physical characteristics of objects need to be observed and discriminated with systematic thoroughness, using all the externally oriented senses.

Concepts   The concepts useful for learning mathematics are needed also in learning science, and some other intriguing ones in addition. All the differential *attributes of objects* previously learned as discriminations need to be used for establishing concepts. *Yellow* becomes not just the color of an object, but the name of a class of (yellow) objects. *Round* becomes not just a characteristic of a ball, but the name of a class of objects that may include coins, cans, drawn circles, and many sizes of spheres. *Smooth* becomes not simply the feel of a water-washed rock, but a class of characteristics applicable to silk, cream, polished wood, a baby's skin, and many other things. Similarly, *near* is not just a position of the hand, but a class of distinctions along a gradient of distances from the individual observer that may be occupied by any sorts of objects (as distinguished, of course, from another set of distinctions called *far*).

Still other concepts must be established on the basis of previously learned discriminations. These include such "positional" concepts as *before* and *following, next to* and *separated from, above* and *below, in front of, behind,* among others. There are "directional" concepts like *parallel to, at right angles to, diagonal to,* as well as *vertical* and *horizontal,* which are common to the beginning study of geometry. Also in this category are concepts of common shapes, such as *circle, square, rectangle, triangle, cube, sphere,* and *pyramid.* Finally, there are the fundamental categories of science, which in this phase probably consist of several concepts of *size* (*length, area, volume*), *time* (*minute, hour, day, week*), *force* (as a push or pull), *weight* (as heaviness), and possibly also *mass* (as related to the phenomenon of inertia).

These basic concepts of science do not attain a high degree of abstraction in this early phase of instruction. On the contrary, they are relatable to quite concrete stimulus situations. And it is just this concreteness that is essential if adequate rules are to be learned later. For example, a later rule will be the relation between length and area of a rectangular figure. To learn such a rule, however, the child must already be able to use the concepts *length* and *area* and *rectangular.* (Using them as concepts means simply that he be able to *identify them,* not simply describe or define them.) For members of an entire class of closed figures, he should be able to choose the ones that are rectangular, identify the sides that have differing lengths, and find the region that has the property of area.

The priority in learning for meanings that are concrete (sometimes called "intuitive," although that is not a clear word) is a matter of great importance to instruction in all subjects. It may be, though, that its importance can be illustrated most clearly within the framework of science. College texts in physics, for example, are concerned with teaching the highly abstract rule contained in the statement $F = ma$. Yet it is common to find that the *force* in such a statement must be related for the student to the basic concept *push* or *pull.* There is nothing shameful in this, or even inaccurate. Before he can master a rule, the student must be able to identify the *concept force,* to point to situations in which a force can in fact be observed. Acceleration and mass are other variables in this equation that must be related to concretely referenced concepts before the rule can be learned. The student must master concepts, imprecise and qualitative as they seem to be, before he can be expected to learn rules.

Rule Learning   To return now to early instruction in science, the preceding phase saw the establishment of a variety of fundamental concepts. Is the student now ready to tackle the learning of rules like $F = ma$, or inheritance through dominant and recessive genes? Probably not, unless one is willing to take the dangerous risk of having him learn to parrot verbal sequences. There are some fundamental *rules* he must learn first, because any science is a highly organized discipline. Some kinds of rules are much more basic than others, and at the same time much more generalizable than others, in the sense that they cut across all the specific scientific disciplines. They are used again and again throughout the study of scientific subjects. In the treatment of introductory science commonly seen in junior and senior high school textbooks, they are usually *assumed* to have been learned previously. What kinds of rules are these?

A rather large number of intellectual skills could be named that are common to all sciences, and no attempt will be made here to exhaust the list. These capabilities, however, seem to fall into certain logical categories, and these might well be considered as proper *topics of elementary science* in contradistinction to the disciplines of chemistry, biology, physics, and the like, which will later be studied as specific subjects. The Commission on Science Education, American Association for the Advancement of Science (1967), undertook the development of materials for science instruction in the elementary grades which emphasize the learning of *processes* relevent to science in a systematic manner. Such processes are equivalent to the intellectual skills described in this section and are categorized under the general names of *observing, classifying, measuring, using space-time relations, using number, communicating,* and *inferring.* In the fifth and sixth grades, students of science progress to carrying out more extended activities (referred to as *integrated processes*), which include *formulating hypotheses, defining operationally, manipulating variables, interpreting data, drawing conclusions,* and, as the most complex activity of all, *experimenting.* As planned in the curriculum sequenee, these later activities incorporate within them the simpler intellectual skills that are to be initially acquired in the earlier grades.

The AAAS curriculum, called *Science—A Process Approach,* thus obviously emphasizes the development of the kinds of intellectual skills that are thought to be involved in "doing science." This is one way to conceive the common features of science instruction, which are believed to give support to the subsequent learning of any particular science. It is, however, not the only way of conceiving the common features of science instruction, and others have emphasized the importance of certain widely occurring entities of *knowledge* (that is, of defined abstract concepts) like *interaction, system, equilibrium,* and so on.

It is apparent that the processes (intellectual skills) described here have not frequently been considered suitable topics for introductory science in the elementary grades. What relation do they have, for example, to observations of the growth of a bean plant in a window box, a typical subject for a kind of elementary science instruction frequently in vogue? The growth of plants can readily be employed in the acquisition of the kinds of rules just described. For example, *classification* rules may be exhibited by means of a demonstration containing several kinds of plants growing at different rates. *Measuring* rules have an obvious applicability to the growth of plants. *Space-time* rules may be exhibited by the changes in size of plants in several dimensions, as well as by the differential rates of growth of the components of the plants. Observations on plant growth can readily be turned into an exercise having a *communication* objective, for example, by inquiring whether other students are able to recognize the change in a plant described by a particular student. Finally, there is plenty of opportunity for the acquisition of *inference* rules, distinguishing between the observed events of changes in size and the inference of "growth" or other "changes of state."

If one has the purpose of having young children learn these intellectual skills, it can be done with magnets, with small animals, with simple machines, with growing plants, and with many other phenomena of the natural world. Alternatively, one can begin with the same observations and end up with not-very-useful verbal sequences. For example, first-graders can easily be taught to answer such questions as, "What do plants need in order to grow?" (Sun, earth, and water.) The instructional question becomes, Which kind of capability is a prerequisite for the rigorous study of any science—general principles of the processes of science or general information (chiefly verbal) about the natural world? On reflection, the second of these alternatives seems trivial in importance as compared with the first.

Problem Solving   As is the case with other subjects, problem solving can profitably be employed in instruction to establish both basic and higher-order rules and principles of science. Novel rules of classification can be discovered by students having suitably designed instructions that guide thinking but do not "give the answer." New units of measurement can be originated for objects or events that have not been previously experienced. In fact, virtually all the rules listed above can be taught by means of instruction using discovery methods. It may be that there is a particular value to instruction that emphasizes problem solving for science subjects, in view of the fact that problem-solving strategies play such a prominent role in science activities themselves.

An Example of a Learning Hierarchy in Science   The dependence of learning of "higher-level" rules of a specific science topic on the prior learning of "lower-level" rules that are general to science may be illustrated by an analysis of the topic "Solving physical work problems," illustrated in Figure 19. To be learned are rules that enable the student

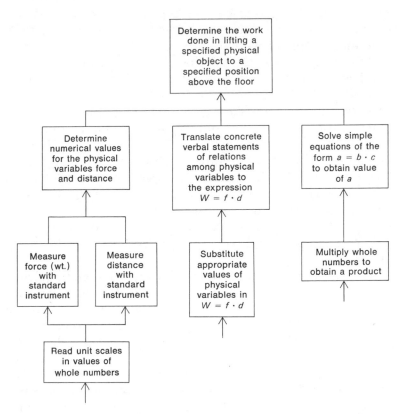

FIGURE 19. Solving physical work problems; a learning hierarchy pertaining to a science topic.

to begin with a problem described to him verbally, or shown to him, such as, "How much (physical) work is done in raising this box to the height of this table?" (The box and table are understood to be physically present in this example.) The student proceeds by translating this physical situation into a mathematical expression for work, choosing and measuring the proper units of force and distance, and then solving the equation to obtain an answer for "amount of work done." Doing this kind of problem, of course, is not intended to represent the only objective of science instruction on the topic of work.

As the figure shows, solving this concretely presented problem depends on prerequisite capabilities of three sorts: (1) determining numerical values for the variables *force* and *distance;* (2) translating concrete verbal problems into mathematical statements; and (3) solving simple equations. Each of these in turn draws positive transfer from still other previously learned capabilities, which have been traced down to a point reasonable for, say, seventh-graders to have attained as starting skills. One could proceed further with the analysis if the topic were to be learned by fourth-graders. In such a case one might come to the level of defined concepts like *force, distance,* and *scale unit,* among others.

Thus it can be seen that rules relevant to a specific science topic require the prior learning of subordinate rules that are *general* to science, in the sense that they deal with the *processes* of obtaining scientific information, whether this is biological, physical, chemical, or whatever. Moreover, these fundamental rules in turn necessitate the learning of prerequisite concepts. It would be possible to show that these latter concepts also depend on simpler forms of learning of the varieties described in previous chapters. Science learning, like mathematics learning, has a hierarchical structure that is crucially supported by a number of concepts and rules that are not content specific; rather, they are general to the study of any and all sciences.

Hierarchies in the Learning of Foreign Languages

The nature of instruction for the learning of a foreign language is of particular interest to the present discussion because such instruction encompasses almost the entire range of learning types. Thus, a challenging task awaits the investigator who attempts to construct a learning hierarchy in this field. There has come to be an increasing awareness during recent times of the necessity for devoting considerable attention to the early parts of language learning, to those capabilities that are generally called skills. Only when such early skills are mastered, it is now generally believed, is the student ready to progress to later stages of language learning.

Basic Types of Learning   The learning of a foreign language must begin with some of the simplest types of learning, the acquiring of $Ss \rightarrow R$ connections and motor chains that copy the *sounds* of the language. The more unfamiliar the foreign language sounds in the native language, the more essential is this phase. Spanish, for example, is often considered "easy," largely because its sounds are relatively similar to those of English; by the same token, Chinese is "difficult." The sounds of the syllables of a word like *gemütlich* are quite different from those in English words; at least, the *ü* and the *ch* are encountered very infrequently as sounds in English. If the learner is expected later to acquire the capability of recognizing and producing these sounds in speech, he must first acquire them as simple $Ss \rightarrow R$ connections (and as parts of motor chains) so that he can generate them himself as voluntary acts.

The precision with which such sounds must be learned in the earliest phase of language instruction has been the subject of some discussion among language educators. It will be clear from the present and following discussion that a "good accent" is *not* the purpose of this phase of language learning. Discrimination learning needs to occur only with the precision that will result in the differentiation of such a sound as *ü* from other confusable sounds, particularly English ones, like *oo* and *uh* and *ee*. To insist on finer differentiations than this (such as "sounding like a native speaker") at this stage of language instruction, although perhaps doing no permanent harm, can certainly delay the progress of acquiring facility in a new language. The degree of precision of discrimination needed in these basic stimulus-response connections is simply that which will enable the *student* to differentiate the sounds in his own utterances.

Verbal Chains   A certain number of common expressions may well be learned as simple chains in order to increase the student's initial confidence in the language. Expressions of courtesy and convenience—for example, *wollen Sie bitte* or *pardonnez-moi* or *wieviel Uhr is es?*—fall into this category.

The most important chains to be learned, however, are the verbal associations between objects and actions on the one hand and foreign words on the other; in other words, in the development of a noun and verb *vocabulary*. As stimuli for these verbal chains, pictures can probably be used to good advantage. It is, after all, the chain (money as physical object) → *Geld* that one wants to establish and not the "translation" chain (English word "money") → *Geld*. However, the importance of the mediating link in such chains is considerable and should not be overlooked. Thus it seems entirely likely that a picture of coins *plus* the English word "gold" as stimuli would be, on the whole, more effective in establishing a verbal chain ending with *Geld* than would the picture alone. There is no reason at all to think that adding the English word to the stimulus complex in this case produces interference, or somehow increases the difficulty of the task. Quite the contrary would seem to be the case—the English word should have a facilitating effect on learning because it can provide a highly useful mediating link in the chain to be learned.

Longer verbal chains may also have considerable importance to later learning of self-generated conversational utterances. To acquire a store of such poetical sequences as *"Wer recht in Freuden wandern will, Der geh' der Sonn' entgegen . . ."* is to have available for ready recall a certain reservoir of expressions and sentence structures that can serve as excellent models from which spontaneous speech can be derived and on which it can be patterned. Prose sequences, of course, can serve the same function equally well.

Concept Learning   The learning of concepts in a foreign language follows much the same course as it does in the native language. Initially, the concept intended by a new foreign word may be most readily conveyed by an English "equivalent." For many nouns and verbs, particularly, this use of an external verbal prompt (the English word) may bring about a very high proportion of the concept learning required. *Fromage* may readily be prompted by the English word "cheese," *écrire* by the English word "write." But, as language scholars are fond of pointing out, such external prompts may be insufficient to convey the "true" conceptual meaning of a foreign word. *Chérie,* for example, may be initially prompted by the English word "dear," but this would be quite insufficient to identify the class of situations in which *chérie* may properly be used. Does one use *chérie* in saying (in French) "dear mother," "dear sister," "dear friend," or is it confined to "dear sweetheart"?

There is no mystery here. Adequate learning of a concept, as mentioned in Chapter 5, requires the learning of discriminations in a *representative variety* of stimulus situations. Accordingly, in order to learn the concept reflected in a new foreign word, one must encounter it and use it in some representative contexts. To the extent that these contexts have been unrepresentative, the concept learned will be an inadequate one. To the extent that a suitable range of stimulus situations is encountered by the learner, the concept learned will be a satisfactory one.

The necessity for an adequate number of contextual examples is particularly apparent for the learning of such words as prepositions and conjunctions. As every beginning student of French knows, *de* does not always mean the same as "of," and *a* means many things besides "to." Again the obvious implication for instruction in these concepts, and many others like them, is to provide a sufficient variety of stimulus contexts in which these small words occur. For such words, although prompting with English probably does no harm when the foreign word is initially encountered, any such procedure is grossly insufficient for the learning of the concept in its full meaning. In order to achieve the latter, the range of situations in which the word occurs must be presented to the learner and responded to by him.

Rule Learning Putting concepts together as connected discourse, whether in understanding spoken speech, in responding to other speakers, or in reading, is a task that obviously requires the use of rules. In traditional language instruction, these are the "rules of grammar and syntax." To learn these rules in verbal form seems a perfectly reasonable thing for a student to do, just so long as the danger of learning "mere verbal sequences" is avoided. If he learns a verbal rule for German such as "*in* in the sense of 'moving into' is followed by an accusative form of the noun," this is a highly useful principle so long as he can identify concretely the concepts that compose it (such as "moving into," "accusative," and "noun") and has not merely memorized it as a verbal sequence.

Some language teachers state a preference for the inductive formulation of rules by students; in other words, for the use of a discovery method of instruction. As pointed out previously, such a method may actually take longer, but seems to have advantages. In practice, the student would be made to encounter a number of contrasting expressions like *in der Welt* and *in die Welt,* and would discover from the context the rule about dative and accusative forms (without necessarily using these technical terms) following the preposition *in.*

In the learning of language rules, a point deserving great emphasis is the importance of prerequisites. And the necessary prerequisites, as has previously been pointed out, are concepts. The contents of the rules that are exhibited in the form of phrases, sentences, and conversations are, of course, the concepts of the foreign language, that is, its *words* in their conceptual form. It should be almost self-evident that ideas cannot be expressed unless one has previously learned their unitary parts. Thus the learning of vocabulary is of considerable importance in facilitating the learning of the rules of grammar and syntax. The greater the number of verbal concepts one knows, the easier it should be to learn the required rules of language structure.

In traditional language instruction, the learning of rules is usually interspersed with the learning of vocabulary. The student learns a little vocabulary, and then practices using a few rules of grammar. It is at least a likely hypothesis, however, that if a student had acquired a sizable vocabulary, the learning of "structure" would proceed quite rapidly. On the other hand, there would seem to be little merit whatsoever, from the standpoint of learning efficiency, in the attempt to teach structure *before* vocabulary. Whatever is learned in this manner cannot be learned efficiently, because the learner is so frequently "at loss for words."

Problem Solving As has already been pointed out, discovery of rules of grammar and syntax is a possible method of learning. At somewhat more advanced stages of foreign language facility, the use of problem-solving situations may also be the best kind of learning condition to employ. A native speaker sets the problem situation by inquiring, "What would you like for dinner?" The student must generate a reply that makes sense not only in being understandable but also in representing the contents of an actual dinner. The setting of many kinds of problem situations of this sort is of great value for acquiring facility in understanding and speaking the foreign language. It need hardly be emphasized again that a reasonably adequate vocabulary is a prerequisite to successful learning by means of such exercises.

A Learning Hierarchy in English

Instruction in one's native language has many points in common with the conditions for learning a foreign language.

This is particularly true in the early stages of education, in which the youngster learns to use the language in communicating and in reading. The learning hierarchy presented here is one that pertains to the early stages of reading. For instruction beyond this initial stage, one would need another entire set of hierarchies having to do with reading comprehension, styles of reading, and so on. Later study of English concerns itself increasingly, as would be expected, with higher-order principles of writing and appreciation of literature. These can be undertaken successfully only after the individual has thoroughly mastered the more fundamental capabilities of English comprehension and expression. However, there is reason to believe that even such complex performances as those that are involved in the study of literature can be analyzed into learning structures which are useful for instruction.

Initial Reading   Figure 20 shows a learning hierarchy applicable to initial reading. This illustrates a portion of the skills that are involved in reading; but it appears to be a very important part. The task to be achieved has been identified by Chall (1968) as *decoding*, the oral pronunciation of printed words constructed according to regular rules. In examining the figure, the reader who has studied this chapter should be able readily to identify various types of learning involved at different levels of the hierarchy.

The objective of this hierarchy, represented in the topmost box, is the application of the relatively complex rule of reading words that conform to regular pronunciation rules (words like "sensational," "prosperity," "fundamentalism" would qualify). An important component of this behavior is illustrated in the next lower box, which is the testing of "trial" pronunciations against familiar English syllable sounds (such as the sound of the oral syllables "fun," "pros," "tion," and "ity," among others). Obviously, there are a number of rules to be learned here, of increasing complexity as the child progresses up the hierarchy of skills.

By glancing down the left branch of the learning hierarchy, it may be noted that one arrives at concrete con-

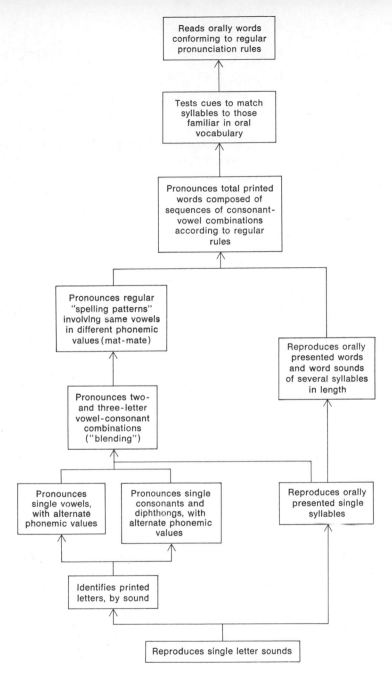

FIGURE 20. A learning hierarchy for a basic reading skill ("decoding").

cepts, such as those involved in responding correctly to (that is, in pronouncing) printed single vowels and single consonants or diphthongs having alternate phonemic values (the concepts of *short a* and *long a, hard c* and *soft c*). These in turn depend upon prior learning of even simpler concepts, the identifying of printed single letters by their sounds. Most basic of all is reproducing single-letter sounds, a capability the child exhibits by repeating orally the same oral letter sound made by his teacher. This capability is pretty close to the single $Ss \rightarrow R$, but may also be considered a simple motor chain.

Longer motor chains are accounted for on the right side of the diagram, where the oral reproduction of single letters is followed by reproduction of syllables, and later by the reproduction of longer strings of syllables that may be actual words. Is this "oral repetition" a necessary part of learning to read? Yes, because it is so obviously a skill subordinate to the pronunciation of *printed* words, which is the next step to be achieved. Thus, the ultimate achievement of *decoding* printed words has a branch concerned with "speaking" that is just as essential as the branch conconcerned with "symbol identification." Many children who begin to learn the decoding process in school can already do the oral speaking tasks. Some, however, cannot, and in such instances this becomes an essential early part of reading instruction.

Later Stages of Reading   The process of decoding is only one of the capabilities involved in reading. Normally, once this skill is mastered, the child can readily progress to other portions of the total complex of reading skills. Additional rules for irregularities in the pronunciation of printed words can be learned. Skills involved in reading comprehension constitute another entire domain of reading capability, including such intellectual tasks as predicting sequences of thought, detecting irrelevant ideas, formulating the main idea, and inferring the meaning of unfamiliar words from context.

An example of higher-level rules involved in reading pertains to the comprehension of sequences of thought. As is well known, the sequences of English are highly predictable. It is not difficult to supply missing words in such a sentence as, "The man's hat was blown off —— —— ———." Although a limited number of alternative forms of completion of this sentence are possible, a great many more are not; hence the probability of completing it in the way it was originally written is quite high (Miller, 1951).

It is these principles of ordering English sentences that are learned by practicing reading with a variety of subject-matter content. As greater facility is achieved, it becomes possible for the reader to attain progressively faster speeds at the task, primarily because he is able to make better and better predictions of what a sentence says without actually looking at every printed word. There are also other higher-order rules to be learned, pertaining to the organization of paragraphs, sections, and chapters. All such principles are quite complex and are typically learned not as formally stated rules but by a process of discovery from the act of reading.

Appreciating Literature   Such skills as have been mentioned previously are involved in the most basic kind of reading, which may be described as the comprehension of the *manifest thought* of printed passages. For the child who begins without the ability to read, reaching this point is in itself a considerable achievement; and for many people it is a stage that is not surpassed during their entire lives. Reading in this basic sense makes possible communication by printed, typed, or written symbols, an activity that is of high value in the pursuit of many of the goals of successful living.

Another major goal in the establishment of reading skills and reading interest is that of appreciating literature. The capabilities involved in such an activity go far beyond those of the basic communication function of reading. In the first place, the student must develop certain *strategies* of reading which do not include reading speed as a goal (see Hall, 1969). In addition, he needs to acquire an intellectual framework that enables him to apply a number of rules which are in the nature of "literary standards" to the interpretation of what is being read. The identification of such rules and their analysis into prerequisite intellectual skills is a challenging task that has not as yet been attempted. Scribner (1967) has suggested that a learning hierarchy of central importance to this task could be built around the idea of "basic literary conflict," which would be analyzed to include the defined concepts of *inevitability, order of importance,* and *order of time,* among others.

LEARNING AND INSTRUCTIONAL SEQUENCES

The four different content examples described in this chapter demonstrate that the topics of school instruction possess hierarchical organizations with respect to required types of learning. Each can be analyzed to reveal prerequisite learnings that grow progressively simpler as one works downward from rules to $Ss \rightarrow R$ connections. The learning of the rules that are usually the clearest *objectives* of instruction requires the previous learning of other rules, and these in turn require prerequisite concepts, discriminations, verbal sequences, chains, and $Ss \rightarrow R$ connections.

The implications for the design of instruction are clear. If learning at any level is to occur with greatest facility, careful attention must be paid to its prerequisites. It will be difficult for the child to learn the definitions (defined concepts) of geometry unless he has previously acquired the concepts of line, angle, triangle, intersection, and so on. It will be difficult for a learner to acquire the rules of any specific science unless he already knows some more basic principles of classifying, measuring, and inferring. It is demonstrably difficult for a learner to construct meaningful utterances in a foreign language unless he has learned the concept words that compose such communications; and it is difficult for him to learn these words unless he has previously learned to say the sounds of the language. Learning to read English comes hard to those who have not first learned to speak many English words. It cannot be said that any of these "shortcut" kinds of learning are impossible, because learning is a marvelous capacity of living organisms that will occur whether one wants it to or not. Nevertheless, shortcuts carry their own handicaps, and typically result in deficiences that show themselves as limitations in ability to generalize the capabilities acquired.

The fundamentals of instruction are not clearly conveyed by such expressions as "reading, writing, and arithmetic." The most general capabilities are much more fundamental than these. In subjects like mathematics and science, the most basic capabilities are to be found in the discriminations, chains, and concepts that make up the activities of observing, counting, drawing, and classifying. In languages, native and foreign, they include the basic forms of learning that characterize the acquisition of word sounds, the discrimination of these sounds, and the mastery of verbal concepts. The systematic planning of instruction in the elementary school grades in terms of such capabilities would probably have a marked positive effect on facility of learning the more advanced principles of all school subjects.

GENERAL REFERENCES

Learning Prerequisites

Ausubel, D. P. *Educational psychology: A cognitive view.* New York: Holt, Rinehart and Winston, 1968. Chap. 5.

Gagné, R. M. The implications of instructional objectives for learning. In C. M. Lindvall (ed.), *Defining educational objectives.* Pittsburgh: University of Pittsburgh Press, 1964. Chap. 4.

Gagné, R. M. Problem solving. In A. W. Melton (ed.), *Categories of human learning.* New York: Academic Press, 1964.

Knight, F. B. Some considerations of method. In G. M. Whipple (ed.), *National Society for the Study of Education, Twenty-ninth yearbook. Report of the society's committee on arithmetic.* Bloomington, Ill.: Public School, 1930. Chap. 4.

The Structure of Selected Subjects

Brooks, N. *Language and language learning: theory and practice.* New York: Harcourt, Brace & World, 1959.

Commission on Science Education. *Science: a process approach. Commentary for teachers.* Washington, D.C.: American Association for the Advancement of Science, 1968.

Congdon, A. R. *Training in high school mathematics essential for success in certain college subjects.* New York: Teachers College, Columbia University, 1930.

Durrell, D. D. *Improving reading instruction.* New York: Harcourt, Brace & World, 1956.

Fries, C. C. *Linguistics and reading.* New York: Holt, Rinehart and Winston, 1963.

National Council of Teachers of English, Commission on the English Curriculum. *The English language arts for today's children.* New York: Appleton-Century-Crofts, 1954.

National Council of Teachers of English, Commission on the English Curriculum. *The English language arts in the secondary school.* New York: Appleton-Century-Crofts, 1956.

National Council of Teachers of Mathematics. *The learning of mathematics, its theory and practice. Twenty-first yearbook.* Washington, D.C.: The Council, 1953.

UNESCO. *The teaching of modern languages.* New York: Columbia University Press, 1955.

10 Readiness for Learning

Previous chapters described the conditions necessary for the establishment of different types of learning, and the last chapter illustrated how several of these types may form hierarchies that describe the conditions for sequences of learning events. It is appropriate at this point to step back a bit from the models that have been depicted to see how specific events of learning fit into the larger picture of *instruction*. A system for instruction is, after all, composed of a relatively complex set of interconnected activities, of which only a portion comprise the establishment of conditions for learning *per se*. A number of arrangements need to be made to insure that instruction is effective, both before the specific event of learning occurs and afterwards.

To begin with, we shall be concerned in this chapter with the general topic of *readiness for learning*. As this phrase implies, there are certain conditions that precede the learning event itself and that operate to determine the probability of its occurrence. Generally speaking, these are preconditions of learning (see Gagné and Bolles, 1959), and they include *attentional sets, motivation,* and the state of *developmental readiness*. Together these may be considered the most important factors that can be influenced by an instructor to prepare for learning to occur. Obviously, each of them refers to an internal state of the learner, a state that can itself be established by management of the external environment of the individual.

As noted in Chapter 3, every act of learning requires an apprehending phase, which is critically dependent upon attention. But how does one insure that attending will occur when needed? One way is to arrange for the stimulus situation to contain elements of novelty, change, intensity of stimulation, and so on. To make continuing provision for such external "attention-getters" would, however, be an impossible task for instruction as it occurs in the schools over any reasonable period of time. Evidently, then, there must be a means by which attending is internally controlled, and which enables the learner to select the stimuli to be apprehended at the appropriate time. Such an internal state is usually called a *set* (see Hebb, 1966, pp. 82–102), and one having the function described here may be termed an *attentional set*. The gaining and maintenance of attention, and the lengthening of what the first-grade teacher calls the span of attention, are instructional questions that concern the presence or absence of an attentional set.

A second kind of internal state, probably possessing a higher degree of stability, is that of *motivation*. The importance of this factor to the educational enterprise is widely recognized. In the present context of readiness, the essential questions to be answered may be put as follows: How does one motivate the individual to undertake the task of learning? How does one keep the learner interested in continuing the learning exercise, as well as in seeking further learning after completing it? Obviously, such questions imply that some state internal to the learner, which functions as a precondition of the events of learning themselves, needs to be established and maintained.

Still a third precondition for learning must be accounted for, particularly since it is now receiving such widespread attention and investigation. This is the condition of *developmental readiness* for accomplishing particular types of learning tasks. How such internal conditions can best be described is not a matter that can be confidently stated at the present time. It may be that the answer may best be sought in *stages of maturation*, innately determined by patterns of neural growth (see Gesell, 1928). A child of seven, for example, may be able to undertake learning tasks impossible to a four-year-old because of differences between them in their stage of nervous system maturation, analogous to the obvious differences in their other bodily structures. Alternatively, the kinds of learning that can be accomplished may be limited by the existence of certain *cognitive schemata*, developed by a process of adaptation, which is the essence of the ideas put forward by Piaget (see Flavell, 1963; Phillips, 1969). Contrasting with these views is the notion that, beyond a certain early age (perhaps three), developmental readiness for learning is primarily determined by previously acquired intellectual skills, and therefore by the *cumulative effects of learning and learning transfer* (see Gagné, 1968).

Following sections of this chapter deal in turn with each of these three main determinants of learning readiness—attention, motivation, and developmental "stage."

ATTENTION

The young child must initially learn certain $Ss \rightarrow R$'s and chains that govern his own behavior in observing the stimuli that constitute the external conditions of learning. He must learn to continue to direct his sense organs toward the source of stimulation, to discriminate the essential features of that stimulation, to maintain the internal cues that determine sequences of action, and to continue an activity that he has begun in the face of distractions, some of which may come from his own body. All of these capabilities appear to fall reasonably within the category of attentional sets. Learning appropriate kinds of attentional sets seems to be understandable in terms of the basic kinds of learning, connections and chains, described in earlier chapters. If one sets out to see that they are learned, one finds he is dealing primarily with the manipulation of reinforcement conditions, much as they are described by Skinner (1968).

Some important categories of attentional sets have been distinguished by Hewett (1968) in his account of instructional practices applicable to children who are deficient in these skills to begin with. A brief summary is as follows:

Attention. Initially, the child may not have learned to observe the stimuli that are an essential part of the learning event. For example, before he begins to learn to read, he must look at the printed letters rather than out the window. He must follow the teacher's finger when she points out differences in the letters. Hewett suggests the use of actual tangible rewards (like small candies) in establishing this very basic attentional skill. Later, symbolic rewards, such as check marks, become effective.

Response. The child may make the initial observation of the stimulus but fail to make a response. But since children tend to be generally responsive, it is usually not difficult to get them to engage in activities that they like to do and that they can do successfully. One can then organize this activity into a chain, in which the new response is accomplished first, followed immediately by the familiar, pleasing accomplishment. Hewett also suggests that the newly acquired chain may be further reinforced by the social effects it has on classmates (Johnny is doing something he couldn't do before!).

Order. This capability is simply one of carrying out a sequence of actions (chain) by following verbal directions. Acquisition of this kind of attentional set may be achieved by starting with short chains and building up longer ones, or alternatively, by having the child practice completing tasks with designated steps leading to a conclusion. Here again the procedure for learning follows closely that described previously for chain learning, in which reinforcement is provided by task completion.

Exploration. The child needs to learn to notice many

aspects of his environment. As an attentional set, this capability expands upon simpler observation by encompassing attention to a number of properties of the environment at once, and perhaps through multisensory channels. Acquiring such behavior may be carried out with reinforcement emphasizing variety and novelty of stimulation, as the child is encouraged to make broader and more intensive explorations of his environment.

Obviously, these types of attentional sets are most important to establish in young children, as preconditions for further learning. Hewett (1968) describes an "engineered classroom" in which many ingenious devices and procedures are used to establish these capabilities in children who initially lack them. Most people surely acquire such sets at an early age, and usually without special provisions for their learning. Absence of some of these capabilities, however, may well be a part of the picture presented by children who are designated as "culturally disadvantaged."

These very basic prelearning capabilities may be viewed as a part of the larger class referred to as cognitive strategies. While it may seem to overdignify such simple attentional functions to call them "strategies," they nevertheless logically belong to the category of intellectual skills that govern the individual's own information-getting behavior, in this case his attentional behavior. Thus, attentional sets appear to be a part of the much larger group of intellectual strategies called "mathemagenic behaviors" (Rothkopf, 1968) or "self-management behaviors" (Skinner, 1968).

MOTIVATION FOR LEARNING

The motivation of human behavior is such a large and complex subject that only a small portion of it can be treated here. Of course, it is of great interest to everyone, not only to the psychologist, who studies motivation intensively, to find out what varieties of motives exist, how they originate and develop within the individual, and how they determine the "force" and direction of human behavior. Many investigations of motivation have been and are being made, and there are many books on the topic (McClelland, Atkinson, Clark, and Lowell, 1953; Hall, 1961; Cofer and Appley, 1964).

It will be apparent to the reader that the present work cannot deal with the topic of motivation in any except a fairly restricted sense. This is not because its importance is unrecognized. In fact, many students of the educational process are convinced that the problem of controlling, developing, and utilizing existing motivation is quite the most serious issue faced by the schools. This broad conception of the motivational problem includes a consideration of the motives that make the student want to seek knowledge, to utilize his talents, to desire self-fulfillment as a human being, to relate to other people in a satisfying manner, and to become an effective member of society. Such goals as these are of tremendous importance to any system of education. The exploration of the motivational development they require is a subject deserving a separate volume.

In this chapter it will be possible to deal only with those varieties of human motivation that are most highly relevant to the process of learning and the procedures of instruction. Before discussing these specifically, it will be desirable to speak of two specific varieties of motivation that seem to represent two contrasting extremes, and that also seem to be outside the scope of the present treatment.

Motivation To Attend School

With respect to the practical problem of providing instruction to students, it is evident that they must want to place themselves in the environment where such instruction occurs in order to be able to be affected by it. Young children sometimes have rather weak motivation to attend school, preferring the familiar environment of home and mother. Such lack of motivation is often a concern of the kindergarten teacher, as it is of parents. Usually, social motives of conformity to group pressures, as well as other motives of curiosity about the new environment and perhaps pleasant rivalries with new children, gather sufficient strength to overcome the negative effects of this motivation to avoid school.

Negative motivation toward a school environment is not entirely lacking in older children either. For example, studies of lower-class children (Riessman, 1962) have emphasized the fact that these students may consider going to school a kind of "sissy" occupation, dominated by females who extoll the virtues of neatness, cleanliness, orderliness, and so on. In essence, this was Huckleberry Finn's attitude toward school. It is noteworthy, however, that these same children do not have negative motivation regarding learning or the value of an education (Wilson, 1959), but only toward school attendance.

If learning of traditional subjects is to take place in schools, it is evident that the problem of establishing positive motivation toward school attendance is both real and important. Nevertheless, it is not a kind of motivation that can be directly treated here. Ensuring positive motivation toward school is something that must be dealt with to a large extent in terms of the family and the community. If the student's family accepts and values the school, the chances are that he will also. If there are community pressures for school attendance, these will be reflected in the individual's behavior. For purposes of the present discussion, the desire or willingness to attend school must be assumed.

The Resolve To Learn

Far at the other extreme of an ordered set of motives is the kind of motivation that may be called a resolve to learn. Some discussions of the problem of motivation speak of "motivation to learn" as if this were a specific kind of resolve by means of which the student could say to himself, "I must learn this," and learning would then follow. But if there is this kind of specific motivation, it does not appear to be very effective. A number of studies have shown that under many circumstances learning occurs about as well when such a resolve is absent as when it is present: this has been the general finding in investigations of "incidental learning" (Postman, 1964).

But such a specific resolve needs to be carefully distinguished from motivation to *achieve*, which, as later discussion will show, is of tremendous importance to successful learning. If the student's "motivation to learn" means that he resolves *to be able to do something*, a something that can be achieved as a *result* of learning, then this is positive motivation of a substantial character.

In general, then, subsequent sections will attempt to discuss the kinds of motivation relevant to successful learning; but in doing so, they will avoid the twin extremes of "motivation to attend school," on the one hand, and the specific "resolve to learn," on the other.

Motivation To Engage in Learning

What makes an individual want to undertake learning? How can one establish the kind of motivation required for the student to be selectively attentive to the stimulus events that will bring about the change in behavior that is the sign of learning?

Hewett's (1968) description of practical procedures that can be used to insure readiness for learning continues on from basic attentional sets into the realm of motivation. Assuming that these fundamental sets can be successfully established, the child may subsequently develop readiness that is *social* in nature: working with other children and relating appropriately to the teacher become essential for effective learning. The child comes to be motivated by a desire to gain the approval of others, to avoid their disapproval, and to establish a position of social esteem among his peers. Beyond this, there is the acquisition of motivation for *mastery*, involving the learning of intellectual skills that enable him to function independently. Reinforcement for such learning is provided by accuracy and completeness of accomplishment of tasks the child undertakes. Occupying the highest level of Hewett's proposed developmental sequence is motivation for *achievement*. This calls for the development of true self-motivation, in which the successful mastery of more and more difficult tasks becomes a source of self-satisfaction and generates a desire for greater improvement. When students attain this level of functioning, they have all the readiness needed to be true self-learners.

Other investigators who have described practical motivational programs are Bereiter and Englemann (1966, pp. 81–91) and Mager (1968). Despite specific differences in detail, there are many resemblances in the approach recommended by these authors and those of Hewett. For example, emphasis is given to the rewarding of behavior that initially approximates the desired behavior, rather than waiting until exactly the correct response is made. Providing the student with information that enables him to judge his own success and failure is another suggestion that is commonly put forth. And finally, the idea of proceeding in steps, or "stages," from very concrete rewards to those that require a sense of satisfaction derived from self-imposed standards is a frequently recommended procedure. None of these techniques, of course, provides a magic key to the insurance of student interest in learning. However, if they are understood as readiness states that are themselves subject to learning, and likely to be acquired according to principles of reinforcement contingencies (see Skinner, 1968, pp. 160–168), they can be of great value in establishing the necessary preconditions for school learning.

Task Motivation   Although the existence of social motivation, often related to *affiliative needs,* is generally recognized, some writers consider it of considerably lesser importance to school learning than the motivation of *task mastery and achievement.* Ausubel (1968, pp. 363–433) reviews the evidence concerning various forms of social motivation and points out that these do not always constitute a dependable basis for learning readiness. In contrast, he believes the advantages of achievement motivation for learning lie, first, in the fact that such motives are intrinsic to the task itself, and hence the reward (the attainment of new knowledge or skill) is capable of wholly satisfying the underlying motive. Second, achievement is ego-enhancing, because the status achieved by the individual is in proportion to his achievement or competence level, affecting directly his self-esteem and feelings of adequacy.

This view of motivation also emphasizes the power of intrinsic and positive motives, including curiosity and exploration, as well as mastery. Such "cognitive" motives may be the most important kind of motivation in school learning. Consideration of their potential effects leads Ausubel (1968, pp. 365–366) to make the following statement:

> The causal relationship between motivation and learning is typically reciprocal rather than unidirectional. Both for this reason, and because motivation is not an indispensable condition of learning, it is unnecessary to postpone learning activities until appropriate interests and motivations have been developed. Frequently, the best way of teaching an unmotivated student is to ignore his motivational state for the time being, and to concentrate on teaching him as effectively as possible. Some degree of learning will ensue in any case, despite the lack of motivation; and from the initial satisfaction of learning he will, hopefully, develop the motivation to learn more. In some circumstances, therefore, the most appropriate way of arousing motivation to learn is to focus on the cognitive rather than on the motivational aspects of learning, and to rely on the motivation that is developed from successful educational achievement to energize further learning.

It is interesting to note that despite great differences from Ausubel in his theoretical point of view toward school learning, Skinner (1968, pp. 145–168) holds an essentially similar view about the importance of motivation intrinsic to the performance of the task itself. Skinner states that the problem of motivation for the schools is not a matter of imparting motivation but rather of arranging the conditions for study and learning so that they will be reinforcing. The teacher must often invent and use "contrived proximate reinforcers," not only to aid in the imparting of knowledge but also in getting the student to acquire diligent behavior of the learning-readiness variety ("precurrent self-management behaviors").

Achievement Motivation   Motivation to achieve is carried much beyond the idea of "task mastery" by some theorists. These writers propose that individuals may acquire, to a greater or lesser degree, a persisting trait of striving to achieve that provides motivation for a great many of their activities, including those pertaining to school learning.

McClelland (1965) describes twelve propositions, derived from a variety of sources, that have been employed in studies designed to heighten the achievement motivation of groups of businessmen, and more recently, groups of disadvantaged students. It is McClelland's view that a combination of techniques, including those leading to clear definition of individual goals, perception of self-improvement, an increasing trend toward the assumption of responsibility for one's performance, and a supportive social environment, can lead to the acquisition of persisting motivation for achievement. It appears a distinct possibility that beneficial effects may be obtained by a program designed to increase this "general" form of achievement motivation in certain categories of students, for example, those who drop out of high school.

Another theory about achievement as a general motivational state is that of White (1959), who describes the concept of *competence*. In White's view, competence motivation has a broadly based biological origin, related to such sources of motivation as exploration, activity, and manipulation, as they have been studied in animal behavior. Many investigators of motivation have expressed the need to identify a similar source of positive motivation, variously termed "mastery," "ego-development," "a sense of industry," and "dealing with the environment." White maintains that many activities of the child must be explained, not through the operation of need satisfactions (like hunger, thirst, and so on) but through the persistence of activities that constitute effective interaction with the environment, and that are accompanied by a "feeling of efficacy." In other words, the human individual is so constituted that he has a need to master his environment, in some small or large way, throughout his life.

Competence motivation can obviously be put to use in the educational process. When the situation is properly arranged for learning, mastering the problem of multiplying two-place numbers or of constructing passive forms of sentences or of producing a white precipitate from a mixture of solutions will provide a rewarding experience to the learner, according to this conception. The problem is not primarily one of "learning new motivation," according to this view. Rather, it is one of cleverly arranging situations for learning in such a way that competence will be displayed and the feeling of efficacy experienced.

It can be seen, therefore, that several possible explanations have been advanced to account for the operation of motivation that is either intrinsic to, or closely related to, the performance of learning tasks. Perhaps such motivation is simply an example of the shifting of control from one task activity to another through reinforcement contingencies; perhaps it is learned as a persisting general state of motivation to achieve; or perhaps it is an innately determined drive for competence. Any of these theories, or all of them, may be right to a degree. It is perhaps most significant, though, that their practical implications are very similar: the learner can be rewarded, and his subsequent learning can be enhanced, by the accomplishment of learning tasks that are within his capabilities. Achievement, successful interaction within the learning environment, and mastery of the objectives of an educational program can themselves lead to persisting satisfaction on the part of the learner and can therefore become a most dependable source of continuing motivation. Something like this conception must evidently be a strong component in the development of a "continuing self-learner"; and such development is often stated as one of the most important goals of education.

DEVELOPMENTAL READINESS

The third essential element that sets the stage for an act of learning is the readiness of all the cognitive states and processes that enter into such an act. Limitations of the performance of a human being often can be directly related to processes of growth. At a given age, for example, the child may be unable to perform some particular act because he is not tall enough or not strong enough. Similarly, it appears that a certain amount of neurological growth must occur before he can walk or talk. If one attempts to have him learn to carry out these activities before he is maturationally ready, one finds it impossible. From observations such as these on young children has come the idea of developmental readiness and the associated notion of "stages of development."

Is it possible that the child must reach a particular stage of developmental growth before he can learn? Many studies have indicated that simple types of learning can occur with the very young infant, and a few investigations have shown signal learning to occur before birth. For practical purposes, it may apparently be assumed that if the conditions for learning of simple connections are properly established, learning of this variety will occur, even in the youngest children.

There are obvious differences in the intellectual "power" displayed by children of different ages. It appears to be much easier for a child of seven, say, to learn the meaning of a new word than it is for a child of four. Similarly, a youngster of eleven may readily learn to use the abstract rules involved in inferring the kinship structure of a primitive society, whereas the seven-year-old may not. When attempts are made to have children learn intellectual skills that are beyond their stage of development, the result is highly predictable. Although some learning may indeed occur, the objectives are typically not achieved within any reasonable periods of time.

Does the existence of these limitations of developmental readiness imply that the more complex forms of learning (concept learning, rule learning, problem solving) are conditional upon stages of neurological growth? There are many who hold this view. Piaget (1952), for example, proposes the stages of cognitive operation called sensori-motor, pre-operational, concrete operational, and formal operational. The differences in intellectual performance he observes in various tasks at various ages are, according to his theory, reflections of differences in the intellectual skills of logical thinking. At a particular age, the growing child may be able to perform certain kinds of intellectual tasks because he has attained a developmental stage in which he can think logically when dealing with concrete events. At the same time, he may be unable to display the operations of logical thought that are necessary to solve problems involving symbolic representations of events.

The alternative view to be described here is, very simply, that differences in developmental readiness are primarily attributable to differences in the number and kind of *previously learned intellectual skills*. At any given age, a child may be unable to perform a particular intellectual task because he has not acquired the specifically relevant intellectual skills as prerequisites to that task. According to this view, limitations of intellectual growth do not prevent a young learner from solving an abstract problem, or from learning new higher-order rules that are symbolically represented. Such learning may be readily accomplished if the learner has acquired, or will undertake to acquire, the intellectual skills that are prerequisite to the task. Prerequisite skills may be derived according to the method described in the previous chapter. It is recognized, of course, that learning such skills may take some time. Can the abstract rules of calculus, such as those of minima and maxima, be learned by fourth-graders? The answer is yes, if they first attain the developmental readiness implied by the skills prerequisite to such learning, which, of course, include many of the concepts and operations of algebra. (This hypothetical example does not imply, of course, that such learning *should* be undertaken; only that it *could* be.)

Cumulative Learning

Developmental readiness for learning any particular new intellectual skill is conceived as the presence of certain specifically relevant subordinate intellectual skills. If the individual is to engage in problem solving to acquire a new higher-order rule, he must first have acquired some other, simpler rules. These in turn depend for their acquisition on the recall of other learned entities, rules, or perhaps concepts. As we have seen in previous chapters, concepts in their turn depend for their learning on the recall of other prerequisites, the discriminations which are specifically related to them, and so on. Viewed from the other end, the learning history of the individual is *cumulative* in character. The $Ss \rightarrow R$ connections and chains that are learned form a basis on which concepts are built. Concepts contribute positive transfer to the learning of rules; and the latter support the learning of more complex rules and problem solving. Among the rules acquired are those special kinds that are called cognitive strategies, which enable the individual to attack many kinds of problems, regardless of their particular content.

Learning has the specific effects of establishing the particular capabilities necessary for the performance of any intellectual task. It also has *cumulative* effects. When an individual has learned a particular rule, for example, he has established a capability that can transfer to the learning not only of a single higher-order rule but also to several others as well. As a specific instance, learning rules regarding the factors of numbers up to 100 may be shown to contribute to the learning of higher-order rules, say, in adding fractions. The factor rules are also prerequisite to other mathematical tasks, such as completing ratios or simplifying equations. When learning of the latter tasks is undertaken, these subordinate rules of number factors do not have to be learned all over again. They are already available in the learner's memory. Learning is cumulative, then, because particular intellectual skills are likely to be transferable to a number of higher-order skills and to a variety of problems to be solved. As the individual develops, he continually increases his store of intellectual skills. This means that the possibilities of combination of these learned skills, in transferring to the learning of higher-order capabilities, increases exponentially. These cumulative effects of learning are the basis for observed increases of intellectual "power" in the growing human being.

An Example of Cumulative Learning

The effects of cumulative learning may be illustrated in a task of liquid conservation, similar to that used by Piaget (Piaget and Inhelder, 1964) and by other investigators who have been interested in studying aspects of his theory (see Bruner, 1966). The task to be performed is illustrated in Figure 21. When the liquid in a container shaped like A is poured into container B (top row), many children below age 7 are inclined to say that the taller container has more liquid. In another variant of the task, children at this age level tend to say that the volume in the shallower container (second row), exhibiting a larger surface area, is "more." Thus a few children at age seven are "conservers" in this task, while most are "non-conservers." To Piaget, these differences in performance reflect a critical point in intellectual development, marking the difference between a pre-operational phase of thought and a concrete operational phase. The kind of logical operation particularly relevant to such a task is considered to be the *multiplying of relations* (recognizing that an increase in height may be compensated by a decrease in width). Such operations are in turn dependent on those that appear at an earlier stage of develop-

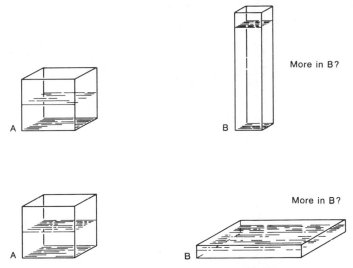

FIGURE 21. Two tasks of "conservation of liquid" in rectangular containers. (From R. M. Gagné, Contributions of learning to human development. *Psychol. Rev.,* 1968, **75,** Figure 2, p. 183. Copyright 1968 by the American Psychological Association and reproduced by permission.)

ment, particularly *reversibility* (carrying out an inverse operation).

From the standpoint of a cumulative learning theory, performance of this conservation task may be accomplished when the individual has acquired the specific intellectual skills that are relevant to it. The set of intellectual skills required may be derived in the manner described in the previous chapter, to yield a learning hierarchy shown in Figure 22.

It may be noted, first of all, that this particular hierarchy has been derived under the assumption that the children to be tested are uninstructed in mathematical concepts of volume, specifically in the relation volume equals height times width times length. Obviously, one *could* construct a learning hierarchy which proposed that children learn this exact mathematical relation in order to perform the final task. This possibility was not followed in the present in-

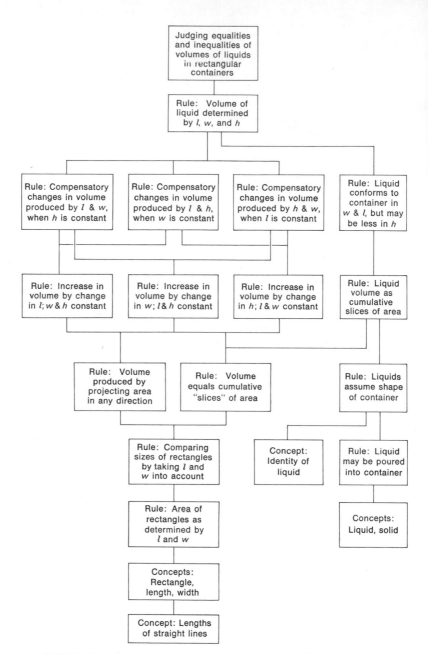

FIGURE 22. A learning hierarchy which shows the cumulative learning of intellectual skills leading to the task of judging equalities and inequalities of liquid volume in rectangular containers. (From R. M. Gagné, Contributions of learning to human development. *Psychol. Rev.,* 1968, **75,** Figure 3, p. 184. Copyright 1968 by the American Psychological Association and reproduced by permission.)

stance in order that fewer assumptions about prior learning could be made.

According to the figure, reading from the top down, the child needs to have learned the rule that volume of a liquid in rectangular containers is determined by length, width, and height. Volume will be changed if any of these is altered. Proceeding one step further in the analysis, we find three rules about compensatory changes in two dimensions when the third dimension remains constant. (The fact that Piaget considers compensatory multiplying of relations essential to this task is noteworthy.) If the width of a liquid remains the same in two different containers, the two can have the same volume if a change in height in one is compensated by a change in length in the other.

In order for a child to learn these complex rules, the figure says, he must have learned three other rules, relating to change in only one dimension at a time. For example, if height is increased while width and length remain constant, volume will increase. The learning of these rules is in turn supported by the prior learning of still other rules. One is that volume of a container is produced by accumulating "slices" of the same shape and area. A second is that volume can be projected from area in any direction, up or down, to the front or back, to the right or left. Following these, one can identify considerably simpler rules, such as those of comparing areas of rectangles by compensatory action of length and width, and the idea that length and width determine area. If one chooses to trace the hierarchy still further downward, he encounters the concepts of rectangle, length, width, and an even simpler one, the concept of length of a line.

In its right-hand branch, the hierarchy describes the intellectual skills having to do with liquids in containers. Included here are rules having to do with changes in shape of liquid in containers and liquid volume as cumulative slices of area. This branch is necessary because at the level of higher-order rules, the child must distinguish the volume of the liquid from that of the container. It is notable that this branch also includes the concept of liquid "identity"—that is, matching a liquid poured from one container to another as "the same liquid." This sort of concept of identity is generally considered to be arrived at very early in the intellectual development of the child, as shown, for example, by Bruner's (1966, pp. 183–192) evidence.

These, then, are the subordinate intellectual skills, each of which can be learned, that are hypothesized to lead to the capability of judging equalities and inequalities in rectangular containers. It is worth noting that studies of children's performance in such tasks have sometimes undertaken to train the children directly on the final task, and have generally reported limited success. Some more recent studies, however, have followed the suggestion of the cumulative learning model by setting out to have children learn subordinate skills (see Kingsley and Hall, 1967; Le François, 1968; Bearison, 1968). Such investigations have found that children can learn relevant subordinate skills and that such learning makes possible transfer of learning to conservation tasks. While more evidence is surely needed, it is particularly noteworthy that "ability to conserve" has been clearly related in these studies to the mastery of prerequisite intellectual skills.

The cumulative learning theory may be seen to propose a conception of "what is learned" (or "what develops") in marked contrast to Piaget's theory. The latter states that performing conservation tasks depends on the development of logical processes, such as "reversibility," "seriation," and "compensation." The proposal of the cumulative learning theory, in contrast, is that development results from the learning of relatively specific intellectual skills having to do with liquids, containers, volumes, areas, lengths, and heights. Specifically, it is supposed that the child does not acquire an ability like "compensatory multiplying of relations" all at once at some particular stage of his development. Instead, he acquires through learning the specific intellectual skill of "identifying equal volumes given compensatory changes in length and width, height remaining constant." In addition, and at approximately the same time, he may acquire a number of other intellectual skills such as those shown in Figure 22. If the necessary specific capabilities are learned, by being taught in some systematic fashion, the child will be able to perform the conservation task.

Do the intellectual capabilities of the child remain as specific as this? Of course they do not. The reason is because of the existence of the well-known property of learning, transfer of learning. Suppose, for example, a child has learned to judge equalities and inequalities of liquids in rectangular containers. Suppose, further, that one undertook then to have him learn, in addition, to judge volumes of liquids in cylindrical containers. Presumably, such learning could be based upon another different learning hierarchy, which would have certain skills in common with that of Figure 22, but would also have some new ones dealing with areas of circles and volumes of cylinders. Having learned to judge volumes in *both* kinds of containers, a learner would then have some intellectual skills of great value for *generalizing* to still other problems. One might, for example, try him on the entirely new problem of judging volumes of liquids in irregularly shaped containers. Since he would already know how to equate volumes in rectangular and in cylindrical containers, it would perhaps not be too difficult for these skills to transfer to the new problem, composed of shapes that were partly and roughly rectangular and partly and roughly cylindrical. Transfer of previously learned skills to the entirely new problem seems highly predictable.

Once a learner has acquired a repertoire of learned specific skills, it is not difficult to realize that his performance of conservation-type problems would become progressively easier, because an increasing number of these subordinate skills would exhibit transfer of learning to any new conservation task one might devise. At some stage in his development, one might then choose to speak of the child as a conserver, or to say that he has acquired a general principle of conservation. To categorize his stage of development in this manner may have some value. However, it does not appear to be at all a necessary inference, in contrast to a finding that the child has learned a variety of relatively specific conservation skills applicable to volume, substance, weight, number, and other physical properties.

It is surely to be expected, then, that intellectual skills of whatever type, although they may be learned as relatively specific entities, will generalize through the mechanism of learning transfer to the learning of many other skills and to the solving of many previously unencountered problems. Readiness for new learning is thus a matter of a stage of development, to be sure. But the stage of development for any learner depends first upon what relevant prerequisite skills he has already learned, and, second, upon what capabilities he has yet to acquire in order to meet the particular objective set for him. Stated simply, the stage of developmental readiness of any learner is determined by what he already knows and by how much he has yet to learn in order to achieve some particular learning goal.

SUMMARY OF READINESS FACTORS

Learning in the school typically takes place within a set of events called *instruction*. Even before these events are put into effect, however, the learner must have been prepared for learning. He needs to have a *readiness for learning*, which has been established by a number of additional events that precede the instructional period itself by various intervals of time. The three major factors comprising learning readiness are (1) attentional sets; (2) motivation; and (3) developmental status.

An attentional set is an internal state of the learner, assumed and maintained temporarily, which enables him to select and apprehend stimuli that are appropriate to the learning being undertaken. Although "attention" serves as a general name, it seems probable that several varieties of such sets exist. For example, attending to the source of the stimulus, making specifically appropriate responses, carrying out a sequence by following verbal directions, and exploring the environment have been distinguished as separate manifestations of attentional set. Such prelearning capabilities appear to belong to the more general category of cognitive strategies, which govern the individual's information-getting behavior. Evidence concerning how they are learned strongly suggests that "contingencies of reinforcement" govern their acquisition.

Motivation is the second requisite component of learning readiness. The motivation of human behavior is a large and complex subject, and attention here must center on those two kinds of motives that are specifically relevant to learning. One is social and includes needs for affiliation, social approval, esteem, and others related to these. Such motives are undoubtedly involved in significant ways in insuring that the student interacts in appropriate ways with the teacher and with other students. The second category of motivation is task mastery and achievement, emphasized by many investigators as of signal importance in the learning of intellectual tasks. In general, such motivation is conceived to be itself enhanced by experiences of success in achieving the specific objectives of learning tasks.

Some motivational theorists go beyond the notion of mastery of specific tasks in their treatment of "achievement-type" motivation. There is, for example, the suggestion that a general motivational state oriented toward achievement may be of relevance to school learning. A variety of shades of meaning can be found in this conception, with a variety of names such as "need for achievement," "mastery," "competence," and "effectance." Regardless of these differences, it appears that these theorists would agree that the learner can obtain reward from achievement and that success in accomplishment can lead to further enhancement of subsequent learning.

The attainment of a state of intellectual development is a third factor in learning readiness. Theories enjoying widespread acceptance are based upon the idea that stages of neurophysiological growth impose certain limitations upon the kind and degree of cognitive development that can occur. Piaget's view, for example, is that processes of adaptation, involving interaction with the environment, determine the appearance of certain intellectual capabilities in the child, within certain general stages categorized as sensori-motor, preoperational, concrete operational, and formal operational. These stages represent periods of development of the operations of logical thought. A large amount of observational data, collected by Piaget and his co-workers as well as by other investigators, attests to the conformity of patterns of development of normal children to this model.

It is also possible, and not inconsistent with existing evidence, to view intellectual development as being primarily attributable to the cumulative effects of learning relatively specific intellectual skills. According to this view, which is most consistent with the theoretical position presented in this book, children learn to deal intellectually with particular concrete problems. The resulting intellectual skills possess the property of transferring to other problems having certain components in common. As these skills continue to accumulate, they have the potentiality, through the process of learning transfer, of generating other skills of increasing degrees of abstractness and generality. Accordingly, readiness for new learning may be seen as depending upon the repertoire of intellectual skills possessed by the individual, which have been previously learned and which are relevant to the new learning task to be undertaken.

The educational implications of this latter view are both clear and simple. Children can learn any intellectual thing we want them to learn, provided they have learned the prerequisites. If one is concerned to have an individual learn some new rules or solve some new problems, one first makes observations to see what he already knows. This is a description of his degree of learning readiness. Next, one undertakes to have him acquire the intellectual skills that take him, in the manner described in Chapter 9, from his current "stage" to the point at which he is able to learn the new capability. In the course of such learning, it will usually be found that a variety of other new potentialities for learning have been developed, because of the tendency of learning effects to accumulate by transfer.

GENERAL REFERENCES

Learning Attentional Sets
Hewett, F. M. *The emotionally disturbed child in the classroom.* Boston: Allyn and Bacon, 1968.

Motivation
Ausubel, D. P. *Educational psychology: A cognitive view.* New York: Holt, Rinehart and Winston, 1968. Chap. 10.
Bandura, A., and Walters, R. H. *Social learning and personality development.* New York: Holt, Rinehart and Winston, 1963.
Cofer, C. N., and Appley, M. H. *Motivation: Theory and research.* New York: Wiley, 1964.
DeCecco, J. P. *Human learning in the school.* New York: Holt, Rinehart and Winston, 1963. Chap. 2.
Hall, J. F. *Psychology of motivation.* Philadelphia: Lippincott, 1961.
McClelland, D. C., Atkinson, J. W., Clark, R. A., and Lowell, E. L. *The achievement motive.* New York: Appleton-Century-Crofts, 1953.
Skinner, B. F. *The technology of teaching.* New York: Appleton-Century-Crofts, 1968. Chap. 7.

Developmental Readiness
Flavell, J. H. *The developmental psychology of Jean Piaget.* Princeton, N.J.: Van Nostrand, 1963.
Hunt, J. McV. *Intelligence and experience.* New York: Ronald, 1961.
Inhelder, B., and Piaget, J. *The growth of logical thinking from childhood to adolescence.* New York: Basic Books, 1958.
Piaget, J. *The origins of intelligence in children.* New York: International Universities Press, 1952.
Piaget, J., and Inhelder, B. *The early growth of logic in the child.* New York: Harper & Row, 1964.
Phillips, J. L., Jr. *The origins of intellect: Piaget's theory.* San Francisco: Freeman, 1969.

11 | The Design of Instruction

Previous chapters have described one of the principal ways in which programs of education need to take into account the conditions of learning—namely, by insuring that certain *internal* conditions of the learner are present. The attainment of new capabilities by human learners requires a systematic plan for the acquiring of prerequisite discriminations, concepts, or rules. Learned capabilities become most readily generalizable when they are soundly based on previously mastered entities.

The three factors that are considered essential in establishing readiness for learning—attention sets, motivation, and stage of cognitive development—were described in Chapter 10. These, it may be said, complete the roster of internal conditions necessary for learning. These are the states that must be present in the learner at the time a learning event occurs, and for which the manager of instruction must make suitable preparations.

In this chapter, we turn our attention to the second category of conditions surrounding the learning event, the *external* conditions of learning. These include the arrangement and timing of the stimulus situation surrounding the learner at the time learning occurs. To a most significant degree, they include the kinds of *verbal communications* that are made to the learner.

THE EVENTS OF INSTRUCTION

Control of the external events in the learning situation is what is typically meant by the word "instruction." These are the events that are manipulated by the teacher, the textbook writer, the designer of films or television lessons, the developer of self-instructional programs. It is possible, of course, to look on instruction as a mysterious art, impossible of being analyzed in these terms. This point of view, however, is in opposition to the one taken in this volume, as will already be apparent. Instead, the present approach attempts to classify the parts of the instructional situation and to describe the kinds of control to which they may be subjected in bringing about learning. The description of conditions for various types of learning contained in Chapters 4 through 8, as well as the general conditions outlined in Chapter 3, should make possible the derivation of general principles of *control over external events* that are related to the types of learning being undertaken, but at the same time independent of the specific content to be taught.

We have spoken of the external conditions of learning, and now we wish to discuss the external events of instruction. What is the relation between the two? The external conditions for any particular type of learning, as they have been previously referred to, are only an abbreviated form of the events of instruction. They are, in a sense, the crux of the matter so far as instruction is concerned. At the same time, they are only one component in a total sequence of events that is usually understood to constitute instruction. The external conditions of learning are definitely a part of the total set of instructional events, but they are not all that happens in instruction.

Instruction may be seen to comprise a set of separate events, each of which has a distinct effect upon the learner.

They engage his attention, they provide him with information and feedback, they present the essential stimulus for learning, they stimulate his recall, they insure that he gets practice in what he has learned. As a total set of events, they usually begin a few minutes before the time of actual learning and come to an end some time afterward. Their general function is to insure that the timing and sequencing of events internal to the learner is proper for the occurrence of learning, and also for retention and transferability of what is learned. The specific functions of these different events that are components of instruction may be described briefly as follows:

1. *Gaining and controlling attention.* An external stimulus arouses the appropriate attentional set.

2. *Informing the learner of expected outcomes.* Communication, usually verbal, tells the learner about the kind of performance he will be able to do after he has learned.

3. *Stimulating recall of relevant prerequisite capabilities.* The learner is reminded of the relevant intellectual skills, and also verbal knowledge, he has previously learned.

4. *Presenting the stimuli inherent to the learning task.* The particular stimuli to which the newly learned performance will be directed are displayed.

5. *Offering guidance for learning.* Usually by verbal communciations the learner's thinking is directed by prompts or hints until the essential performance is achieved.

6. *Providing feedback.* The learner is informed of the correctness of his newly attained performance.

7. *Appraising performance.* Opportunity is provided for the learner to verify his achievement in one or more situations.

8. *Making provisions for transferability.* Additional examples are used to establish increased generalizability of the newly acquired capability.

9. *Insuring retention.* Provisions are also made for practice and use of the new capabality so that it will be remembered.

Any or all of these events may form a part of the instructional situation. Typically, they occur in approximately the order listed, although there is no absolute requirement about this order. As is implied, however, the critical learning occurrence transpires between events 5 and 6 in this list. One could hardly expect, therefore, that events transpiring prior to 5 could be temporally switched with those occurring after 5.

As will be evident in subsequent descriptions of the events of instruction, these events are often initiated and controlled by means of verbal communications to the learner (see Gagné, 1969). Such communications may be given the general name of *verbal directions*. Their function is not "instruction," in a strict sense (since this word is used to apply to the total set of events accompanying learning), but rather that of telling the learner what to do at any given point in time. In this sense, they are like the directions printed on packages to tell purchasers how to open them. The latter may say, "First, pull the tab, then press with the thumb," cr something like that. In a similar way, verbal directions to the learner may tell him, "First do this, then do that," or, "First remember the word meaning apple, then the word meaning tree, then write them down as one word." Of course, the events of instruction *can* be controlled without verbal directions, and they may have to be with a young child who does not understand the words. But typically, verbal communication is the preferred mode.

Gaining and Controlling Attention

One function for verbal directions is to direct attention to the object or characteristic that is to become the stimulus in a learned connection. With the simpler forms of learning, it is common for the instructor to say, "Now watch this!" while holding up or pointing to a stimulus object or event. "Look at this," "What do you see here?" "Notice this part," or "Listen carefully" are some of the many examples of verbal communications used by a teacher to direct attention to some specific stimulus. Such directions are particularly common when simple kinds of learning are being undertaken.

Although verbal statements are perhaps the most commonly used means of directing attention, there are, of course, other ways. Gestures made by the teacher can be equally effective. The sudden movement of an object is another kind of event likely to direct attention to it. When illustrations are used as a part of instruction, a variety of means of directing attention are available, including over-printed arrows, circles, or contrasting colors. Animated techniques in motion pictures provide many additional ways of directing the viewer's attention to relevant stimuli.

In the acquisition of concepts and principles, since the content itself is represented verbally, methods must be sought to distinguish this content from the verbal directions that focus attention, as well as from directions performing still other functions. It is common to find the concepts to be learned italicized, underlined, or printed in bold type for the purpose of focusing attention. Similarly, rules may be set apart from the remainder of a text by being printed in different type style or size. A variety of other devices can be used for directing attention toward the content to be learned, including setting the latter apart by means of color or by use of a surrounding "box," as is done in many modern textbooks.

Informing the Learner of Expected Outcomes

Another function of verbal directions in the learning situation is to give the learner information about the class of responses to be expected when learning is completed. If he is beginning to learn about reproduction, for example, some such instructions may be used: "There are several different ways in which living organisms reproduce themselves. What you will be learning is how to describe each of these ways and to give some actual examples of them." Or, if he is learning to add decimals, instructions may say, "What you will learn is how to add the numbers such as 124.27 and 16.743 to obtain the sum 141.013."

Telling the learner what is to be his performance when learning is complete is a function of directions that seems to be of considerable importance to the learning process. It cannot be said with certainty why this is the case. Such instructions may provide continuing "direction" to learning, in the sense suggested by Maier (1930). This may mean that they establish a *set* that is "carried in his head" by the learner throughout the period of learning and that makes it possible for him to reject extraneous and irrelevant stimuli. The use of "advance organizers" as studied by Ausubel (1960) may also be considered as performing a similar function for the learning of meaningful verbal material. Another possibility is that directions telling the learner about expected performance enable him to match his own responses with a response class he remembers, and thus to know when he is correct—a reinforcement function. For example, the performance expected in adding decimals, the learner knows, must be an expression that contains a decimal point and otherwise has the general form of 141.013. It cannot be of the form 141013, nor 141 1/77.

Under many circumstances, the clearest kinds of directions about expected performance following learning may be those that actually show the learner, before learning begins, what such a performance looks like. Is this "telling him the answer"? Obviously, it is not really doing this, because one ordinarily expects him to learn a whole class of performances, not just the single one used to illustrate that class. However, if in fact the learner can acquire all he is supposed to learn by simply being told about this class, surely this is economical learning! Presumably, keeping the learner in the dark serves no useful function in such instances.

Stimulating Recall of Relevant Prerequisites

Verbal directions may tell the learner to recall something he has learned previously. When a chain is being acquired, recall of the links may be stimulated in the proper sequence by verbal means. "Wrap the string around the package," "Twist the ends," "Turn the package over," and similar verbal instructions may be used in establishing the chain involved in tying a package. Recall may also be stimulated in connection with the learning of concepts. The verbal instruction, "This is a button" may be used to recall a single verbal association that has previously been learned before proceeding with instruction that exposes new varieties of buttons along with the verbal response "button." And a most important use of directions to induce recall accompanies the learning of rules of various orders of complexity. Before acquiring the rule, "Sodium is a metal," it is necessary for the learner to recall what "sodium" is and what a "metal" is; each of these concepts may be made recallable by suitable verbal directions to "remember."

Two different kinds of directions can be used to induce recall of previously learned entities, and either may be preferable in particular instances. When a relatively simple rule is being learned, it may be sufficient for verbal directions to stimulate *recognition* of what has previously been learned. This would be the case with such instructions as, "You remember what sodium is and you remember what a metal is." When more complex rules are being acquired, it may be desirable for the directions to require *reinstatement* of the concepts subordinate to rules rather than simply recognition of them. Thus, in the learning of such a rule as that involved in identifying and drawing the separation of a plane by a simple closed curve (see Figure 11), it may be desirable for directions to require the *reinstatement* of subordinate rules by saying "Draw a simple closed curve," and, "Which one of these represents a plane?" The learning of the higher-order rule can then proceed satisfactorily with the assurance that the necessary subordinate rules are available for immediate recall.

The necessity for recall of previously learned entities immediately prior to the new act of learning is probably a reflection of the importance of the factor of *contiguity* in learning. As indicated in previous chapters, the establishment of chains, concepts, and rules is made easy when it is certain that the necessary subordinate capabilities are highly "available" in memory, so that they can be recalled in close temporal contiguity to the new set of connections being acquired. In contrast, the attempt to learn when some "piece of content" cannot be recalled results in lengthy delays and frustration to the learner. The use of verbal instructions in inducing recall is accordingly a highly important feature of the total instructional process.

Presenting the Stimulus Situation

The objects and events that are an inherent part of the stimulus situation for learning, naturally enough, vary according to what is being learned. The desired content of instruction will determine whether the stimulus situation is primarily composed of foreign words, of collections of rocks, or of geometrical shapes. But the general forms taken by stimuli, whether objects, pictures, or printed texts, are importantly determined by the *type of learning* that must be undertaken. To deal with this question adequately, therefore, it is necessary to consider the stimulus situation applicable to the types of learning described in previous chapters. For this purpose it will be possible to begin with stimulus-response learning (type 2); it may be assumed that the requirements of the stimulus situation for signal learning (type 1) may be satisfied by the introduction of a signal (almost any physical stimulus will qualify).

The Stimulus Situation for the Learning of Ss → R's and Chains   In learning a stimulus-response connection, the stimulus with which the response is to be associated must be presented in such a way that it is perceived by the learner. If the individual is to learn to grasp a pencil, one needs simply to be sure that he sees this physical object and also feels it. A second aspect of stimulation that needs to be present comes from the kinesthetic sense, that is, stimulation generated by muscular action. As indicated in Chapter 4, this latter part of the total stimulation must be present if a voluntary act is being learned. Many studies provide evidence that trying to establish a motor act by having the instructor guide or push the moving member is quite ineffective for learning (Carr, 1930). Learning to print or write script provides an example in the school; the student must practice "doing it himself." Only in this way can the necessary stimulation from his own muscles be made to occur dependably as a part of the total stimulus situation.

As these examples imply, the presence of kinesthetic stimulation is equally necessary when single $Ss \rightarrow R$'s are being linked into chains. In this case, however, the primary purpose is not to establish the individual links but to connect these links in a proper sequence. The stimulation for each following link needs to include the kinesthetic feedback from the immediately preceding link if the chain is to be learned most effectively. Verbal chains are no exception; the stimulation provided by hearing and feeling oneself say word number 1 furnishes an important portion of the cue to saying word number 2, and so on.

The Stimulus Situation for Discrimination Learning   The basic requirement for discrimination learning is that the stimuli be associated with different responses so that they will not be confused with one another. In some instances, all the stimulus objects may be presented at once. For example, if the student is being asked to learn to distinguish leaves of oak, maple, elm, birch, and poplar, samples of each of these leaf types may be shown all at once on a table. Under such circumstances, it is possible for the student to learn in a circumscribed time interval that the maple leaf has a shape that differs from the oak leaf; that the elm leaf is distinguishable from the birch; and so on.

Under other circumstances, particularly when the number of discriminations to be made is large, it may be necessary to present the stimuli in sequence, because they cannot all be looked at effectively together. Identifying twenty children in a schoolroom is an example. The important requirement continues to be one of "contrast practice," in which the learner not only has a chance to learn that one object is an X and another a Y but also that the first is *not a Y* and the second is *not an X*. Sometimes the stimuli are grouped into highly similar subsets in order to make easier this kind of differentiation. In formal terms, as was stated in Chapter 6, the primary purpose of "contrast practice" is to overcome the effects of interference.

The Stimulus Situation for Concept Learning   The stimuli for the learning of concept categories are the objects (or events) selected to *represent* the class being learned. For example, if the concept *triangle* is to be learned, it is necessary to represent a variety of these in order for the child to acquire a concept broad enough to apply to all triangles. Similarly, if the concept *reflex* is being acquired, the variety of such events must not be limited to the knee jerk, but needs to include a reasonable variety of reflexes having different bodily sites.

The stimuli for concept learning *may* be words, and this is particularly the case when defined concepts are to be learned. Educated adults often acquire concepts whose stimuli have been words; thus, an adult may acquire a fairly adequate concept of meiosis by reading about it or by looking it up in a dictionary. It is noteworthy, however, that even with sophisticated learners a few pictures may greatly facilitate the acquisition of such a concept. Youngsters, too, are able to acquire the concept *triangle* verbally from words such as "three points not in the same straight line, joined by three line segments," and this method can be used provided it is clear that the subordinate concepts *point, line, juin*, and *line segment* have previously been learned. As will be apparent, such learning is actually a matter of acquiring a defined concept by learning a rule, with the added effect that the rule thus learned can also be stated verbally. However, as previously noted, this is not the simplest way to learn a concept, and in many cases it is not the best way. A variety of pictured triangles provides the most direct stimulus approach to the learning of *triangle* as a concrete concept.

The Stimulus Situation for Rule Learning   The stimuli for learning rules are most often verbal ones. The major part of the content that makes up an academic curriculum is thus set apart from most simpler forms of learning by being presented via verbal communication. The early grades of school may be considered as having the primary purpose of furnishing the student with the basic language skills that will make it possible for him to learn rules. Determining the temperature of boiling water or demonstrating the effects of English taxation on the American colonies are the kinds of rule-governed learning objectives that abound in the curriculum of elementary and secondary education. Verbal statements of the sort, "Water boils when its temperature reaches 212 degrees F" are often typical stimuli for the learning of rules. Presumably, it is not the fact that such statements are English sentences, which is their essential characteristic, but the fact that they contain verbal stimuli arousing concepts in close contiguity with each other. The rule concerning water, for example, is a sequence of the concepts *water, boil, temperature, reach, 212, degrees*, and *F*. As previously emphasized, such a sequence of contiguous concepts is highly effective for learning, provided all the concepts it contains have been previously learned and can be recalled.

There is nothing impossible about learning rules without using verbal stimuli; it is simply a more roundabout process. For example, one can imagine a person learning some rules of checker-playing without a word being spoken, over a period of time in which he participates in a number of games. Under such circumstances, the individual may "put together" rules by saying them to himself. But obviously the rules of the game, as well as the strategies of the game, can be learned much more rapidly by using verbal stimuli that present verbal statements of principles pertaining to "moves," "pieces," "jumps," "kings," and so on.

The stimuli for learning, then, are dependent on what kind of learning is going to be required and not simply on what content is to be taught. For simple forms of learning, stimuli are those features of stimulus objects that are to serve as cues to the responses in $Ss \rightarrow R$ connections. In discrimination learning, contrasting stimuli presented during "contrast practice" are necessary for the establishment of connections that differentiate among these stimuli. For concrete concepts, a variety of stimulus objects is needed to represent the class being learned. And for defined concepts and rules, verbal stimuli presented in the proper sequence are usually employed to arouse the concepts that are being combined to form them.

Offering Guidance for Learning

Guidance for learning may take a number of forms, depending to a large extent on the type of learning involved. Practically, learning guidance is often in the form of a verbal communication, although this need not always be the case. When the simple connection of lifting the paw is being learned by the dog, the master is providing guidance when he first lifts the dog's paw into the proper position. Guidance of a nonverbal sort may also be provided by diagrams when a child is first learning to print letters or to draw figures.

The learning of motor and verbal chains is often accompanied by a form of learning guidance called *prompting*. For example, if the child is learning to spell words having the common suffix "-ate," the suffix may be initially suggested by the stimulus "a-e," as in the word "infla-e." Subsequently, the cues may be reduced ("faded") as in the word "summa____," and finally eliminated for the word "dict___." As has been mentioned in previous chapters, "extra" verbal cues are often used to aid the learning of discriminations and concrete concepts.

Still another way in which verbal communications are employed as a part of instruction is to *guide discovery* of defined concepts and rules to be acquired. Many rules are learned simply by being stated in verbal form, as in, for example, "Current flows in the direction of higher to lower electric potential." When the method of discovery is employed, a sequence like the following might become a part of instruction: "Remember that a given point in a circuit may have a greater potential than another point. In which direction would you expect current to flow?" The first of these statements is designed to stimulate recall. The second is a question asking the student to discover the rule governing the flow of electric current. It is an example, then, of a verbal instruction having the function of *guiding* discovery.

Directions that guide the learner's discovery are very often in the form of questions. Of course, more than one question may be needed, in contrast to the rather simple example just given. In general, questions used for this purpose do not include all the language needed in the "answer," but they may include some of it, and they are certainly designed to suggest the kind of answer required. Guidance provided by this kind of verbal communication is a method familiar to every teacher. It has been found to be effective in experimental studies of rule learning (Gagné and Brown, 1961; Gagné, Mayor, Garstens, and Paradise, 1962), although the question of how much or how little guidance is most effective has not received a satisfactory answer as yet. Presumably, the effect of such verbal questioning is to channel the thinking of the learner in such a way that the extreme incorrect hypotheses he may try out implicitly are eliminated from consideration. The effect of guidance may be, therefore, to speed up the learning, since the learner does not waste time on discovered rules that are wildly wrong. At the same time, even though guided, he does actively generate the rules himself, rather than simply responding to them in prestructured verbal form.

Feedback from Learning

Learning is not something that just happens to the individual, at least so far as most of its varieties are concerned. Typically, the learner is attempting to achieve some performance, and his motivation toward this achievement may be of critical importance. Accordingly, some means or other must be provided during instruction for him to perceive the results of his activity, to receive from the learning environment some feedback that enables him to realize that his performance is "correct."

Simple Forms of Learning   According to a considerable body of evidence (Kimble, 1961, pp. 140–156), feedback from the execution of desired responses in stimulus-response learning needs to occur within a few seconds if learning is to progress rapidly. When an animal is acquiring a simple connection like pressing a lever or running along a pathway, acquisition is fastest when the reinforcement (usually in the form of a food pellet) is given immediately following a successful response. As the delay is lengthened within a range of thirty seconds or so, learning takes place more slowly. However, it is possible for animals to learn simple acts of this sort when the delay in reinforcement is a minute or longer. Observations of learning under such feedback conditions have suggested the strong possibility that the animals are actually learning chains, made up of links that they themselves supply and that fill the gaps between their correct response and the occurrence of reinforcement. In other words, chain learning is a means available to an animal to acquire connections under conditions of delay in reinforcement (Kimble, 1961, pp. 196–198). This kind of event, therefore, may serve to emphasize the importance of immediate feedback, rather than to disaffirm it.

Feedback in the Learning of Concepts and Rules   It is quite apparent that the learning of concepts and rules takes place in human beings under conditions in which reinforcement, however it may be characterized, bears not the faintest resemblance to a pellet of food. In the most typical instance, the learner makes a response that reflects his newly acquired capability and then is "told" whether he is right or wrong. However, this does not mean that the words "right," "wrong," "correct," "incorrect" have to be used. In the classroom, supplying the correct response may be followed by the teacher's going on to the next point in the lesson. Many other kinds of subtle cues may be employed—a nod, a smile, a glance; there is no need to specify what all the possibilities are. Presumably, the learner needs to have previously learned that these events signify that his response has been a correct one. This can be assumed under most circumstances, since he probably has learned it quite early in his life.

The usefulness of frequent feedback during the acquisition of rules, or of a set of interrelated rules, should not be overlooked. The designers of programmed instruction frequently point to the importance of confirming responses each step of the way. Many instructional programs are composed of single sentences containing blanks to be filled by the learner and a printed answer that may then be checked against this response. When entire topics are being learned, feedback for the correct accomplishment of each subtopic can probably be of considerable value for the efficiency of learning.

When rules are being learned, feedback need not always come from the external situation, but may arise from other concepts or rules recalled by the learner himself. In other words, there are many instances in which the learner knows he is right because of an internal check that he can apply to the responses he has produced. For example, in completing the chemical equation

$$HCl + NaOH \rightarrow H_2O + NaCl$$

the compounds on the right are (let it be assumed) familiar ones whose chemical composition has been previously learned. Furthermore, the number of atoms of each element involved in the equation is the same on the right as on the left. Thus a learner who managed to discover how to complete this equation would be pretty confident about its being correct without being told. Of course, he might like to have further verification at a later time. But the point is that he has been able to use recalled rules in supplying his own reinforcement within a short time after the completion of his response.

It may be that the internal checking the learner is able to do in the learning of rules and hierarchies of rules is an important source of reinforcement in learning. If immediacy of feedback is necessary for learning, as suggested by studies of simpler forms, self-checking may be the best way to insure it. Even though the "knowledge that one is right" may occasionally turn out to be incorrect when further verification against external standards is made, the effect of such self-checking can furnish some immediate satisfaction that may speed learning.

Performance Appraisal

Still another event providing feedback over longer sequences of instruction takes the form of an "appraisal exercise" or "test" given at the end of instruction on a topic. If the learner has been informed of the performance expected at the end of learning, it is desirable that this expectation be fulfilled by permitting him the opportunity of checking his performance against an external standard. If appraisal procedures become customary, it is reasonable to suppose that they will have an important effect on the student's motivation to continue learning. Obviously, a "test" given mainly for motivational purposes should have nothing about it that is obscure to the learner or deliberately hidden from him. If the objective of instruction is to add decimals, the appraisal should be of his capability of adding decimals; if he is learning to balance chemical equations, then the appraisal should concern balancing chemical equations; and so on. There should be no attempt to measure other aspects of his behavior simply because he is "taking a test." Of course, testing sometimes has other purposes than this, but the initial appraisal test needs to be a straightforward attempt to assess exactly what the student has learned in the immediately preceding exercise. As such, it can be a source of feedback of value to retention of what has been learned, and to the continuation of positive motivation for learning.

Making Provision for Transferability

Once an intellectual skill has been acquired, it needs to be put to use. Most statements of educational objectives emphasize the broad applicability of learned capabilities, rather than specific performances. Thus, it is generally considered desirable that the student learn not only to recognize structurally correct English sentences but to apply this knowledge to compositions that he himself generates. Similarly, a goal of science instruction is not simply having the student state a concrete example of a scientific principle but also making it possible for him to apply this principle in novel situations, and perhaps even to design an experiment to test a principle of his own devising. Obviously, instruction must include provisions for meeting such goals as these, which demand the *transfer of learning*.

What kinds of events support and encourage the transfer of learning? First, it may be noted that transfer requires a suitable design of the learning hierarchy itself, which needs to include the kinds of subordinate capabilities that are relevant to the range of performances for which instruction is designed. As for the conditions of instruction themselves, some evidence suggests the importance of *variety* of settings and examples (Gagné and Rohwer, 1969, pp. 408–410) in facilitating transfer of learning to new problems. It would be fair to say, however, that additional evidence of the effectiveness of this variable is greatly needed. Perhaps the most dependable factor in the instructional situation for insuring transfer of learning is the thorough learning of the original concept or principle.

Insuring Retention

It would seem reasonable that certain kinds of instructional events could be instituted to increase the probability of retention of what is learned. In the case of simpler types of learning, such as motor and verbal chains, there is considerable evidence that the variable whose effects outweigh all others in importance for long-term retention is *amount of practice* during initial learning (see Underwood, 1964).

When one considers concept and rule learning, however, it is not at all clear that the variable of amount of initial learning is of such importance. If a concept or rule has been completely learned (in the sense that it can be applied to a novel example), it is entirely possible that additional practice may have no appreciable effect on its retention. Insofar as meaningful verbal knowledge is concerned, Ausubel (1968, pp. 83–123) summarizes a considerable body of evidence tending to show that the effects of interference, which are prominently found in the verbatim retention of verbal chains, are not prominent in their effects on retention of meaningful materials. He suggests, instead, that one must predict retention of such materials on the basis of (1) availability of relevant anchoring ideas; (2) the stability and clarity of these ideas; and (3) the distinguishability of new material from its anchoring ideas. Thus his suggestion is, so far as instruction is concerned, that events be included which carefully relate the new verbal material to previously acquired knowledge. The aim of such events is to make the new material readily *subsumable* under previously learned ideas and at the same time *distinguishable* from them.

THE PROCEDURES OF INSTRUCTION

The instructional process as a whole may be thought of as a set of procedures designed to bring about the kinds of events just described. Once the structure of a learning sequence has been planned in accordance with the prin-

ciples of Chapter 9, the task of instruction for *each* intellectual skill becomes one of gaining and controlling attention,
informing the learner of expected outcomes, and so on. Each
of these functions is essential; should any one of them be
omitted, learning would occur only with difficulty.

How do these procedures fit together in a typical instructional exercise? This can be illustrated by an analysis of
an instructional sequence in elementary science, entitled,
"Inferring the Presence of Water Vapor in Air." This exercise has the objective, for the child, of learning to identify
an inference, namely, that the liquid accumulating on a
cold surface exposed to the air comes from the air. From
the instruction provided, it is expected that the child will be
able not only to state the inferred principle, but will be able
to tell the operations and steps in reasoning that make possible the checking of the inference. The analysis of instruction for this exercise is given in Table 2.

This table makes it clear that each step in the instructional process can be accounted for in terms of the principles
previously described in this chapter and others. There are
several reasons why this analysis should be informative for
an understanding of instruction. First, it is made apparent
that an exercise of this sort has an *objective* to begin with,
and is completed only when that objective is reached, that
is, when students are able to display the performances implied by the objective. Second, the analysis helps to pinpoint
the exact *stage at which learning occurs*. Some learning may
occur at step 5, although recall of a previously learned principle may be more likely for some students. Step 11, however, is clearly the point at which one can expect students
to be able to state and carry out the principles of interest
they are supposed to be learning. As a third and related
matter, the analysis given in the table serves to emphasize
that a substantial amount of recall must *precede* the act of
learning itself. Verbal directions are used to stimulate recall
in steps 4, 6, 7, 8, 9, and 10. And finally, the point is well
illustrated that learning is not really complete when the required principles are elicited on the first occasion, as in

TABLE 2

THE INSTRUCTIONAL PROCESS FOR AN EXERCISE ON
"INFERRING THE PRESENCE OF WATER VAPOR IN AIR"

INSTRUCTIONAL EVENT	FUNCTION
1. Teacher directs attention to clouding of windows on a cold day; the ring of water left by a glass of ice water; the cloud left by breathing on a mirror. Questions students about why these events happen.	1. Establishment of *achievement motivation,* based on curiosity and the desire to display knowledge to other children and to parents.
2. Children are given tin cans and ice cubes.	2. Providing *stimulus objects.*
3. Students are told to put the ice cubes in the cans, and to watch what happens to the outside of the cans.	3. Completion of stimulus situation. *Verbal directions* to focus attention.
4. Students are asked to describe what they see. "Fog"; "drops of water"; "large drops running down"; "ring of water at base of can."	4. *Verbal directions* to stimulate *recall* of previously learned concepts. *Feedback* provided.
5. Students are asked what they can infer from their observations. "Liquid is water from the air."	5. Learning of a principle by discovery; for some students, this may be recall. *Feedback* provided.
6. Other alternatives are pointed out to students. Could it be some other liquid? Could it come from the metal of the can? *How can one test an inference?*	6. *Verbal directions* to inform the learner of the expected *outcome* of instruction (how to test this inference).
7. "How can we tell whether this liquid is water?" ("Taste it.")	7. *Verbal directions* requiring *recall* of previously learned principle.
8. "If the water comes out of the metal, what should happen when it is wiped off?" ("Can should weigh less.")	8. *Verbal directions* requiring *recall* of previously learned principle.
9. Students are asked, if the water comes from the air, what should happen to the weight of the can after the water collects on it. ("Can should increase in weight.") Direct observation is made of increase in weight of can by ice, by weighing on an equal-arm balance.	9. *Verbal directions* requiring *recall* of previously learned principles.

TABLE 2 (cont.)

INSTRUCTIONAL EVENT	FUNCTION
10. Students are asked to recall that steam consists of water droplets and water vapor (an invisible gas). Air can contain water vapor.	10. *Verbal directions* requiring *recall* of previously learned principles.
11. Students are asked to state (a) what they observed; (b) what they inferred; and (c) how they checked their inference.	11. Learning of the principles of distinguishing observation and inference, and of operations required to check inferences. *Feedback* provided.
12. Students are asked to make and test inferences in two or three other new situations, and to describe the operations and reasoning involved. These might be (a) water evaporation; (b) the extinguishing of a candle in a closed cylinder; (c) the displacement of water by gas in an inverted cylinder.	12. Additional *examples* of the principles learned, for the purpose of ensuring their recall and generalization.
13. Another new situation is presented to the students and they are asked to describe it in terms of (a) what they observed; (b) what they inferred; (c) how they checked their inference.	13. *Appraisal* providing *feedback*.

Based on an exercise of the same name occurring in Commission on Science Education, *Science: A process approach, Part 4.* Washington, D.C.: American Association for the Advancement of Science, 1963.

step 11. This must be followed by some *additional examples* of the principle, as well as by an *appraisal* that informs the learner of his own success in achieving a new capability.

Designing instruction for initial learning is thus seen to be a matter of setting up a total set of circumstances within which learning can be embedded. Many preparations need to be made for the act of learning, and together these constitute what is known as *instruction.* These procedures have the functions of establishing motivation; and in addition, of controlling the external situation in terms of the presentation of the stimulus, the verbal direction of behavior, and the provision of learning feedback.

The Management of Instruction

The modifications brought about in the human individual by the educational system are the result of the process called learning. To be sure, the individual does grow and mature in a physiological sense during the years from five to twenty. But the changes that make him a productive member of society happen because of a process of learning that interacts with this process of maturation. The growing itself cannot be affected or altered very much. The learning, in contrast, is easily affected by almost every interaction the individual has with his environment, physical and social. To appreciate how prone to learning the human individual is, it would perhaps be wise to start with the notion that he is learning all the time.

Since learning is such a pervasive and enduring process, it is not entirely unreasonable to ask whether an educational system is necessary at all. Why not let the individual grow up, watch what others do, become curious about the world, discover principles for himself, and thus with a minimum of fuss become a "well-educated" man? This is not a completely ridiculous idea, for it is quite conceivable that a certain number of individuals who are inherently bright enough, and who are simply told where to find things when they are looking for them, can in fact become knowledgeable and capable adults. But it seems quite certain that only a few unusual individuals could actually accomplish this feat. The amount of knowledge modern man must have to be even a moderately successful and satisfied citizen is growing all the time. And for the person who is not an intellectual giant, that is, for 98 percent of the population, the system of "educating oneself" simply will not work. By implication, the fundamental reason for an educational system is to *manage instruction* so that learning will occur most efficiently.

How well is instruction managed by our present educational system? During recent years, there have been many complaints that learning is not very efficiently dealt with. Periodically, a sample is taken of what high school graduates know about history or about arithmetic, and the amount of knowledge revealed is often astoundingly low. Frequently, college professors testify to the inadequate mastery of language skills among their entering students. During recent years, university scholars have increasingly participated with other educators in projects designed to revise and reform the curricula of the earlier grades of school—not simply to bring them up to date, but to incorporate in them a range of intellectual content that they have not previously possessed. Frequent suggestions are made to introduce content subjects in the elementary grades that have for years been thought suitable only for the junior and senior high school years.

These and other events raise the question as to just how efficiently learning *can* be managed by an educational system. Judged by the needs for intellectual competence in the modern world, is our system of education doing a fraction of what it might? Have our schools become, relatively speaking, mainly community organizations for the care and socialization of the young rather than institutions for the building of intellectual competence? Can they become the means for insuring intellectual freedom?

In most conceptions of the educational system, the teacher is the *manager of the conditions of learning*. What he says to the student comprises the verbal communications and also the verbal stimulus content of the learning situation. What he points to or has the student look at in the surrounding environment becomes a part of the stimulus situation for learning. This managing function of the teacher does not change when the system is made more complex by incorporating certain technological improvements. Providing the student with verbal content by means of books speeds up the whole process of learning, once the skill of reading has been acquired. Using pictures, filmstrips, or motion pictures makes possible the representation of a great variety of objects and events that cannot be directly seen from one geographical spot. Records and tape recordings can provide auditory stimulation of languages, music, and other sounds beyond the capabilities of a single teacher. In more complex educational systems, then, the teacher may be aided by a number of gadgets, and also by a number of other people. But the essential function remains one of managing the conditions of learning.

The management of learning is surely not an easy function to perform. It requires many decisions, each of which affects in some way or other the conditions of learning and, therefore, the "input" to the student. The objective of this management is to insure that learning will be efficient, that is, that the greatest change in the student's behavior will occur in the shortest period of time, and that this change will lead progressively to increased self-management of further learning. The first kind of decision about learning pertains to the *planning* of suitable conditions for learning.

Defining Objectives for Learning

It is logical to suppose that the initial step in deciding on the conditions for learning is defining objectives. In terms of the system model, this means that for any given occasion on which the system is to perform its mission, there needs to be a decision about the *nature of the change in behavior* sought. Only if this is done will it be possible to infer what kind of input needs to be made to the learner, that is, what kind of learning situation needs to be established to bring about this change.

The Nature of Objectives   A number of writers have emphasized the importance of defining the objectives of learning in terms of *observable human performances* (Gagné, 1964b; Lindvall, 1964; Tyler, 1949). As Mager's (1962) work shows so effectively, to say that a student at the end of a learning session will be expected to *know* something, or to *understand* something, or to *appreciate* something provides an unsatisfactory basis for the planning of the learning situation. These kinds of verbs, which occur so frequently in works on the "objectives of education" (French, 1957; Kearney, 1953)

may, to be sure, furnish an agreeable starting point for thinking about the problem. But they are quite inadequate as concluding statements on the basis of which decisions about
learning can be made. The idea that a high school student
should "understand probability," for example, is a good general statement with which many educators and parents
might agree. But it is only the beginning so far as the formulation of defined objectives is concerned. Does it mean,
for example, "stating in numerical terms the probability of
choosing a black bean from a set composed of n black beans
and m white beans"? Or does it mean "deriving a general
expression for the probability of n events taken m at a
time"? Or perhaps, "identifying the probability of a hit by
a baseball player with a batting average of 220"? Or possibly
all these?

It may be noted that each of the latter kinds of statements
of objectives carries the air of objectivity with it. One of
the evident reasons for this is the use of a certain kind of
verb, which describes *overt action*. The verbs are "state"
(which means make a verbal statement of), "derive" (which
means make a sequence of logically consistent statements
beginning with certain assumptions), and "identify" (which
means simply point out or choose correctly). One has little
difficulty in realizing from these statements what it is that
can be observed about the student's performance which
would lead to the conclusion that the objective had been
attained. Quite in contrast are verbs like "understand" or
"know," which simply set the stage for these "objective" objectives, and cannot themselves be unambiguously observed.

There are, then, obvious differences between statements
of objectives that are ambiguous, and true *definitions* of objectives, which are not. What are the characteristics of a
definition of an objective? Such a definition is a verbal statement that communicates reliably to any individual (who
knows the words of the statement as concepts) *the set of
circumstances that identifies a class of human performances.*
There is little room for disagreement about such definitions,
excluding sematic ones, which can be made rare. By means
of this sort of definition one individual should be able to

identify the same human performance as some other individual. In other words, these are "operational definitions." The kind of statement required appears to be one having the following components:

1. A *verb* denoting observable action (draw, identify, recognize, compute, and many others qualify; know, grasp, see, and others do not).

2. A description of the *class of stimuli* being responded to [for example, "Given the printed statement $ab + ac = a(b + c)$"].

3. A word or phrase denoting the *object used for action* by the performer, unless this is implied by the verb (for example, if the verb is "draw," this phrase might be "with a ruling pen"; if it is "state," the word might simply be "orally").

4. A description of the *class of correct responses* (for example, "a right triangle," or "the sum," or "the name of the rule").

Using these criteria, it becomes a relatively straightforward task to make adequate definitions of objectives. For example, a mathematical objective might be: "Given a printed statement of the form $ab + ac = a(b + c)$, containing numerals, states the name of the principle exhibited." In the field of English, one could have this objective: "Completes sentences of the form, 'The people gave _____,' when given the instruction 'supply a direct object.'" In a foreign language, an example of an objective could be: "Speaks grammatically correct French sentences to questions of the form '*Qu'est-ce que vous avez?*' '*Qu'est-ce qu'il a?*' and so on, using familiar nouns." Instruction in biology might include as an objective: "Distinguishes, in written description, between *mitosis* and *meiosis*, in terms of the kinds of cells in which they occur."

When instructional objectives are derived and defined in this manner, it becomes readily possible to observe the human performances to which they refer. Moreover, it is possible to assess (or measure) the attainment of these objectives. Thus, as will be seen in a later section, the problem of measuring many of the outcomes of instruction can be approached in a fairly straightforward manner.

Perhaps the most important implication of this method of defining objectives is that the *type of learning* to be undertaken, and the required *conditions for learning*, are tremendously clarified. For example, if the objective is "distinguishes ascending from descending patterns of musical tones," it is fairly clear that the capability for this performance must be acquired as a *discrimination*. If the objective is "identifies similes in passages of English literature," it is apparent that a *defined concept* must be learned. If the objective is "demonstrates a test of Archimedes' principle (using materials that have not been employed in instruction on this principle)," then of course, *rule learning* is called for. "States the scientific problem connecting dew and boiling water" might well call for the learning of a *strategy*, as well as some higher-order rules.

The relevant set of decisions for instruction deriving from the definition of objectives are those that determine the type of learning to be employed in attaining these objectives. As described here, such decisions are obviously highly specific. They can usually not be made for an entity of learning as large as a "topic." Instead, they need to be made for each of the individual learning acts that collectively make up a topic, arranged in a hierarchical manner (Chapter 9). The beginning objectives in a topic are likely to imply the learning of *concrete* and *defined concepts*. The later objectives are more likely to be *rules* of considerable complexity. A decision to teach an entire topic under the same kind of learning conditions would evidently be both harmful and inefficient. What is needed is an analysis of the objectives that make up a topic, and a set of decisions about each of them as to the most effective conditions for learning.

Determining the Learning Structure

If decisions concerning what conditions of learning need to be made for each act of learning within a topic, then obviously the topic must first be analyzed to determine its composition. This is the process of analysis that leads to the specification of learning hierarchies such as those described in Chapter 9.

Analysis of a topic begins with the statement of the terminal objective—the performance or performances one expects the student to be able to exhibit after the learning of that topic has been completed. Once this objective has been satisfactorily defined, one can proceed to identify a subordinate set of subtopics, each an individual learning act, that must be considered prerequisites for the learning. Each of these subtopics in turn may be subjected to the same process of analysis, until one has arrived at performances that the students are known to possess, at which point the analysis stops. Each *subordinate* objective, then, is derived by systematically applying to the *next higher objective* the question, "What must the student already know how to do, in order to learn this performance?" (Gagné, 1965). The description of what the student must know—in other words, the prerequisite capabilities he must have—identifies the subordinate objectives.

Choosing the Conditions for Instruction

The choice of conditions for instruction in each topic and subtopic results in a *design* for instruction that determines its effectiveness in a crucial manner. Conditions can be predesigned (and thus, in a sense, become a part of planning) or they can be designed on the spot to meet each instructional situation as it arises. These two methods need to be examined somewhat more closely.

Two Methods of Design   The most fundamental question affecting the design of the instructional situation is the extent to which it may be predesigned for the individual learner and the extent to which it must be created while instruction proceeds. The writer of a technical book, for example, usually makes the implicit assumption that he is predesigning the instructional situation—that a learner who interacts with the printed matter on the pages of his book will in fact achieve the objectives he has in mind, whether or not they are explicitly stated. In contrast, the writer of a book called *Brief French Grammar* is making quite a different assumption. He is, in a sense, stating only the objectives of instruction and assumes that the design of the conditions of instruction will be made by a teacher during the time the latter is interacting with a student. The first example illustrates intentional *predesign* of the conditions of instruction. In the second example, the teacher engages in *extemporaneous design*.

Extemporaneous design of the conditions of instruction, during interaction with a student or students, is undoubtedly considered by many teachers one of their most important functions. To be done well, it requires a tremendous amount of knowledge and skill, which may well be possessed by a certain number of members of the teaching profession, but doubtfully by all. There is no evidence at present as to how well this task of extemporaneous design is done. The comparative achievements of students or classes provide no answer to this question, since such achievement is affected by several other factors in the instructional situation, including the student's own self-initiated activities. Everyone remembers one or more "good" teachers, or teachers who have "had an effect" on him, but this appears to be irrelevant evidence. While engaged in the learning process itself, the learner cannot be expected to be able to judge the adequacy of instructional decisions made by a teacher. However, he *is* likely to remember his own motivational changes that resulted from the teacher's efforts, and this is surely a legitimate basis for recalling a teacher favorably.

There is much to be said in favor of *predesign* of the conditions of instruction. First of all, it appears to be completely feasible. Once the objectives of instruction have been defined, and the learning structure of any topic has been determined, the only remaining action needed is the establishment of the conditions required for each type of learning described in Chapters 4 through 8, individually for each learning objective. Such a procedure should, if systematically followed, bring about the required learning in the most efficient possible manner. As the description of each type of learning has made evident, there is nothing difficult or obscure about these conditions. Often they consist mainly in communicating to the learner by means of a verbal statement, as is the case when rules are being taught. Often, too, they depend simply on placing two statements in temporal contiguity so that the learner himself can discover the rule to be learned.

It may be argued that extemporaneous design can better take into account the individual differences of students. One student, because of previous learning or innate constitution, may be able to discover a new principle with a minimum of learning guidance, whereas another may need a great deal of help. The teacher can detect these differences and react to them, making an extemporaneous design that fits the individual learner. But this is an unconvincing argument. First of all, it may be seriously doubted that the typical classroom is a place where the task of designing learning conditions for each individual student can possibly be done. The teacher is simply unable to deal with each student individually in this manner. More likely, the design that evolves extemporaneously is one that goes too slowly for the well-informed student, moves at about the proper pace for the average, and misses the ill-prepared student entirely. Second, it *is* perfectly possible for predesigned instruction to take individual differences into account. The two most important sources of difference are the degree to which prerequisite capabilities are available; and the degree to which "learning guidance" is needed (as when rules are being learned).

Advantages of Predesign of Conditions   The major possibilities of predesigning instructional content to allow for individual differences have been exhibited, not in the classroom or in the textbook, but in *programmed instruction*. It has become increasingly evident to research investigators of this technique that one of its major contributions to instruction is the feature of being adaptable to many varieties of learners (De Cecco, 1964; Glaser, 1965). "Adaptive" instructional programs can be made to select for the student the instructional content he needs in order to have the necessary prerequisites for the learning of each new topic or subtopic. If these prerequisites are present, the student is sent on to the next concept or rule to be learned; if they are not present, then they must be learned first, after which the student is sent on as usual. Amount of learning guidance can similarly be made adaptive to the needs of the individual learner (Gagné, 1963a). There is nothing about predesign as such, therefore, that prohibits the adjustment of the learning situation to the needs of the individual learner. In fact, quite the contrary: adaptive instructional programs take this feature of design as one of the main objectives to be achieved.

The positive advantages of predesign of instructional conditions go beyond this particular feature of adaptation to the needs of the individuals learner. They include the following:

1. The selection of proper conditions may be made as an unhurried choice, rather than in "spur of the moment" decisions.

2. A "quality control" of the choice of instructional conditions is insured and maintained. Quality does not suffer from variations in teacher's skills.

3. Predesign makes possible pretesting. Whether or not a set of learning conditions has been correctly chosen and designed can be determined by trying it out on students, and revising if necessary.

4. Predesign of instructional conditions greatly reduces the necessity for the teacher to use valuable time in extemporaneous design, and thus makes it possible for a proper emphasis to be restored to the teacher functions of *managing instruction, motivating, generalizing,* and *assessing.*

The fourth point should not be taken lightly, since these other functions deserve a great deal of emphasis in education, and are likely to suffer neglect by teachers who are overburdened with the very difficult task of extemporaneous design of instructional conditions. Managing instruction by advising on the choices of what topics to undertake next, and by suggesting suitable sequences of topics to fit the students' interests and objectives, is surely a most important function for the teacher to perform. Motivating students, insofar as this is not completed by parents, can be most effectively done by a wise and understanding teacher. Generalizing knowledge by providing discussions that stretch the imagination and encourage originality is surely an activity whose value is highly recognized and for which teachers would welcome having more time. Finally, the job of assessing the progress and achievements of students is another most essential function that requires the skill and objectivity of the teacher. More time for all of these important teacher activities might well be obtained by reducing the time spent in extemporaneous design of instructional conditions.

External Conditions of Learning   The essential conditions for each *type* of learning need to be incorporated into the events of instruction, typically in presenting the stimulus situation, offering guidance for learning, and providing feedback (events 4 through 6), as described earlier in this chapter. These conditions have been described for each learning type in Chapters 4 through 8 and are recapitulated in brief form in Table 3 (see Gagné, 1967, p. 301). Prerequisite capabilities, to be aroused by stimulating recall (event 3) are also indicated.

Conditions for Transfer of Learning

In general, learning is managed and instituted for broader purposes than simply the modification of particular human performances. It is brought about in order to establish

TABLE 3

SUMMARY OF ESSENTIAL CONDITIONS
APPROPRIATE FOR EACH TYPE OF LEARNING

LEARNING TYPE	PREREQUISITE CAPABILITY	EXTERNAL CONDITIONS OF LEARNING
$Ss \rightarrow R$ Connection	Apprehension of stimulus	Presentation of stimulus so that desired response will be *contiguous* in time and supply *contingent reinforcement.*
Motor Chain	Individual connections	A *sequence* of external cues, stimulating a sequence of specific responses *contiguous* in time; *repetition* for selection of correct response-produced stimuli.
Verbal Chain	Individual connections, including "coding" links	A *sequence* of external verbal cues, stimulating a sequence of verbal responses *contiguous* in time; *repetition* may be necessary to reduce interference.
Discrimination	Individual connections, or chains	Practice providing *contrast* of correct and incorrect stimuli; or, practice providing *progressive reduction* in stimulus differences.
Concrete Concept	Discriminations	Responding to a *variety of stimuli* differing in appearance, belonging to a single class.
Rule, including Defined Concept	Concepts	External cues, usually verbal, stimulate the formation of component concepts *contiguously in a proper sequence;* application is made in *specific examples.*
Higher-Order Rule —Problem Solving	Rules	*Self-arousal* and *selection* of previously learned rules to achieve a novel combination.

capabilities that will be of lasting and general usefulness to the individual. As mentioned earlier in this chapter, there are two major ways in which learned capabilities can be of use. One is in making it possible for the individual to execute some performances that are not directly learned but are in some sense similar to those that are learned. For example, the teacher of physics hopes that certain elements of the scientific method learned in connection with that subject will transfer to the solution of a problem in biology or social science. The capabilities specifically learned in school should enable the student to perform some acts of practical value to him, whether in his everyday life or in connection with an occupation. This *transferability* of what has been learned may be called *lateral transfer*, since it refers to a kind of generalizing that spreads over a broad set of situations at roughly the same "level of complexity."

The second kind of use for learned capabilities lies in making it possible for the individual to learn additional, "advanced," or more complex things, in the sense described in Chapter 9. The student who has learned the subordinate rules involved in finding the capacitance of an electrical system finds that the learning of such a higher-order rule is easier than it would otherwise be. The subordinate capabilities transfer to the higher-order learning and facilitate its occurrence. This may be called *vertical transfer*, since it refers to the effects that learned capabilities at one level have on the learning of additional ones at higher levels. Both kinds of transfer are of importance to instruction.

Lateral Transfer   The kind of observation that leads to the inference that lateral transfer has occurred is as follows. An individual has learned that the relation between two sides of a right triangle may be expressed as $A/B = cos\ \phi$. He now encounters, for the first time, a problem in physics relating to the acceleration of a body rolling down an inclined plane, and he sees that the plane may be treated as a side of a right triangle. Without additional instruction, he proceeds to express the relation he is looking for in terms of the cosine of the angle of inclination of the plane with the horizontal surface on which it rests. This behavior may be contrasted with that of another individual who has *not* learned $A/B = \cos\ \phi$, and therefore does *not* express the relation seen in the inclined plane in that manner. The behavior of the first individual is said to show *transfer of learning* to the extent that the performance is done more readily than it would have been had not the originally learned capability been present (that is, more readily than the second individual was able to do the same thing).

In the case of this kind of transfer, the question of *how much* appears to be a matter of *how broadly* the individual can generalize what he has learned to new situations. Presumably, there are limits to this breadth of generalization, which vary with different individuals. One could perhaps think of a whole range of situations of potential applicability of the cosine relationship that displayed decreasing degrees of similarity to the situation in which the rule had originally been learned. At some point along this dimension of breadth of generalizability, a given individual will fail to transfer his previously learned knowledge. Another individual, however, may be able to exhibit transfer more broadly to a wider variety of differing situations.

The most important conditions for lateral transfer appear to be *internal* to the individual. Apparently, some students are able to relate what they have learned to a wider variety of new situations than are others. Is this because they are "built that way," or because they know more? This question is a difficult one, and its answer is not known at present. Presumably, though, both learned and innate factors are at work.

Assuming that nothing can be done in an educational sense to alter innate differences in breadth of transferability, a good deal can be done concerning the learned factors. The more broadly based a learned capability, the better chance it will have to transfer to new and different situations. Accordingly, the usefulness of any learned capability will be increased if it is practiced in as wide a variety of situations as possible. Finding the cosine of an angle, once learned, has a greater probability of being transferable if it is practiced in situations that are widely different from each other. A similar statement can be made about almost any learned capability. The transferability of foreign words and phrases will be increased if they are practiced in a wide variety of contexts. The transferability of the scientific process of "formulating operational definitions" will be increased if it is practiced in connection with a wide variety of natural phenomena. The implication for the management of instruction is, therefore, quite clear: provision needs to be made for encouraging the learner to apply his knowledge broadly and in as great a variety of new situations as can be devised.

Vertical Transfer   Vertical transfer is observed when a capability to be learned is *acquired more rapidly* when it has been preceded by previous learning of subordinate capabilities. Many examples of this sort of event have been implied by the learning hierarchies described in Chapter 9. In this case, the question of *how much* transfer is a matter of the time taken to learn a higher-order rule by an individual who has learned subordinate capabilities, as compared with the time to learn by one who has not. Alternatively, one can contrast the proportion of individuals learning the higher-order rule in groups of students who have, and who have not, learned the subordinate ones. It is possible to observe such vertical transfer throughout an entire learning structure, as has been done for tasks on the addition of integers (Gagné, Mayor, Garstens, and Paradise, 1962).

The primary *internal* condition for vertical transfer is the *mastery of the subordinate capabilities*. This kind of transfer is very improbable unless the relevant lower-order chains, concepts, or rules have been learned. Learning of these subordinate capabilities must *precede* transfer. The *external* conditions are the same as those that govern the learning of higher-order capabilities and that have been specifically described in the previous section; they include the verbal directions given to guide the learner's behavior and to stimulate recall. The most important prescription for managing the conditions of vertical transfer can be stated as follows: insure that relevant subordinate capabilities have been thoroughly learned before calling on vertical transfer to aid the learning of "advanced" capabilities.

Another internal condition of vertical transfer should be mentioned. This kind of transfer is presumably enhanced by the *variety of previous knowledge* the individual has acquired. The reason for this is that the learning of any particular advanced principle or topic may be approached in various ways, not just in one way. The definition of a *limit* in mathematics, for example, can be introduced in a manner that is based on a number of different subordinate rules. In physics, *mass* can be defined in several different ways and thus made to depend on the previous mastery of different rules. It is possible that these subordinate knowledges may act to enhance each other's effects when a new capability is being learned. For this reason the latter learning may be faster for an individual who has many subordinate capabilities to drawn on than it is for one who has few. Vertical transfer may occur more readily in an individual who knows a lot (of relevant subordinate knowledge) than in an individual who knows a little. At the present time, however, such a statement has a hypothetical character, since it has not been systematically studied.

Teaching for Transfer   Establishing the conditions for transferability of what is learned can be seen to be an educational function of considerable importance. It involves procedures that will have an effect not only on the acquisition of further knowledge, as in vertical transfer, but also on the broad application of learned capabilities to novel and practical situations, as is the case when transfer is of the lateral type. Both these meanings would appear to be included in a phrase like "teaching for transfer," an objective of instruction that has been emphasized by many educational scholars.

It is of prime importance to note that transfer is a phenomenon which depends on previous learning. Educational writers occasionally wax so enthusiastic about the importance of transferability that they are prone to forget this fact. Of course, it is desirable to set up instructional conditions that will "stretch students' minds," "encourage the generalization of knowledge," "challenge students to solve problems in novel situations." Any or all of these objectives enbody transfer of learning. But something must first be learned before it can be transferred. The student who is going to transfer the principles of elastic bodies to the membranes of a living organism must first learn the principles of elastic bodies. One of the major prerequisites for transfer is learning.

The second condition of importance in seeking to assure transfer is the variety of stimulus situations over which the student is encouraged to generalize his knowledge. The more varied these can be made, the more useful will the learned capability become. At lower educational levels, this variety may be achieved by deliberate use of a whole range of natural objects and events in the classroom or on field trips. At higher levels, the function of providing contextual variety can be largely performed by verbal communication, of the sort that may take place in a "discussion group," for example.

Procedures for Assessment

As previously pointed out, the management of learning includes provision for assessment of the capabilities that have been learned. For one thing, properly conducted assessment constitutes an important source of feedback to the learner, and thus is intimately bound up with the learning process itself. And for another, the necessity of planning out a systematic course of instruction in which one performance builds on another means that the attainment of each capability needs to be carefully confirmed before the learner proceeds to the next. In order for the next higher rule to be learned effectively, assessment is needed *within* topic learning (Gagné, Mayor, Garstens, and Paradise, 1962); and it is needed *at the end* of topic learning so that the learner can proceed to related or advanced topics.

Despite the existence of a rather elaborate technology, it cannot be said with confidence that the assessment procedures customarily used in developing typical "standardized" tests are entirely adequate to meet current assessment needs. One important problem that does not appear to have been included in current techniques is a method for assessing human performance in terms of the objectives of instruction. Instead, achievement tests often appear to have the goal of demonstrating how disparate human abilities can be, along undefined dimensions. Now, the existence of individual differences is a well-known fact, and it scarcely seems a worthwhile enterprise at this point to continue to refine the techniques of measuring them with increasing degrees of precision and reliability. In fact, it is a legitimate question as to whether such an attempt can ever succeed any more than it has already.

Assessing the Immediate Outcomes of Learning   The aim of tests designed for the assessment of learning outcomes, in contrast, needs to take quite a different tack. In particular, tests should be designed to assess the immediate outcomes of learning, as exhibited by the learner when he has first attained a new discrimination, concept, rule, or an entire topic. The interest in such tests is not on how different one learner is from another, but rather on the extent to which each learner has achieved the defined objective with which instructional planning began. This distinction has been well described by Glaser (1963) as between tests that are *norm-referenced* and tests that are *criterion-referenced*. The former type is a test whose scores are interpretable only by reference to a distribution of scores obtained from an entire tested group; in other words, the scores express the extent of individual differences. Scores of the latter type derive their meaning by reference to an *external standard (criterion)*. Certainly, it is the latter kind of measure that is needed for assessment of a learner's capability in attaining defined instructional objectives.

Tests of immediate learning outcomes cannot be designed merely by changing the purpose of the total test. Attention must also be paid to the form of each item that the test contains. The item must be designed to measure the objective specifically, not in a general sense. For example, there must be an item to measure "spelling verb forms that double their terminal consonants when made into a gerund by the addition of 'ing,' as sum, summing"; not just a collection of items that measure "spelling."

Consider a test item like the following: "Find the thickness of a pipe whose inner circumference is 9π and whose outer circumference is 21π. (a) 12π; (b) 12; (c) 6π; (d) 6; (e) 3." It is difficult to see how such an item could serve the purpose of assessing *immediate outcomes* of learning a topic in mathematics (although, to be sure, it may be employed for other purposes, as discussed in subsequent paragraphs). The reason is that this item draws on the knowledge of two different higher-order rules, rather than on only one. First, there is the rule relating circumference to diameter. And second, there is the rule, readily exhibited in a drawing, that the outer diameter of a pipe equals the inner diameter plus twice the thickness of the pipe. Should an individual be unable to perform this item correctly, it would not be possible to tell from this failure whether (1) he did not know the first rule; (2) he did not know the second rule; (3) he did not know either rule; or (4) he knew both rules, but because of innate intellectual limitations, was unable to "put them together" in solving a new problem. Thus an item of this sort cannot be used to obtain a direct measure of whether the student has mastered specific objectives. To do this, one needs an item that tests knowledge of the first rule directly and unambiguously, as, "What is the difference in diameter of two pipes, one of which has a circumference of 21π, the other a circumference of 9π?" And in addition, an item is needed to measure the second rule, perhaps one that exhibits a drawing of a pipe in cross section, with values of internal and external diameters shown, asking the question, "What is the thickness of the pipe?"

To assess the immediate outcomes of learning, then, it is necessary to construct a "test" whose items have the following characteristics:

1. Pose questions that reflect directly the defined objective of the learning;

2. Conform to the class of performances that the learner has been told represent the achievement to be reached at the end of a learning session; and

3. Represent this class of performances without being specifically recallable as verbal chains from within the learning session itself (except in those instances in which specific verbal recall is itself the objective).

In other words, measuring specific outcomes of learning cannot be a matter of designing items that are "easy" or "hard," in the sense that they require the use of capabilities other than those which were to have been specifically established by the learning session. It is not the kind of questioning whose general form should be hidden from the student. Such measurement does not have the aim of increasing the contrast among the performances of students. On the contrary, *its purpose is to compare each student's performance with an external standard representing the defined objective.*

It should be clear from this discussion that the primary reason for direct measurement of the outcomes of a learning exercise or session is to insure that instructional objectives have been met. If a student fails to exhibit the performance required on such a test, he needs to undertake additional learning covering the same ground. It is inefficient, even useless, for him to try to proceed to the learning of advanced topics, in view of the hierarchical nature of knowledge, as described in Chapter 9. Whether by "repeating" the same instruction he has been given, or by using a more elaborately "guided" form of instruction, the defined objective must somehow be achieved if subsequent learning is to be even minimally efficient for this student. This kind of test, then, has the aim of determining whether the learning that was supposed to occur has really happened.

GENERAL REFERENCES

Managing Instruction

Ausubel, D. P. *Educational psychology: A cognitive view.* New York: Holt, Rinehart and Winston, 1968.

De Cecco, J. P. *The psychology of learning and instruction: Educational psychology.* Englewood Cliffs, N.J.: Prentice-Hall, 1968.

Hilgard, E. J. (ed.). *Theories of learning and instruction. Sixty-third yearbook, Part I.* Chicago: National Society for the Study of Education, 1964.

Siegel, L. *Instruction: Some contemporary viewpoints.* San Francisco: Chandler, 1967.

Determining Objectives

Bloom, B. S. (ed.), Engelhart, M. D., Furst, E. J., Hill, W. H., and Krathwohl, D. R. *Taxonomy of educational objectives. Handbook I: Cognitive domain.* New York: McKay, 1956.

French, W. *Behavioral goals of general education in high school.* New York: Russell Sage Foundation, 1957.

Kearney, N. C. *Elementary school objectives.* New York: Russell Sage Foundation, 1953.

Krathwohl, D. R., Bloom, B. S., and Masia, B. B. *Taxonomy of educational objectives. Handbook II: Affective domain.* New York: McKay, 1964.

Mager, R. F. *Preparing objectives for programmed instruction.* Palo Alto, Calif.: Fearon, 1962.

The Predesign of Learning Conditions

De Cecco, J. P. *Educational technology.* New York: Holt, Rinehart and Winston, 1964.

Glaser, R. (ed.). *Teaching machines and programmed learning. II: Data and directions.* Washington, D.C.: National Education Association, 1965.

Lumsdaine, A. A., and Glaser, R. (eds.). *Teaching machines and programmed learning: A source book.* Washington, D.C.: National Education Association, 1960.

Markle, S. *Good frames and bad: A grammar of frame writing.* New York: Wiley, 1964.

Pipe, P. *Practical programming.* New York: Holt, Rinehart and Winston, 1966.

Assessment

Dressel, P. L. (ed.). *Evaluation in general education.* Dubuque, Iowa: Brown, 1954.

Ebel, R. *Measuring educational achievement.* Englewood Cliffs, N.J.: Prentice-Hall, 1965.

Lindquist, E. F. (ed.). *Educational measurement.* Washington, D.C.: American Council on Education, 1950.

12 | Resources for Learning

The arrangements of instructional events that are used to bring learning about have been described in the preceding chapter. When these events are wisely planned, they lead to efficient learning; when they are not, learning is inefficient and often ineffective. In conducting instruction, the teacher in a modern school has a variety of resources to call upon. There are not only chalkboards and textbooks but also projectors and tape recorders and television circuits and computers. Furthermore, each and all of these may be introduced at many points in the instructional sequence and used in a variety of ways. They may become parts of, or even to some extent replacements for, the lecture, the recitation class, the discussion group, the demonstration, the laboratory.

The purpose of this chapter is to discuss these resources for learning by describing the functions they can serve in instruction, and thus play a part in the promotion of efficient learning. To do this, it will be desirable first to review in a general way the *kinds of communications* involved in the instructional situation. Following this, it will be possible to consider the purposes that particular "devices" can fulfill in instruction, as well as those they cannot serve. The various kinds of arrangements that the instructional situation can take—the "modes" of instruction—can then be systematically described. The lecture, the class, the tutoring session, the laboratory—each of these modes will be seen to involve different arrangements of instructional media. Finally, the implications of these resources and their modes of usage can be pointed out for the educational system of today and tomorrow.

COMMUNICATION IN INSTRUCTION

The focus of the instructional situation is the student, within whom learning actually occurs. Most of the previous chapters have been concerned with describing the nature of these learning changes and how they are brought about. A slightly different viewpoint will be needed in order to delineate the subject of this chapter, namely, a view over the learner's shoulder. The environment of the learner has many components that are important for learning. Most important among these are the *communications* that are included in the instructional situation.

Communication Components of Instruction

Ignoring for the moment the physical appearance of the instructional situation, it is possible to identify the communication functions performed in instruction by various components. These functions have been mentioned in previous chapters but need to be reviewed here as a basis for a discussion of the *media* that bring them about.

In *gaining and controlling attention*, the vivid or suddenly changing stimulation continues as effective stimulation at any age (see May, 1965). Following suitable learning, such stimuli can be supplanted by oral or printed directions, for example, "Notice the number of electrons in the outer ring" or, "Look at the graph in Figure 23."

Providing a model for expected learning outcomes may be done in many ways. When the model is one comprising human behavior, a presentation of moving pictures appears to be peculiarly appropriate and effective. For many kinds of performances, however, the "model" to be expected following learning is often conveyed by oral or printed communication.

Stimulating recall of prerequisite capabilities, as a part of the sequence of instructional events, is usually accomplished by some form of verbal communication. Examples are such statements as, "Remember how a line is defined" or, "Recall that a singular subject requires a singular verb." Communications having these purposes can be presented either orally or in printed form.

Presenting the stimuli for learning is another communication function. If a chain is being learned, an external cue must be provided for each link, even though these cues may become unnecessary later. If discrimination is to be accomplished, the stimuli to be discriminated must be displayed so that correct connections can become differentiated from incorrect ones. If concepts are being learned, a suitable variety of objects or events representing a class must be displayed. If principles are being acquired, the stimulus objects to which they are expected to apply must somehow be represented to the student. And if problem solving is undertaken, the "problem situation" must similarly be represented and displayed. Obviously, these various stimuli can be presented in many different ways by objects already in the learner's environment, or by means of pictures, printed books, or oral communication.

Offering guidance for learning is done by communications that take various forms depending on the type of learning that is desired. For the learning of chains and discriminations, cues may be provided in the instructional situation to establish a proper sequence of connections or to increase the distinctiveness of stimuli. As learning proceeds, these extra cues may be made to "vanish" when they are no longer needed. Stimuli that function as extra cues may take a variety of forms. For example, they may be pictorial, as when a sequence is depicted in a diagram reading from left to right. Or they may be auditory, as in emphasizing the differences in sound of such French words as *rue* and *rouge*. Verbal stimuli are often employed for both these purposes, as well as for the purpose of furnishing distinctive "coding links" in verbal chains. When rules are being learned, and particularly when learning takes the form of problem solving, communications that suggest the direction of thought often take the form of printed or prose statements.

Appraising learned performances is usually accomplished by placing the learner in representative problem situations that concretely reflect the capability he is expected to have learned. Pictures, still or moving, of such situations are often of considerable value. Verbal communications in the form of questions frequently complete the setting of the problem.

Closely related to assessment is the provision for *feedback* concerning the correctness of the learner's responses. The questions that are asked the learner, followed by his answers, must in turn be followed by information that tells him whether he is right or wrong. Sometimes the provision for this feedback function of the learner's environment is simple to arrange: a foreign word pronounced by the student may sound like one he hears on tape; the color of a chemical solution may indicate the presence of an element he is searching for. At other times it may be considerably more complex, as when the adequacy of a constructed prose paragraph is assessed and various comments are fed back to the student.

Providing for the *transfer* of learned concepts and rules to novel situations may be accomplished in a number of ways. The verbal communication that takes place in a discussion class may be considered to serve this function. The process is often initiated by verbally stated questions of the "problem-solving" variety. An important alternative method is to place the individual within a problem situation more or less directly, without the use of words to describe it. A science demonstration is an example. Motion pictures can be used with considerable effectiveness to initiate problem-solving activities by "getting the students into the situation" in a highly realistic manner.

Means for *insuring retention* may involve any of a variety of media. Often, verbal questions are appropriate. However, it is usually a good idea to match the stimuli used to provide practice with those that will ultimately be used when recall is requested. Remembering what to do in answering the verbal question, "How do you adjust a carburetor?" is not necessarily the same as remembering what to do when confronted with an actual carburetor in need of adjustment. Thus, for many scientific and practical tasks, actual objects or pictures of them often have a particular effectiveness for this instructional function.

It is important to realize, then, that any given medium of communication may perform one or several functions during the course of instruction. Communication is indeed a major part of what happens during instruction. It would be going too far, apparently, to equate communication to instruction, since this would tend to leave out such essential elements as the operation of physical stimuli, as well as of the processes internal to the learner. Nevertheless, communications of various sorts, and with several different functions, make up a large portion of the instructional events that are designed to bring about learning.

Obviously, there are many ways to establish suitable conditions for instruction, and many combinations of objects, devices, and verbal communications may be employed in doing so. One important consideration for the design of effective instruction is that several alternative ways of accomplishing the same function are usually available. For any given function, certain means of interacting with the learner may be more effective than others. Accordingly, the characteristics of various *media for instruction* in performing these functions need to be considered carefully in making a choice.

MEDIA FOR INSTRUCTION

The phrase *instructional media* is used here to refer to the various kinds of components of the learning environment that generate stimulation to the learner—in other words, communicate with him. In this broad sense, the teacher is usually a major source of such stimulation. Besides the teacher, there are various objects and devices, ranging from books to television receivers, that have this general function of providing inputs to the learner. There is no intention here to detract from the teacher's importance by considering his function of stimulus generation along with that of inanimate systems. Naturally, inanimate systems can perform their function effectively only when their stimulus contents are designed by people who also have in mind the purpose of instructing. However, it is illuminating to distinguish all the sources of stimulation for the learner in the situation immediately surrounding him, and thus to include the teacher as one of these.

Some media for instruction have formed a part of the learning environment for many, many years. Besides the teacher, these include printed or written media provided by chalkboards and books, natural objects that are directly imported into the instructional situation, and photographs or drawn representations. Newer media for instruction are motion pictures, whether presented by means of a movie projector or a television system, and teaching machines, which may be considered a means of combining the characteristics of books and pictures with certain other instructional functions. For what purposes are these various media appropriate, and for what purposes are they inappropriate, or at least relatively ineffective?

Objects for Instruction

The stimuli for the instruction of the child in his pre-school years are primarily the objects in his restricted world:

his toys, the furniture in his house, the simple tools he uses, the ground and trees and telephone poles and streets, and, of course, the other human beings with whom he interacts. When he goes to school, the variety of these objects changes somewhat. Now there are special collections of leaves or shells or rocks that display all in one place the individual things he has encountered before. In addition, there are other objects that he has not yet seen before, perhaps new kinds of animals and plants, or specially constructed blocks. The use of objects to present stimuli continues throughout his school years, with the objects themselves growing more refined and complex. Particularly is this true in the science laboratory, where the new objects may be chemicals and solutions, new varieties of animals and plants, and instruments such as balances, microscopes, ammeters, and chronometers.

Instruction needs to be fundamentally based on the stimulation provided by objects and events (that is, changes in objects), assuming, of course, that these objects may be people. As emphasized in Chapter 6, objects and events are the stimuli from which concepts are derived. Although instruction comes to depend heavily on verbal communication, the words merely "stand for" things that may be directly observed. This is the fundamental reason why scientists place such a high value on the laboratory and the field exercise. Scientific knowledge depends ultimately on the direct observation of things and events.

Naturally, the objects used for instruction must be carefully chosen. If multiple discriminations are being established among varieties of rocks, care must be taken to select the samples so that the differential features will be emphasized. If the addition of unit quantities is to be learned, a set of objects (blocks) of sizes graded in these units must be provided. If the concept of magnetic attraction is to be learned, a suitable variety of magnets and pole orientations must be employed. The kind of learning that is contemplated therefore has considerable significance for the choice of objects selected as media for instruction.

Demonstration

Demonstrations consist of actual objects that are typically made to interact with each other so as to display an event or a set of events. Water may be heated to boiling, steel balls may be made to run down inclined planes, oxygen liberated from a chemical reaction may be collected in an inverted vessel, and so on. The event is just as much a stimulus situation as is a display of objects by themselves. In many instances, the events that might otherwise be made to occur by the student's own activity in the laboratory can function to present the needed stimulus situation with equal effectiveness by way of a demonstration. In general, the functions of the demonstration in instruction are basically the same as those discussed for the display of objects.

The Human Model

Special importance inheres in the demonstration of socially interacting behavior by a human model, that is, the parent or teacher. Patterns of interaction with people, the combined total of which is referred to as the personality, seem to be most typically learned in situations involving another human person, often an adult. Learning in such situations is usually referred to as imitation, or modeling (see Bandura and Walters, 1964). Many studies have been conducted on social learning through this medium of the human model. It is clear that children readily learn by imitation such behaviors as aggressiveness, dependency, ways of reacting to frustration, reactions to the opposite sex, self-control, and many particular kinds of moral behavior. Furthermore, it is of considerable interest to note that desirable patterns of social behavior can be learned when children see the "model" rewarded; this phenomenon is called "vicarious reinforcement." Similarly, studies have shown that undesirable kinds of social behavior can be reduced when children observe a model being punished for such behavior.

The importance of learning from demonstrations of desirable social behavior by the human model would be difficult to overemphasize. Presumably, this is the major way in which nonintellectual kinds of capabilities and dispositions become acquired. Of course, as the child develops, he himself gains increasing control over such learning; probably he learns to choose his own models and to administer self-reinforcement and self-punishment. During formative years, however, the influence of models and imitative learning is considerable. If one is concerned about conditions for instruction to establish patterns of social interaction, moral and ethical conduct, and personal values, he can probably not devise an adequate arrangement of such conditions without including the human model. The implications for teaching are obvious: the teacher is often (although not always) the model whose behavior is being imitated by many children.

Oral Communication by the Teacher

There are many situations for which oral communication by a teacher can provide *all* the required instructional functions. But this is not true of every situation. It will be desirable to consider certain of these functions in some detail, along with some important limitations.

Oral communication can serve well such purposes as gaining attention and stimulating recall of prerequisite capabilities. For the early years, it is difficult to find any medium that works as well. For later years of education, printed and pictorial materials may be able to equal the effectiveness of oral communication in performing this function.

In informing the learner of expected learning outcomes, oral communication appears to have no general advantage over other media. The terminal performance may sometimes be communicated more conveniently in printed or pictorial form. For example, if the objective is "computing the normality of chemical solutions," the printed example ".5N" is evidently a good model for the kind of performance required. Oral communication is needed, however, when the terminal performance is itself an oral one, as in constructing sentences in a foreign language, or in making a speech.

Communication of the stimuli inherent to the learning task can often be done orally, but other media may be more appropriate. In advanced forms of instruction, adequate presentation of stimuli can be done verbally. The earth's orbit around the sun can be described rather than being directly observed. The course of passage of a bill through the Congress can be verbally described. Appropriate conversation in a foreign language can be orally communicated. But there are real limitations to the use of oral communication for presenting stimuli. The science teacher would feel grossly handicapped if he had to depend solely on oral communication to describe wave motion. The description of a town meeting may not be as satisfactory a stimulus for learning as the direct observation of a town meeting, or a filmed record of one.

In offering guidance for learning, oral communication may be particularly effective in the early years. For example, the chains involved in the printing or writing of letters may be prompted by teachers' oral directions, for example, "First, a long line down," "Next, a line across near the top," and so on. Prompting can also be done well by printed means once the student has learned to read, as is shown in many self-instructional programs (Klaus, 1965). As for guidance in problem solving, the following is an example. Asked to demonstrate the truth of the statement

$$8 \times 3 + 16 = 5 \times 8,$$

the student's thinking may be guided by such questions as, "Can you think of another name for 16?"—and others as needed—to enable him to arrive at the expression

$$8 \times 5 = 8 \times 5.$$

Again it is true that such guidance can also be given by printed means, and some self-instructional programs do this quite effectively.

Feedback to the learner is often furnished by oral communication. For young children, a good deal of the teacher's conversation may consist of statements of "yes," "good!" "that's right" as the students attain successive goals of instruction. At later ages, the necessity for such "oral reinforcement" becomes greatly reduced, since the student is able to match his own performance with an external standard, or one that he himself supplies.

The teacher often undertakes to carry out the function of appraising performance by means of oral questioning. But there are certainly limitations to this method. The attainment of concepts and principles can also be measured by means of printed statements, and often requires the use of pictures or diagrams.

Questions that initiate the process of providing for transfer can be presented orally. If students have learned the principles of distribution of powers among legislative, executive, and judiciary components of government, a question like the following can be asked: "What possible means could there be of legislative restraint on judicial powers?" A demonstration using actual objects or pictures is another possibility for setting the stage for knowledge transfer. In continuing the process, oral discussion is often employed.

All of these functions, then, *can* be done by oral communication, and perhaps this is the reason why the model of the teacher and student talking to each other while seated on a log seems so appropriate for the instructional situation. But many of the functions can be done just as well by other means, as by the display of print and pictures. And certain subjects require something other than oral communication: much of science and mathematics cannot be taught without recourse to stimulation that includes actual objects and events.

Printed Language Media

Books, pamphlets, and leaflets are also a traditional part of the instructional situation. In the later periods of education, the amount of dependence on books as media of instruction is very high relative to dependence on other media. It is noteworthy, however, that oral discussion still has an instructional function at the level of postgraduate education. An experienced university scholar may derive most of his instruction from the printed media of books and learned journals; yet he finds it necessary to discuss with his colleagues the ideas he gets from books. At the other extreme of the educational scale, printed communication can accomplish very little; the presentation of actual objects accompanied by oral communication is the typical mode of instruction for children in the elementary grades. Accordingly, learning the skill of reading is the crucial event that determines the increasing dependence on printed media from the early grades of school onward.

Assuming that the student possesses the necessary prerequisite knowledge, instruction by means of a book is usually a remarkably rapid and efficient process. Although no figures are available, the amount of time required for oral communication must surely be three or four times as much as that needed for instruction by means of a book. For the vast range of subject matter that is taught following the primary school years, printed communication can certainly be the major medium of instruction, and often is. When pictures and diagrams are combined with printed text (as, for example, in a good high school physics text), the dangers of excessive verbalism can largely be overcome, and the book can impart a great deal of instruction in a relatively short time when used by a suitably prepared student who can read. At this level of schooling, in fact, whatever ineffectiveness books possess as instructional media may often be attributed to difficulties that are not inherent in the medium itself: either the student has not acquired the necessary background knowledge or he has not learned how to read, or both.

There are, however, other limitations of the printed medium. These have to do with the ways in which the sentences on the printed page are functioning in the instructional situation. Many textbooks, after all, are poorly written from the standpoint of establishing the proper conditions for learning. For example, does the printed text introducing a topic direct attention to the proper stimuli? Does it inform the learner of the nature of the performance to be learned? Does it use prompts, where these are appropriate, or guide the direction of the student's thought? Does it assess the attainments of learning at frequent intervals, and provide for feedback to the learner? Many printed texts would score quite low on their performance of these necessary instructional functions. What happens, usually, is that the learner performs these functions himself by the time he has as much experience as a college student has. But it is perhaps too much to expect that a fifth-grader will have acquired this much sophistication about self-instruction through reading. The deficiencies of ordinary printed texts as instructional media often become markedly clear to people who try writing self-instructional programs.

The potentialities of printed texts for instruction are very high, and it is doubtful that they have been well exploited as yet. Designing a printed text that will efficiently instruct a ten-year-old is not simply a matter of matching his vocabulary. Primarily, it is a matter of *organizing* the statements in such a way that they will perform the instructional functions that have previously been described. Unless one is simply "telling a story" (which may be the case for some sorts of subject matter like history), it is doubtful that the proper sequence of printed statements is much like a story at all. Each sentence has a purpose, and sets of sentences are organized in such a way that learning will occur most readily. The reader will perhaps be able to identify the instructional functions of the following sequence of printed statements applicable to Figure 23.

1. Look at the pictures.
2. How is the pressure at the bottom of a vessel full of liquid related to the shape of the vessel?
3. Remember that pressure is the ratio of a force to (what?).

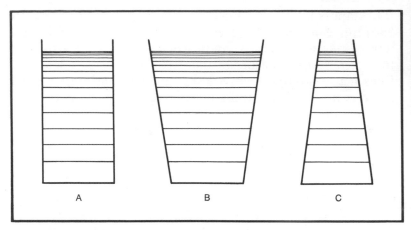

FIGURE 23.   Vessels of different shapes, each containing a liquid.

4. In a vessel whose walls flare outward, where is the force of the central cylindrical portion of the water exerted? Where is the force of the water outside this central cylinder exerted?

5. The areas of the bottoms of the vessels are equal.

6. What can you say about the pressure at the bottom of the two vessels (A) and (B)?

7. State the relationship in general terms. (ANSWER: The pressure at the bottom of the vessel of liquid is not affected by the shape of vessel.)

8. Now look at the other vessel, with walls flaring inward (C).

9. Etc.

It will be apparent that not many textbooks are written with this kind of organization of instructional functions. As will be seen later, "instructional programs" often are. Both, of course, are examples of printed media.

Pictures

As implied by the previous example, the most important function of pictures and diagrams as media of instruction is to display the stimulus situation. For the earliest years, this function may be most effectively performed by actual objects and events. Children have to learn the chains that link the pictures as stimuli with appropriate responses. Once these have been acquired, pictures greatly extend the range of stimulus situations that can be brought into the classroom. Another function well performed by pictures is that of prompting. For example, motion picture sequences can be effectively used as a source of external stimuli for instruction in tying knots, as well as for many other kinds of procedural chains (Roshal, 1961).

Still pictures take many forms as media of instruction. They may appear on the pages of books, accompanying printed material. They frequently are used by the teacher to accompany oral instruction, in the form of enlarged prints, slides, filmstrips, or transparencies. The question as to whether one of these physical forms of still picture is "better" than another for instruction is surely not a sensible one, unless confined to the issue of whether one form can be seen better than another. A picture is a picture, and the educational question of interest is simply whether it can perform some particular instructional function better than something else, like printed statements. When the function is presenting a stimulus situation, there often is nothing feasible that can do the job a fraction as well as a picture.

Presenting the stimulus situation for problem solving, and thereby introducing group discussion, is a specialized function that often calls for a picture. Such is the case, for example, in presenting a science problem that is to be solved by the novel application of previously learned principles. Similarly, a picture may be used to pose a problem of creative description in a course in English. Over a tremendous range of educational subject matter, the uses of pictures are many, and it is not surprising that for some purposes a picture is worth an unlimited number of words.

The limitations of pictures in performing instructional functions are equally apparent. There are many occasions on which they cannot be effectively used to inform the learner of the performance to be expected as a result of learning. They cannot readily be used by themselves to guide the learner's thinking, or to assess his performance, or to provide him with feedback. Although none of these functions of pictures should be considered impossible, they are much more frequently performed by some kind of verbal communication. There are, then, a number of instructional functions that are better executed by words than by pictures.

Motion Pictures and Television

Although these two media of instruction are often discussed separately, there is no important reason for doing so. Logistically, of course, different arrangements are required to employ them as a part of instruction. But from the standpoint of instructional functioning, they are the same. Each can display *events*, rather than simply objects, and also *sequences of events*. "Moving pictures" is a good general name for the combined instructional medium they represent.

The relation between moving pictures and still pictures is analogous to that between demonstrations and objects. Demonstrations can present events as stimulus situations, rather than simply the objects that participate in these events. The advantage of moving pictures in performing this function is that they enormously extend the range of stimulus situations that can be brought into the classroom. Films and television can display not only balls rolling down inclined planes, but many other kinds of events, both real and imagined: the motions of planets around the sun, the flow of blood through capillaries, the motion of molecules in a container of gas, the actions of satellite particles surrounding an atomic nucleus. They can show political and economic institutions in operation, and re-create for the student the events of history. Their potentialities as part of the conditions of instruction seem as yet only partially realized.

Basically, what moving pictures do in a highly effective way is to present the stimulus situation to the learner. For those instances in which commonly available objects are used in a demonstration, this may not seem a very valuable function. But there are many demonstrations that require expensive equipment or space, and these can be well executed by means of films. (Examples can be found in the series of films produced by the Physical Sciences Study Committee for courses in high school physics.) For presenting problem situations whose solutions are not shown, but which are to be the subject of later class discussion, moving pictures are also excellent media. Their potential for this purpose currently remains largely unexploited, although such films have been made for use in courses in leadership and teacher training.

What other functions can be performed by moving pictures? They can provide the external prompting needed to learn chains and procedures (Lumsdaine, 1963). In certain instances, they are effective in communicating to the learner the kind of terminal performance expected; this is particularly true when a complex motor skill is to be learned. Sequences of pictures may also be used to provide feedback to the learner. If in the course of viewing a demonstration in physics, the learner predicts that one object will exert more force than another, a filmed sequence can then confirm that this is true (see Gropper, 1963).

Moving pictures are seldom used by themselves to perform instructional functions. A sound track is added. When this is done, the range of functions which can be performed is greatly increased, since all of the feats performed by oral communication supplement the stimulus-presentation function. In other words, the teacher is in effect put on the sound track. The oral communication thus provided is capable of directing the student's activities, describing the performance to be learned, guiding the thinking process, questioning for assessment purposes, and providing feedback. With such a combination of talents, the sound motion picture should be a truly marvelous instrument for instruction! Unfortunately, the sound film that exploits these potentialities to their full extent is a great rarity. To a considerable degree, the reason may be that the content and sequencing of such films are governed by production considerations borrowed from the field of theatrical motion pictures (Lumsdaine, 1963). Except for highly specialized subjects (such as knot tying, micrometer reading), it is probably fair to say that sound motion picture film that systematically uses the various instructional functions of moving pictures and oral communication in their proper places has yet to be made.

Teaching Machines

Teaching machines do not represent a truly distinct medium for instruction, but rather a combination of media. Just as the sound motion picture is considered a combination of moving pictures and oral communication, a teaching machine in its typical form combines printed communication with still pictures. This combination of media is also present in a good textbook, and it is in fact quite reasonable to compare a teaching machine to a book. One can consider a teaching machine as a "programmed" book, which is sometimes automated as well.

The "programmed" feature of the teaching machine, however, is likely to make it differ considerably from the usual textbook. In its simplest form, a teaching-machine program contains printed statements in "frames," each of which performs a *single* instructional function. When it is appropriate, the learner responds to a frame by answering a question asked therein, or by filling in a blank to complete a statement. In this way, assessment of the learner's progress is frequent, and the feedback to him is equally frequent. A good teaching-machine program is one that performs each instructional function meticulously, and in an order similar to that described in Chapter 8. There is every reason to suppose that good self-instructional programs are highly effective, as they have many times been shown to be (Glaser, 1965; Schramm, 1964).

To a limited degree, self-instructional programs can foster transfer of knowledge, or at least pave the way for it. Knowledge transfer can be "built into" a teaching-machine program, just as it can into a good textbook or sound film (Kersh, 1965). The technique of doing this is mainly one of presenting the student with a variety of problems requiring the application of principles after he has mastered these principles. Limitations to the variety of problems is in this instance imposed by the designer of the program, and accordingly is not determined by the student's own questions. Again in the case of this medium it is apparent that the well-conducted discussion performs a function that cannot quite be reached by a predesigned program, that is, of inducing the broad generalizing of a variety of individual ideas, and at the same time providing the critical means by which these generalizations can be refined and made more powerful.

DESIGNING INSTRUCTION USING MEDIA

How is one to decide which media to use for which instructional purposes? This question has been the subject of much research over a period of many years (see Campeau, 1967; Lumsdaine and May, 1965). Some of the conclusions that can be drawn from this research may be valuable as an introduction to the problem.

First, no single medium is likely to have properties that make it best for all purposes. When effectiveness of one medium is compared with another for instruction in any given subject, it is rare for significant differences to be found. Lectures have been compared with reading, lectures with motion pictures, pictures with text, and many other kinds of comparisons have been made without revealing clear superiority for any given medium. At any given time, a medium may enjoy unusual popularity, as has been the case, for example, with television, teaching machines, and computerized instruction, at one period or another. Sometimes one medium is found by research to have an advantage for one subject matter only to be shown to have none for some other subject matter. Over a period of years, researchers have learned to be skeptical of single instances of reported statistical superiority of one medium versus another.

Most instructional functions can be performed by most media. The oral presentation of a teacher can be used to gain and control attention, but so also can the use of paragraph headings in a textbook, or an animated sequence in an instructional motion picture. The learner can be informed of the expected outcomes of instruction by a printed text, by an oral communication, or in some instances by a picture or diagram. Recall of prerequisite learned capabilities can be done by oral communication, by means of a sentence or picture in a text, or by a movie or television pictorial sequence. Similar remarks could be made about every one of the functions of instruction described in this chapter. It is possible, of course, that additional research of an analytic nature may yet reveal some important special properties of single media that make them peculiarly adapted to one instructional function or another. Up to now, however, the most reasonable generalization is that all media are capable of performing these functions.

In general, media have not been found to be differentially effective for different people. It is an old idea that some people may be "visual-minded" and therefore learn more readily from visual presentations, while others may be "auditory-minded," and therefore learn better from auditory presentations. While a number of studies have been conducted with the aim of matching media to human ability differences, it is difficult to find any investigations from which one can draw unequivocal conclusions (see Hoban, 1960). If this idea has validity, it has not yet been demonstrated. A possible exception is this: several studies have shown that pictorial presentations may be more effective than printed texts for those who have reading difficulties or small vocabularies. This is hardly a surprising result, and it seems wise to refrain from overgeneralizing its significance.

In view of these findings, which serve the purpose of "clearing the air" in discussing media, how is one to proceed in designing instruction with media or in making the most effective use of available media? The suggestion to be made is that decisions about media should probably be made in sequential stages, choosing the best alternatives at each stage. The process described here is much like that of Briggs, Campeau, Gagné and May (1967).

1. *Stage 1*. The initial key to the question of which media is a consideration of the learning task, that is, the objectives of the learning. A properly defined set of objectives provides information on the nature of stimuli to which the learner is expected to respond, after he has learned. Such stimuli are those *inherent to the learning task*. For example:

a. An objective in a course in physics might be demonstrating Ohm's law. If one expects the student to show how resistance in an electric circuit varies with current and voltage, it would seem reasonable to use actual objects and events as the medium for instruction. In other words, one might set up instruction in a laboratory. If the student has sufficient prior acquaintance with such objects and events, a pictorial presentation could perform the same function.

b. An objective in an English course might be editing written paragraphs for correctness of structure and clarity of expression. Obviously, what has to be presented here are incorrect and unclear paragraphs, and printed language has to be the medium. However, it may be of importance in such an instance to arrange for frequent and prompt feedback to the learner as he makes his corrections. Thus one might choose to have a teacher convey this feedback in the presence of printed language given in a text or projected on a screen.

c. In a foreign language course, an objective might be making appropriate responses to personal questions asked by a speaker in the foreign language. Here again, the medium required is quite evident—it is oral language. The learner must be presented with the questions in oral form, and the printed form will not be an adequate substitute.

2. *Stage 2.* Having determined which medium "fits" the stimuli of the task to be learned, one can then proceed to check the characteristics various media may have in performing other instructional functions. In doing so, however, the medium chosen for each function is expected to be contingent upon the choices already made in stage 1 and not independent of the learning task itself. What medium or media may be used to gain attention for this particular learning task? Perhaps a picture of a voltmeter would be adequate for the learning of Ohm's law, whereas a printed statement would be less effective. What medium can best be used to recall previously learned capabilities? Perhaps some orally presented sentences or phrases would work best for learning to converse in a foreign language, whereas a picture or text would serve less well. What medium can best be used to guide the learning of new rules of paragraph editing? Perhaps, as already suggested, orally guided instruction would be both convenient and effective, whereas printed instructions would tend to generate interference with the essential task, also printed.

It should be evident that many of the decisions to be made in stage 2 sound like common sense. By this is meant that the choices to be made at this stage result mainly in the rejection of media alternatives that are inappropriate or inconvenient. It should also be apparent, however, that the questions raised by decisions of this stage may yet be greatly illuminated by research which has not yet been accomplished. It seems entirely possible that particular effects of different media in the performance of instructional functions may be found to exist within different varieties of learning tasks.

3. *Stage 3.* Having chosen media that are judged to be most effective for various instructional functions, the next decision is one of synthesizing or integrating them into a

reasonable instructional sequence. At this point, various practical judgments need to be made. For example, if one has found that a motion picture (or television) presentation is likely to be effective for five out of six functions of instruction, but that an actual object would be best for one of the six, it is not unreasonable at this point to substitute a picture for the actual object.

The main point reflected in stage 3 of this procedure is this: Decisions about media involve first the analysis of instructional functions and then a synthesis, not the other way around. Good media decisions are likely to be made by matching instructional functions to media, followed by a cost-conscious synthesis into a total instructional sequence. The suggestion is, one does not first decide to teach a chemistry sequence by means of a motion picture and then represent the events of instruction as best one can in the movie. Instead, one decides what media can best be used for the various events of an instructional sequence and then proceeds to make the practical decision about what medium or combination of media to employ—whether this turns out to be a motion picture, a tape recorder, or a laboratory demonstration.

MODES OF INSTRUCTION

Environments for learning consist of the various communication media arranged so as to perform their several functions by interaction with the student. The particular *arrangements* these media may have in relation to the student are usually called the *modes of instruction*. Certain of these modes are traditional in education and have been used for many years, like the lecture and the demonstration. Others are much newer, but nevertheless are widely used, like televised instruction and sound-film presentations. It will be useful here to examine some of the most distinctive modes of instruction, in order to see if "what is going on" can be adequately described and understood in terms of instructional functions. Of course, there are many variations in the arrangements of media even within a given mode, and it will not be possible to describe all of these. Typical events must be considered in each case.

The Tutoring Session

By a "tutoring session" is meant an interchange between a student and his "tutor," which has been preceded by reading by the student, and will be followed by more reading. This appears to be the fundamental character of the mode as practiced, for example, in English universities. However, this kind of tutoring session should not be confused with something that is often called a "cram" session, or even with a "special instruction" session, in which most of the time may be spent in oral communication by the teacher.

The tutoring session as here defined is not like the situation of the student and teacher on opposite ends of a log. Instead, the student has to a large extent done his own learning, primarily by reading books. The tutor's function is, first, to guide the student's thinking by answering the questions he has formulated on the basis of his reading. Second, the tutor conducts an assessment of the student's performance, attempting to judge what he has "gotten out of" his reading. Third, the tutor provides feedback to the learner on the basis of this assessment. And finally, he performs what is, strictly speaking, not an instructional function but a management function: he tells the student what he should read next. In other words, he recommends the direction of further learning that the student is to undertake. In this mode of instruction, then, it is apparent that most of the functions of instruction are performed by the student himself.

Americans should probably not be overly inclined to disparage such a system of instruction, which has, after all, worked very well for many generations. Instead, the important question might well be, what does it take to make such a mode effective? One answer appears to be, it takes a great deal of prerequisite, disciplined learning, including the capability of getting the most out of reading. It is difficult to argue that such a system is not a very good one for college instruction, and there appears to be no great amount of evidence to suggest that the typical system of American colleges and universities is any better. In fact, it may be that the American system of lectures and classes has arisen in part because students entering colleges have *not* acquired enough background knowledge and skill in reading to make it possible for such a system to work. Perhaps the more time-consuming stimulation of oral communication must be used because college students are not really well enough prepared to manage learning for themselves. At any rate, it is interesting to speculate about the extent to which the tutoring mode, accompanied by student reading, could be successfully used in American schools and colleges.

The limitations of the tutoring mode relate to the age at which it can be used, and to the amount of prerequisite knowledge and skill it requires of the student. Obviously, one would not employ this mode in the elementary grades, when students have not learned to read, much less to engage in self-directed study. But some sort of adaptation of the system might well be appropriate, even in the junior high years, if the materials assigned for study were self-instructionally designed, that is, if they were "programmed" for learning. Were such materials available, it would be possible for the teacher to expect the student to use them by himself, and then to follow such "self-study" periods by tutoring sessions devoted to questioning, discussion, assessment, and feedback to the learner. Developments and tryouts of such combinations of instructional modes may be expected to occur in the near future.

The Lecture

The lecture, consisting of oral communication on the part of the teacher, is an extremely common mode of instruction in American schools. It is a very familiar mode to college teachers, and to a large extent also, to secondary school teachers. Junior high teachers might be surprised and even offended at the suggestion that their classroom behavior also includes a great deal of "lecturing," interspersed, naturally, with periods of assessment. Yet such is the case.

A lecture can accomplish, or try to accomplish, a number of different instructional objectives. Among these are the following:

1. It can establish and augment motivation to achieve. Everyone has heard lectures that inspire interest in the subject talked about, both in school and out. For the college and secondary school student, particularly, a lecture that relates events of interest to the broader and larger objectives of an intellectual discipline can be of great educational value.

2. It can inform learners of the expected outcomes of learning. For example, part of a lecture on English writing might be devoted to the styles of good writers. But one probably would not expect a whole lecture to be concerned with such a function—at least not a whole series of lectures.

3. It can attempt to provide prompting and guidance to learning. But in most instances, the lecture does this very badly indeed. Some students do not have the prerequisite knowledge, others are inattentive, others may be bored. Most may be taking notes, which, so far as anyone knows, is an entirely useless activity quite unrelated to learning. The notion that one can import the essential oral communication functions from the teacher-log-student situation into the lecture hall is not very sensible. A certain number of verbal chains may be acquired in note taking, which can, to be sure, be recalled for examinations. But that is about all one can expect.

There are other limitations to the lecture as an instructional mode. Except for those instances in which the stimuli to be presented are verbal (as in certain subjects like English, philosophy, history), the lecturer must use media besides oral communication—objects, demonstrations, pic-

tures. Assessment cannot be done in a lecture, nor can feedback be provided to the student. All in all, the use of the
lecture might best be confined to the functions of motivating
students and informing them of expected accomplishments.
As a means of establishing conditions for learning, the lecture leaves much to be desired.

The Recitation Class

The recitation class is an instructional mode that has a
long history in American schools. It has been depreciated by
a generation of educational writers, probably for quite the
wrong reasons. In the older tradition, the recitation class
was a session in which the teacher "heard" the students
perform what they had presumably learned through previous self-study, the latter being done either in the school or
as homework. In other words, the recitation class is a mode
devoted to assessment and feedback, and to very little else.
It is true that the kind of assessment conducted, in classrooms of an earlier age, often consisted of the recitation of
verbal sequences of varying lengths. But there needs to be
a distinction made between *what* was being assessed, on the
one hand, and *how* this function was carried out, on the
other. It is recognized nowadays that the learning of verbal
sequences is not always a desirable objective for instruction,
and the criticism of "recitation exercises" on these grounds
can be justified. But the conduct of "assessment exercises"
to determine what the student has learned, and to provide
him with a means of knowing what he has attained by learning, is an entirely reasonable mode for instruction.

The recitation class is another mode that depends for its
effectiveness on self-instruction carried out by the student.
Students in such a class are expected to be "prepared"; if a
substantial proportion of them are not, the exercise has little
value, since it simply has the effect of differentiating those
who have mastered a learning assignment and those who
have not. If previous learning has in fact been accomplished,
then the questioning conducted by the teacher can have the

effect of providing feedback to all the students, accomplishing a review at the same time.

The limitations of the recitation class arise not from the class exercise itself but from the prerequisite learning that is left to the student. The purposes of instruction are not served simply by differentiating "bright" students who have found the learning assignment easy and "less bright" students who have not. If this mode is to function effectively, there must be some assurance that all members of the class can in fact learn the material assigned prior to the class meeting, within certain reasonable time limits. The recitation itself provides few clues as to the reasons why the required learning may be easy or difficult. Here is another situation in which teaching-machine programs, which are designed to be learnable by students of a wide range of abilities, may serve a particularly useful function. If the assigned learning takes the form of programmed instruction, whose content has been determined to be at the proper "level," then the succeeding recitation class can proceed readily with its valuable functions of assessment and feedback, with the assumption that all students are roughly equally well "prepared."

The Discussion Class

In the discussion class, the kinds of questions posed by the teacher are different from those of the recitation class. The questions assume that the knowledge required has been attained, and are designed instead to search out the nearest and the remotest implications of what has been learned. Very often, a discussion is begun by introducing a problem situation that has not been encountered during the preceding learning. If the class is in science, the question might be asked, "How would an astronaut go about determining the acceleration of a freely falling body on another planet?" If the class is in English, a newly published poem of a young poet might be presented and a discussion begun of its meaning or meanings. The oral communication that follows may originally occur between teacher and student, but for greatest effectiveness should probably progress to interactions between students. It should be emphasized particularly that the purpose of this communication is *not* to assess: differences in prerequisite knowledge among the participating students merely serves to detract from the value of the exercise. The purpose of the discussion is to make a public exploration of new ideas, of analogies, of similarities and differences among various branches of knowledge. Although novel ideas are to be encouraged, they should also be subjected to the discipline of public evaluation by other students.

The technique of conducting a successful discussion is a subtle art of the teacher, and it is not possible at the present time to specify in detail how it can best be done. This much should be said, however: the questions that are asked are not designed to elicit "facts" or "information," but rather to generate hypotheses within the students. During the course of the discussion, it is the leader's (teacher's) function to make frequent checks to see that this purpose is continually emphasized. The point of such discussion is not whether students "know the answers," but to a large extent whether they "ask the right questions."

Discussions cannot be successful unless the members of the group have previously acquired at least a certain minimum of prerequisite knowledge. A discussion of gravitational forces on distant planets cannot get off the ground unless the students know some fundamental principles about gravitational forces. A discussion of procedures of the United States Congress is similarly impossible unless the students have previously learned the principles of congressional powers and actions. Prerequisite learning *must be assumed*, regardless of how it may have been accomplished. Otherwise the discussion rapidly degenerates into an entirely inefficient attempt to have some students "catch up" with others. Again it is apparent that the prerequisite learning for any particular discussion may be done by self-instructional means, perhaps with the use of a teaching-machine program. At the high school and college level, of course, students may be able to manage their own self-instruction by means of conventional books.

A successful discussion class can be a great delight to both students and teacher. This is as it should be, since knowledge generalization is bound to be intellectual fun. Perhaps in part because of this fact, some educational writers have proposed that the discussion class (or something like it) ought to be the prototype for learning in the school. But an important limitation should be noted. As previous chapters have shown, the discussion class is *not* primarily concerned with learning at all, but with the transfer (generalizing) of what has already been learned. To make discussion the major kind of instructional exercise would therefore be deliberately to ignore the critical prior requirement of insuring that learning occurs. To get learning to happen is still the basic problem. The conditions that bring learning about are not those of the discussion class. The major requirement of successful discussion, with its resultant effect on knowledge transfer, is certainly prior learning.

The Laboratory

In its most general sense, the laboratory is an instructional mode whose purpose is to present a stimulus situation that brings the student into contact with actual objects and events. Although familiarly associated with education in science, the laboratory in this broad meaning can equally well be a part of instruction in almost any subject. A laboratory period in a foreign language may present the stimuli of connected discourse in the language spoken by a native speaker. A laboratory in mathematics may begin with a complex problem requiring a variety of applications of mathematical principles for its solution. A laboratory in English writing can be designed to produce a description of some displayed object or event that is "tested" for its effectiveness in communicating. Sometimes the laboratory must be cast in the form of a field trip, as is often the case in geology and in social science. In contrast to other instructional modes, the laboratory uses actual objects and events for stimuli, rather than verbal communications about them. Of course, in language study, these events may themselves be verbal in form; but in this case they are stimuli to be responded to directly, rather than things to be "read about."

The laboratory has a fundamental importance in science instruction, as it does in other subjects. To learn Ohm's law as the verbal expression $E = IR$ into which certain numerical values can be substituted is an entirely inadequate objective for science instruction, as most science teachers are well aware. Ohm's law is a principle that combines certain concepts. Understanding of these concepts requires that they be tied in a stimulus sense to certain events in the learner's environment which can be directly observed. Accordingly, the laboratory is designed to make it possible for the student to observe and measure changes in voltage produced by changes in resistance (such as those associated with length of conducting wire). When the concepts *voltage, current,* and *resistance* are given objective meanings, Ohm's law likewise acquires a materiality that it would not otherwise have, and that is essential for further learning of other higher-level rules.

In addition, the laboratory can undoubtedly serve as a mode for teaching certain strategies and methods of science. Among these are the procedures of *formulating hypotheses, making operational definitions, controlling and manipulating variables, conducting experiments, designing "models,"* and *interpreting data.* To do all these things well naturally requires that exercises for the laboratory present the kinds of situations that will entail the use of previously acquired knowledge on the part of the student. They should have some novelty in them, so that they will not become simply exercises in "following a procedure," or in performing routines. The design of laboratory exercises having these functions is indeed a challenging task.

Homework

Most instruction in schools of today is likely to include "homework" as one mode on which considerable dependence is placed. Whereas homework assignments used to begin in about the ninth grade, the trend has been toward including them as a part of instruction well down into the elementary grades. Homework takes several forms, and may attempt to do several different things, with varying degrees of effectiveness:

1. Self-instruction on a prescribed topic, as a chapter in a textbook, the translation of a foreign language passage, the reading of a poem, may constitute homework. The effectiveness of such assignments obviously depends on the feasibility of self-instruction for the student. If the material employed makes self-instruction easy (as in the case of teaching-machine programs or programmed texts), such assignments may be quite effective even in the early grades. High school students have presumably acquired enough self-study capabilities so that reading a chapter of history, or a short story, may accomplish the required learning.

2. Practice in a variety of examples of previously learned rules is another common type of homework assignment. Examples at the end of chapters in mathematics and science texts are often used in this manner. Provided the rules have in fact been learned, such assignments can be quite effective. If the rules have not been mastered, the student may get "stuck" and be unable to instruct himself in the required rules. Should this happen frequently, one may expect homework to become a source of negative motivation for such a student.

3. Homework assignments sometimes take the form of "projects" in which the student is asked to organize a variety of activities for himself in such a way as to lead to the development of a product, like a report, a demonstration, or the description of an experiment. Some project assignments are reasonable and feasible, but some are obviously

not. For example, asking a sixth-grade child to read a book and write a review of it is obviously reasonable if the book is written at a suitable vocabulary level, and such an exercise may result in some effective learning. But asking such a child to do a project requiring a scientific experiment is obviously unreasonable because the child does not have the requisite background knowledge to design and carry out such an experiment. It may even be doubted whether assignments of this latter sort are reasonable for ninth- and tenth-graders in today's schools, and for the same reason. Many "science" projects turn out to be concerned with trivial applications of well-known scientific principles. Although projects of this sort may have some motivational effects, their value as a part of science instruction appears highly doubtful at best.

On the whole, the most important function of homework would appear to be self-instruction in topics that can be presented by means of printed books, perhaps containing pictures and diagrams where necessary. This mode of instruction can perform a highly important and essential role when used in conjunction with other modes, such as the tutoring session, the recitation class, or the discussion class. Insofar as these latter modes require *prior learning*, the homework assignment is a means of providing it.

An additional implication is that homework needs to be carefully planned in two respects. First, its assignments should be integrated with preceding assessments to insure that prerequisite knowledge has been attained, and with the subsequent conduct of classes that assume homework learning has been effective. Second, homework assignments need to be of a nature that *all* students can readily master. Their purpose is not to distinguish between bright and dull students; rather, it is to insure that all students have attained a specified set of prerequisite knowledges. These requirements of the homework assignment strongly suggest that the teaching-machine program or programmed self-instructional text should have outstanding usefulness for this purpose.

The Design of Instructional Modes

Modes of instruction are organizations of media to accomplish certain instructional purposes. The modes discussed here are simply those that are best known, or that have been longest in use. But many kinds of organization are possible, including some that use relatively new media, and it would not be correct to suppose that traditional ones are necessarily best. Tryouts of novel forms of media combination and organization may be expected to lead to improved exploitation of the principles governing the conditions of learning. Consider, for example, the potential effectiveness of the following sequence utilizing several media to teach the topic "Reflection and Refraction of Light":

Step 1: A *demonstration* is used, with accompanying oral communication, to teach definitions of concepts (angle of incidence, angle of reflection, angle of refraction, image, virtual image, and so on).

Step 2: A chapter of *programmed instruction* is assigned as the medium for learning the rules (the laws of reflection and refraction, images formed in a plane mirror, dispersion and deviation of light, and so on). Interspersed within the program are exercises designed to establish generalizability of the rules.

Step 3: An *assessment exercise* is conducted by the teacher, primarily to determine that the required principles have been attained. If students have not acquired these principles, they will not be able to undertake the next step.

Step 4: A brief *motion picture sequence* is used to show a novel instance of reflection, or of refraction, or both. This introduces a *discussion* designed to answer the question, "How would one go about investigating the problem shown in this film?"

Step 5: An *assessment of knowledge transfer* may now be carried out by presenting (verbally or pictorially) to students several additional "problems" of reflection and refraction.

Certain favorable characteristics may be predicted for such a combination of instructional media. The use of the demonstration serves to insure that concepts will be soundly based upon observations of concrete objects and events. The acquisition of principles can occur in a manner that incorporates careful design of the conditions of learning, using the medium of programmed instruction, and therefore capable of individualizing the instruction. Assessment is used to insure that all students have mastered the necessary prerequisites for a discussion, which can be introduced by means of pictures representing a real situation, avoiding the danger of excessive verbalization of the problem. Discussion can expand and refine the knowledge previously acquired, and insure its transfer to novel problems. A final assessment can then verify the generalizability of what has been acquired.

Many other arrangements of media are possible for instruction; it is not proposed that this example would necessarily serve best for all purposes. The real point to be made is that the use of a variety of instructional modes is both feasible and potentially effective. The traditional modes are not necessarily either the best or the worst, for any given purpose. What is needed in each case is thoughtful design and management of the learning environment. This requires decisions that match the requirements of the conditions needed to present the proper stimulus for learning, and further to perform other instructional functions, as described in the previous section. If this approach is taken, it will be apparent that there are technological aids for any mode of instruction, designed to meet many different educational objectives.

GENERAL REFERENCES

Principles of Instruction
Bandura, A., and Walters, R. H. *Social learning and personality development.* New York: Holt, Rinehart and Winston, 1964.

De Cecco, J. P. *Human learning in the school.* New York: Holt, Rinehart and Winston, 1963.

Gage, N. L. (ed.). *Handbook of research on teaching.* Chicago: Rand McNally, 1963.

Glaser, R. (ed.). *Training research and education.* Pittsburgh: University of Pittsburgh Press, 1962.

Siegel, L. *Instruction: Some contemporary viewpoints.* San Francisco: Chandler, 1967.

Teaching Machines and Programmed Instruction

De Cecco, J. P. *Educational technology: Readings in programmed instruction.* New York: Holt, Rinehart and Winston, 1964.

Glaser, R. (ed.). *Teaching machines and programed learning, II: Data and directions.* Washington, D.C.: National Education Association, 1965.

Lumsdaine, A. A., and Glaser, R. (eds.). *Teaching machines and programmed learning: A source book.* Washington, D.C.: National Education Association, 1960.

Schramm, W. *The research on programed instruction.* Washington, D.C.: U.S. Department of Health, Education and Welfare, 1964. (OE-34034)

Stolurow, L. M. *Teaching by machine.* Washington, D.C.: U.S. Department of Health, Education and Welfare, 1961. (Cooperative Research Monograph No. 6, OE-34010)

Motion Pictures and Television in Instruction

Gropper, G. L. Why is a picture worth a thousand words? *A V Communic. Rev.,* 1963, **11,** 75–95.

Lumsdaine, A. A. Instruments and media of instruction. In N. L. Gage (ed.), *Handbook of research on teaching.* Chicago: Rand McNally, 1963. Pp. 583–682.

May, M. A., and Lumsdaine, A. A. *Learning from films.* New Haven, Conn.: Yale University Press, 1958.

Roshal, S. M. The instructional film. In G. Finch (ed.), *Educational and training media: A symposium.* Washington, D.C.: National Academy of Sciences-National Research Council, 1960. Pp. 114–121.

References

Adams, J. A. *Human memory.* New York: McGraw-Hill, 1967.

Ausubel, D. P. The use of advance organizers in the learning and retention of meaningful verbal material. *J. educ. Psychol.*, 1960, **51,** 267–272.

Ausubel, D. P. *The psychology of meaningful verbal learning.* New York: Grune & Stratton, 1963.

Ausubel, D. P. *Educational psychology: A cognitive view.* New York: Holt, Rinehart and Winston, 1968.

Ausubel, D. P., and Blake, E. Proactive inhibition in the forgetting of meaningful school material. *J. educ. Res.*, 1958, **52,** 145–149.

Bandura, A., and Walters, R. H. *Social learning and personality development.* New York: Holt, Rinehart and Winston, 1963.

Barnes, J. M., and Underwood, B. J. "Fate" of first-list associations in transfer theory. *J. exp. Psychol.*, 1959, **58,** 97–105.

Bearison, D. J. The role of measurement operations in the acquisition of conservation. Paper presented at Annual Meeting, Eastern Psychological Association, April 1968.

Bereiter, C., and Engelmann, S. *Teaching disadvantaged children in the preschool.* Englewood Cliffs, N.J.: Prentice-Hall, 1966.

Berlyne, D. E. *Structure and direction in thinking.* New York: Wiley, 1965.

Bloom, B. S. (ed.), Engelhart, M. D., Furst, E. J., Hill, W. H., and Krathwohl, D. R. *Taxonomy of educational objectives. Handbook I: Cognitive domain.* New York: McKay, 1956.

Bousfield, W. A. The occurrence of clustering in the recall of randomly arranged associates. *J. gen. Psychol.*, 1953, **49**, 229–240.

Briggs, L. J., Campeau, P. L., Gagné, R. M., and May, M. A. *Instructional media*. Pittsburgh: American Institutes for Research, 1967. Monograph No. 2.

Briggs, L. J., and Reed, H. B. The curve of retention for substance material. *J. exp. Psychol.*, 1943, **32**, 513–517.

Brooks, N. *Language and language learning: Theory and practice*. New York: Harcourt, Brace & World, 1959.

Brown, J. S. *The motivation of behavior*. New York: McGraw-Hill, 1961.

Bruner, J. S. The act of discovery. *Harvard Educ. Rev.*, 1961, **31**, 21–32.

Bruner, J. S. On the conservation of liquids. In Bruner, J. S., Olver, R. R., and Greenfield, P. M. *Studies in cognitive growth*. New York: Wiley, 1966.

Bruner, J. S., Goodnow, J. J., and Austin, G. A. *A study of thinking*. New York: Wiley, 1956.

Campeau, P. L. Selective review of literature on audiovisual media of instruction. In Briggs, L. J., Campeau, P. L., Gagné, R. M., and May, M. A. *Instructional media*. Pittsburgh: American Institutes for Research, 1967. Monograph No. 2.

Carr, H. Teaching and learning. *J. genet. Psychol.*, 1930, **37**, 189–219.

Chall, J. S. *Learning to read: The great debate*. New York: McGraw-Hill, 1967.

Cofer, C. N. (ed.). *Verbal learning and verbal behavior*. New York: McGraw-Hill, 1961.

Cofer, C. N., and Appley, M. H. *Motivation: Theory and research*. New York: Wiley, 1964.

Cofer, C. N., and Musgrave, B. S. (eds.). *Verbal behavior and learning: Problems and processes*. New York: McGraw-Hill, 1963.

Commission on Science Education. *Science: a process approach*. Part 4. Washington, D.C.: American Association for the Advancement of Science, 1963.

Commission on Science Education. *Science: a process approach. Teachers guide*. Washington, D.C.: American Association for the Advancement of Science, 1963.

Congdon, A. R. *Training in high school mathematics essential for success in certain college subjects*. New York: Teachers College, Columbia University, 1930.

De Cecco, J. P. *Human learning in the school*. New York: Holt, Rinehart and Winston, 1963.

De Cecco, J. P. *Educational technology*. New York: Holt, Rinehart and Winston, 1964.

De Cecco, J. P. *The psychology of learning and instruction: Educational psychology.* Englewood Cliffs, N.J.: Prentice-Hall, 1968.

Deese, J. From the isolated verbal unit to connected discourse. In C. N. Cofer (ed.), *Verbal learning and verbal behavior.* New York: McGraw-Hill, 1961.

Deese, J. On the structure of associative meaning. *Psychol. Rev.,* 1962, **69,** 161–175.

Deese, J., and Hulse, S. H. *The psychology of learning,* 3d ed. New York: McGraw-Hill, 1967.

Dewey, J. *How we think.* Boston: Heath, 1910.

Dixon, T. R., and Horton, D. L. (eds.). *Verbal behavior and general behavior theory.* Englewood Cliffs, N.J.: Prentice-Hall, 1968.

Dressel, P. L. (ed.). *Evaluation in general education.* Dubuque, Iowa: Brown, 1954.

Duncan, C. P. (ed.), *Thinking: Current experimental studies.* Philadelphia: Lippincott, 1967.

Durrell, D. D. *Improving reading instruction.* New York: Harcourt, Brace & World, 1956.

Ebbinghaus, H. *Memory: A contribution to experimental psychology.* (Transl. by H. A. Ruger.) New York: Teachers College, Columbia University, 1913.

English, H. B., Welborn, E. L., and Kilian, C. D. Studies in substance memorization. *J. genet. Psychol.,* 1934, **11,** 233–260.

Estes, W. K. The statistical approach to learning theory. In S. Koch (ed.), *Psychology: A study of a science;* Vol. 2. *General systematic formulations, learning, and special processes.* New York: McGraw-Hill, 1959.

Fagerstrom, W. H. *Mathematical facts and processes prerequisite to the study of the calculus.* New York: Teachers College, Columbia University, 1933.

Ferster, C. B., and Skinner, B. F. *Schedules of reinforcement.* New York: Appleton-Century-Crofts, 1957.

Flavell, J. H. *The developmental psychology of Jean Piaget.* Princeton, N.J.: Van Nostrand, 1963.

French, W. *Behavioral goals of general education in high school.* New York: Russell Sage Foundation, 1957.

Fries, C. C. *Linguistics and reading.* New York: Holt, Rinehart and Winston, 1963.

Gage, N. L. (ed.). *Handbook of research on teaching.* Chicago: Rand McNally, 1963.

Gagné, R. M. The acquisition of knowledge. *Psychol. Rev.,* 1962, **69,** 355–365.

Gagné, R. M. Learning and proficiency in mathematics. *Math. Teacher,* 1963, **56,** 620–626 (a).

Gagné, R. M. The learning requirements for enquiry. *J. Res. Science Teaching*, 1963, **1**, 144–153 (b)

Gagné, R. M. Problem solving. In A. W. Melton (ed.), *Categories of human learning*. New York: Academic Press, 1964 (a).

Gagné, R. M. The implications of instructional objectives for learning. In C. M. Lindvall (ed.), *Defining educational objectives*. Pittsburgh: University of Pittsburgh Press, 1964 (b).

Gagné, R. M. The analysis of instructional objectives for the design of instruction. In R. Glaser (ed.), *Teaching machines and programed learning. II: Data and directions*. Washington, D.C.: National Education Association, 1965.

Gagné, R. M. The learning of principles. In H. J. Klausmeier and C. W. Harris (eds.), *Analyses of concept learning*. New York: Academic Press, 1966 (a).

Gagné, R. M. Human problem solving: Internal and external events. In B. Kleinmuntz (ed.), *Problem solving: Research, method, and theory*. New York: Wiley, 1966 (b).

Gagné, R. M. Instruction and the conditions of learning. In L. Siegel (ed.), *Instruction: Some contemporary viewpoints*. San Francisco: Chandler, 1967.

Gagné, R. M. Contributions of learning to human development. *Psychol. Rev.*, 1968, **75**, 177–191 (a).

Gagné, R. M. Learning hierarchies. *Educ. Psychologist*, 1968, **6**, 1–9 (b).

Gagné, R. M. Learning and communication. In R. V. Wiman and W. C. Meierhenry (eds.), *Educational media: Theory into practice*. Columbus, Ohio: Merrill, 1969.

Gagné, R. M., and Bassler, O. C. Study of retention of some topics of elementary non-metric geometry. *J. educ. Psychol.*, 1963, **54**, 123–131.

Gagné, R. M., and Bolles, R. C. A review of factors in learning efficiency. In E. Galanter (ed.), *Automatic teaching: The state of the art*. New York: Wiley, 1959.

Gagné, R. M., and Brown, L. T. Some factors in the programming of conceptual learning. *J. exp. Psychol.*, 1961, **62**, 313–321.

Gagné, R. M., Mayor, J. R., Garstens, H. L., and Paradise, N. E. Factors in acquiring knowledge of a mathematical task. *Psychol. Monogr.*, 1962, **76**, No. 7 (Whole No. 526).

Gagné, R. M., and Paradise, N. E. Abilities and learning sets in knowledge acquisition. *Psychol. Monogr.*, 1961, **75**, No. 14 (Whole No. 518).

Gagné, R. M., and Rohwer, W. D., Jr. Instructional psychology. *Ann. Rev. Psychol.*, 1969, **20**, 381–418.

Gagné, R. M., and staff, Univ. of Md. Math. Project. Some factors in learning non-metric geometry. *Monogr. soc. Res. Child Develpm.*, 1965, **30,** No. 1, 42–49.

Galanter, E. H. (ed.). *Automatic teaching: The state of the art.* New York: Wiley, 1959.

Gardner, J. W. *Excellence.* New York: Harper & Row, 1961.

Gesell, A. Infancy and human growth. New York: Macmillan, 1928.

Getzels, J. W., and Jackson, P. W. *Creativity and intelligence.* New York: Wiley, 1962.

Gibson, E. J. A systematic application of the concepts of generalization and differentiation to verbal learning. *Psychol. Rev.,* 1940, **47,** 196–229.

Gibson, E. J. Retroactive inhibition as a function of degree of generalization between tasks. *J. exp. Psychol.,* 1941, **28,** 93–115.

Gibson, E. J. Intra-list generalization as a factor in verbal learning. *J. exp. Psychol.,* 1942, **30,** 185–200.

Gibson, E. J. Perceptual learning. In R. M. Gagné and W. R. Gephart (eds.), *Learning research and school subjects.* Itasca, Ill.: Peacock, 1968.

Gilbert, T. F. Mathetics: the technology of education. *J. Mathetics,* 1962, **1,** 7–73.

Glaser, R. (ed.). *Training research and education.* Pittsburgh: University of Pittsburgh Press, 1962.

Glaser, R. Instructional technology and the measurement of learning outcomes. *Amer. Psychologist,* 1963, **18,** 519–521.

Glaser, R. (ed.). *Teaching machines and programed learning, II: Data and directions.* Washington, D.C.: National Education Association, 1965.

Glaser, R. Concept learning and concept teaching. In R. M. Gagné and W. J. Gephart (eds.), *Learning research and school subjects.* Itasca, Ill.: Peacock, 1968.

Goodnow, J. J. Determinants of choice-distribution in two choice situations. *Am. J. Psychol.,* 1955, **68,** 106–116.

Goss, A. E. Comments on Professor Noble's paper. In C. N. Cofer and B. S. Musgrave (eds.), *Verbal behavior and learning: Problems and processes.* New York: McGraw-Hill, 1963.

Gropper, G. L. Why is a picture worth a thousand words? *A V Communic. Rev.,* 1963, **11,** 75–95.

Grose, R. F., and Birney, R. C. (eds.). *Transfer of learning.* Princeton, N.J.: Van Nostrand, 1963.

Guilford, J. P. *The nature of human intelligence.* New York: McGraw-Hill, 1967.

Guthrie, E. R. *The psychology of learning.* New York: Harper & Row, 1935.

Guthrie, J. T. Instruction versus a discovery method. *J. educ. Psychol.,* 1967, **58,** 45–49.

Guttman, N., and Kalish, H. I. Discriminability and stimulus generalization. *J. exp. Psychol.,* 1956, **51,** 79–88.

Hall, D. Four kinds of reading. *New York Times Book Review Section,* January 26, 1969.

Hall, J. F. Retroactive inhibition in meaningful material. *J. educ. Psychol.,* 1955, **46,** 47–52.

Hall, J. F. *Psychology of motivation.* Philadelphia: Lippincott, 1961.

Harlow, H. F. The formation of learning sets. *Psychol. Rev.,* 1949, **56,** 51–65.

Harlow, H. F. The development of learning in the rhesus monkey. *Amer. Scientist,* 1959, **47,** 459–479.

Harlow, H. F., and Harlow, M. K. Learning to think. *Scient. Amer.,* 1949, **181,** 36–39.

Hebb, D. O. *A textbook of psychology,* 2d ed. Philadelphia: Saunders, 1966.

Hewett, F. M. *The emotionally disturbed child in the classroom.* Boston: Allyn and Bacon, 1968.

Hilgard, E. R. (ed.). *Theories of learning and instruction, 1964. Sixty-third yearbook.* Chicago: National Society for the Study of Education, 1964, Part I.

Hilgard, E. R., and Bower, G. V. *Theories of learning,* 3d ed. New York: Appleton-Century-Crofts, 1966.

Hilgard, E. R., and Humphreys, L. G. The retention of conditioned discrimination in man. *J. gen. Psychol.,* 1938, **19,** 111–125.

Hill, W. F. *Learning: A survey of psychological interpretations.* San Francisco: Chandler, 1963.

Hoban, C. F. The usable residue of educational film research. In *New teaching aids for the American classroom.* Stanford, Calif.: Stanford University Institute for Communication Research, 1960.

Hovland, C. I. "Inhibition of reinforcement" and phenomena of experimental extinction. *Proc. Nat. Acad. Sci.,* 1936, **22,** 430–433.

Hovland, C. I. The generalization of conditioned responses. I. The sensory generalization of conditioned responses with varying frequencies of tone. *J. gen. Psychol.,* 1937, **17,** 125–148.

Hull, C. L. The concept of the habit-family hierarchy and maze learning. *Psychol. Rev.,* 1934, **41,** 33–54, 134–152.

Hull, C. L. *Principles of behavior.* New York: Appleton-Century-Crofts, 1943.

Hunt, J. McV. *Intelligence and experience.* New York: Ronald, 1961.

Inhelder, B., and Piaget, J. *The growth of logical thinking from childhood to adolescence.* New York: Basic Books, 1958.

James, W. *Principles of psychology.* New York: Holt, Rinehart and Winston, 1890.

Jenkins, H. M., and Harrison, R. H. Effect of discrimination training on auditory generalization. *J. exp. Psychol.,* 1960, **59,** 246–253.

Jenkins, J. J. Mediated associations: paradigms and situations. In C. N. Cofer and B. S. Musgrave (eds.), *Verbal behavior and learning.* New York: McGraw-Hill, 1963.

Jensen, A. R. An empirical theory of the serial-position effect. *J. Psychol.,* 1962, **53,** 127–142.

Jensen, A. R. Discussion of Dr. Rothkopf's paper. In R. M. Gagné and W. R. Gephart (eds.), *Learning research and school subjects.* Itasca, Ill.: Peacock, 1968. Pp. 134–141.

John, E. R. *Mechanisms of memory.* New York: Academic Press, 1967.

Johnson, D. M. *The psychology of thought and judgment.* New York: Harper & Row, 1955.

Jones, H. E., and English, H. B. Notional *vs.* rote memory. *Amer. J. Psychol.,* 1926, **37,** 602–603.

Karplus, R. Beginning a study in elementary school science. *Amer. J. Physics,* 1962, **30,** 1–9.

Katona, G. *Organizing and memorizing.* New York: Columbia University Press, 1940.

Kearney, N. C. *Elementary school objectives.* New York: Russell Sage Foundation, 1953.

Keller, F. A., and Schoenfeld, W. N. *Principles of psychology.* New York: Appleton-Century-Crofts, 1950.

Kendler, H. H. The concept of the concept. In A. W. Melton (ed.), *Categories of human learning.* New York: Academic Press, 1964.

Kendler, H. H., and Kendler, T. S. Effect of verbalization on reversal shifts in children. *Science,* 1961, **141,** 1619–1620.

Kersh, B. Y. Programing classroom instruction. In R. Glaser (ed.), *Teaching machines and programed learning, II: Data and directions.* Washington, D.C.: National Education Association, 1965.

Kimble, G. A. *Hilgard and Marquis' "Conditioning and learning."* New York: Appleton-Century-Crofts, 1961.

Kimble, G. A. *Foundations of conditioning and learning.* New York: Appleton-Century-Crofts, 1967.

Kingsley, R. C., and Hall, V. C. Training conservation through the use of learning sets. *Child Developm.,* 1967, **38,** 1111–1126.

Klaus, D. Programing techniques. In R. Glaser (ed.), *Teaching machines and programed learning, II: Data and directions.* Washington, D.C.: National Education Association, 1965.

Klausmeier, H. J., and Harris, C. W. *Analyses of concept learning.* New York: Academic Press, 1966.

Knight, F. B. Some considerations of method. In G. M. Whipple (ed.), *National Society for the Study of Education, Twenty-ninth Yearbook. Report of the society's committee on arithmetic.* Bloomington, Ill.: Public School, 1930. Chap. 4.

Koffka, K. *The growth of the mind,* 2d ed. New York: Harcourt, Brace & World, 1929.

Köhler, W. *The mentality of apes.* New York: Harcourt, Brace & World, 1927.

Köhler, W. *Gestalt psychology.* New York: Liveright, 1929.

Krathwohl, D. R., Bloom, B. S., and Masia, B. B. *Taxonomy of educational objectives. Handbook II: Affective domain.* New York: McKay, 1964.

Krueger, W. C. F. Rate of progress as related to difficulty of assignment. *J. educ. Psychol.,* 1946, **37,** 247–249.

Lashley, K. S. In search of the engram. *Sympos. Soc. exp. Biol.,* 1950, **4,** 454–482.

Leavitt, H. J., and Schlosberg, H. The retention of verbal and of motor skills. *J. exp. Psychol.,* 1944, **34,** 404–417.

Le François, G. A treatment hierarchy for the acceleration of conservation of substance. *Canad. J. Psychol.,* 1968, **22,** 277–284.

Lindquist, E. F. (ed.). *Educational measurement.* Washington, D.C.: American Council on Education, 1950.

Lindvall, C. M. (ed.). *Defining educational objectives.* Pittsburgh: University of Pittsburgh Press, 1964.

Lorge, I., Tuckman, J., Aikman, L., Spiegel, J., and Moss, G. Problem solving by teams and by individuals in a field setting. *J. educ. Psychol.,* 1955, **46,** 160–166.

Lovell, K. *The growth of basic mathematical and scientific concepts in children.* New York: Philosophical Library, 1961.

Lumsdaine, A. A. Instruments and media of instruction. In N. L. Gage (ed.), *Handbook of research on teaching.* Chicago: Rand McNally, 1963. Pp. 583–682.

Lumsdaine, A. A., and Glaser, R. (eds.). *Teaching machines and programmed learning: A source book.* Washington, D.C.: National Education Association, 1960.

Lumsdaine, A. A., and May, M. A. Mass communication and educational media. *Ann. Rev. Psychol.*, 1965, **16**, 475–534.

McClelland, D. C. Toward a theory of motive acquisition. *Amer. Psychologist*, 1959, **66**, 297–333.

McClelland, D. C., Atkinson, J. W., Clark, R. A., and Lowell, E. L. *The achievement motive.* New York: Appleton-Century-Crofts, 1953.

McGeoch, J. A. *The psychology of human learning.* New York: McKay, 1942.

McGeoch, J. A., and Irion, A. L. *The psychology of human learning.* New York: McKay, 1952.

Mager, R. F. *Preparing objectives for programmed instruction.* Palo Alto, Calif.: Fearon, 1962.

Mager, R. F. *Developing attitude toward learning.* Palo Alto, Calif.: Fearon, 1968.

Maier, N. R. F. Reasoning in humans: I. On direction. *J. comp. Psychol.*, 1930, **10**, 115–143.

Mandler, G. Association and organization: Facts, fancies, and theories. In T. R. Dixon and D. L. Horton (eds.), *Verbal behavior and general behavior theory.* Englewood Cliffs, N.J.: Prentice-Hall, 1968. Pp. 109–119.

Mandler, J. M., and Mandler, G. *Thinking: From association to Gestalt.* New York: Wiley, 1964.

May, M. A. *Word-picture relationships in audio-visual presentations.* Washington, D.C.: Bureau of Research, Office of Education, U.S. Dept. of Health, Education and Welfare, 1965. (Project 5-0999)

Melton, A. W. Learning. In W. S. Monroe (ed.), *Encyclopedia of educational research.* New York: Macmillan, 1940.

Melton, A. W. The taxonomy of human learning: overview. In A. W. Melton (ed.), *Categories of human learning.* New York: Academic Press, 1964 (a).

Melton, A. W. (ed.). *Categories of human learning.* New York: Academic Press, 1964 (b).

Mill, J. *Analysis of the phenomena of the human mind.* (Ed. by A. Bain, A. Findlater, and G. Grote; ed. with additional notes by J. S. Mill.) London: Longmans, 1869.

Miller, G. A. *Language and communication.* New York: McGraw-Hill, 1951.

Miller, G. A. The magical number seven, plus or minus two: Some limits on our capacity for processing information. *Psychol. Rev.*, 1956, **63**, 81–97.

Miller, N. E. Liberalization of basic S-R concepts: Extensions to conflict behavior, motivation, and social learning. In S. Koch (ed.), *Psychology, a study of a science,* Vol. 2. New York: McGraw-Hill, 1959.

390 References

Miller, N. E. Laws of learning relevant to its biological basis. *Proc. Amer. Philos. Soc.*, 1967, **111**, 315–325.

Mowrer, O. H. *Learning theory and behavior.* New York: Wiley, 1960 (a).

Mowrer, O. H. *Learning theory and the symbolic processes.* New York: Wiley, 1960 (b).

Murdock, B. B., Jr. The retention of individual items. *J. exp. Psychol.*, 1961, **62**, 618–625.

National Council of Teachers of English, Commission on the English Curriculum. *The English language arts for today's children.* New York: Appleton-Century-Crofts, 1954.

National Council of Teachers of English, Commission on the English Curriculum. *The English language arts in the secondary school.* New York: Appleton-Century-Crofts, 1956.

National Council of Teachers of Mathematics. *The learning of mathematics: its theory and practice.* 21st Yearbook. Washington, D.C.: The Council, 1953.

Newman, E. B. Forgetting of meaningful material during sleep and waking. *Amer. J. Psychol.*, 1939, **52**, 65–71.

Noble, C. E. Meaningfulness and familiarity. In C. N. Cofer and B. S. Musgrave (eds.), *Verbal behavior and learning.* New York: McGraw-Hill, 1963.

Northrop, F. S. C. *The logic of the sciences and the humanities.* New York: Macmillan, 1947.

Orlando, R., and Bijou, S. W. Single and multiple schedules of reinforcement in developmentally retarded children. *J. exp. Anal. Beh.*, 1960, **3**, 339–348.

Patrick, C. *What is creative thinking?* New York: Philosophical Library, 1955.

Pavlov, I. P. *Conditioned reflexes.* (Transl. by G. V. Anrep.) London: Oxford University Press, 1927. (Also available in paperback; New York: Dover.)

Penfield, W. Memory mechanisms. *Trans. Amer. Neurol. Assoc.*, 1951, **76**, 15–31.

Phillips, J. L., Jr. *The origins of intellect: Piaget's theory.* San Francisco: Freeman, 1969.

Piaget, J. *The origins of intelligence in children.* New York: International Universities Press, 1952.

Piaget, J. *Construction of reality in the child.* New York: Basic Books, 1954.

Piaget, J., and Inhelder, B. *The early growth of logic in the child.* New York: Harper & Row, 1964.

Postman, L. The present status of interference theory. In C. N. Cofer (ed.), *Verbal learning and verbal behavior.* New York: McGraw-Hill, 1961.

Postman, L. Short-term memory and incidental learning. In A. W. Melton (ed.), *Categories of human learning*. New York: Academic Press, 1964.

Resnick, L. B. *Design of an early learning curriculum*. Working paper 16. Pittsburgh: Learning Research and Development Center, University of Pittsburgh, 1967.

Riessman, F. *The culturally deprived child*. New York: Harper & Row, 1962.

Riley, D. A. *Discrimination learning*. Englewood Cliffs, N.J.: Prentice-Hall, 1968.

Robinson, E. S. *Association theory today*. New York: Appleton-Century-Crofts, 1932.

Roshal, S. M. The instructional film. In G. Finch (ed.), *Educational and training media: A symposium*. Washington, D.C.: National Academy of Sciences-National Research Council, 1960.

Roshal, S. M. Film-mediated learning with varying representation of the task: viewing angle, portrayal of demonstration, motion, and student participation. In A. A. Lumsdaine (ed.), *Student response in programmed instruction*. Washington, D.C.: National Academy of Sciences-National Research Council, 1961.

Rothkopf, E. Z. Two scientific approaches to the management of instruction. In R. M. Gagné and W. R. Gephart (eds.), *Learning research and school subjects*. Itasca, Ill.: Peacock, 1968.

Russell, D. H. *Children's thinking*. Boston: Ginn, 1956.

Saltz, E. Response pretraining: differentiation or availability? *J. exp. Psychol.*, 1961, **62**, 583–587.

Schramm, W. *The research on programed instruction*. Washington, D.C.: Department of Health, Education and Welfare, 1964. (OE-34034)

Schwab, J. J. The teaching of science as enquiry. In *The teaching of science*. Cambridge, Mass.: Harvard University Press, 1962.

Scribner, D. C. *Learning hierarchies and literary sequence*. *Engl. J.*, 1967, **56**, 385–393.

Shaw, G. B. *Adventures of the black girl in her search for God*. New York: Putnam, 1959.

Shulman, L. S., and Keislar, E. R. *Learning by discovery: A critical appraisal*. Chicago: Rand McNally, 1966.

Siegel, L. *Instruction: Some contemporary viewpoints*. San Francisco: Chandler, 1967.

Skinner, B. F. *The behavior of organisms; an experimental analysis*. New York: Appleton-Century-Crofts, 1938.

Skinner, B. F. *Walden Two.* New York: Macmillan, 1948.

Skinner, B. F. Are theories of learning necessary? *Psychol. Rev.*, 1950, **57**, 193–216.

Skinner, B. F. *Science and human behavior.* New York: Macmillan, 1953.

Skinner, B. F. *Verbal behavior.* New York: Appleton-Century-Crofts, 1957.

Skinner, B. F. *The technology of teaching.* New York: Appleton-Century-Crofts, 1968.

Spence, K. W. *Behavior theory and conditioning.* New Haven, Conn.: Yale University Press, 1956.

Staats, A. W. *Human learning.* New York: Holt, Rinehart and Winston, 1964.

Stephens, J. M. Transfer of learning. In C. W. Harris (ed.), *Encyclopedia of educational research.* New York: Macmillan, 1960.

Stolurow, L. M. *Teaching by machine.* Washington, D.C.: U.S. Department of Health, Education and Welfare, 1961. (Cooperative Research Monograph No. 6, OE-34010).

Taylor, C. W. *The second University of Utah research conference on the identification of creative scientific talent.* Salt Lake City: University of Utah Press, 1958.

Taylor, D. W., Berry, P. C., and Block, C. H. Does group participation when using brainstorming facilitate or inhibit creative thinking? *Tech. Rept. No. 1, NR 150–166,* Department of Industrial Administration and Department of Psychology, Yale University, 1957.

Taylor, J. A. The relationship of anxiety to the conditioned eyelid response. *J. exp. Psychol.*, 1951, **41**, 81–92.

Thorndike, E. L. Animal intelligence: An experimental study of the associative processes in animals. *Psychol. Rev. Monogr. Suppl.*, 1898, **2**, No. 4 (Whole No. 8).

Thorndike, E. L. *Animal intelligence.* New York: Macmillan, 1911.

Thorndike, E. L. *Human learning.* New York: Appleton-Century-Crofts, 1931.

Tolman, E. C. *Purposive behavior in animals and men.* New York: Appleton-Century-Crofts, 1932.

Tolman, E. C. There is more than one kind of learning. *Psychol. Rev.*, 1949, **56**, 144–155.

Travers, R. M. W. *Essentials of learning,* 2d ed. New York: Macmillan, 1967.

Tyler, R. W. Achievement testing and curriculum construction. In E. G. Williamson (ed.), *Trends in student personnel work.*

393   *References*

Minneapolis: University of Minnesota Press, 1949. Pp. 391–407.

Underwood, B. J. Studies of distributed practice: IX. Learning and retention of paired adjectives as a function of intralist similarity. *J. exp. Psychol.*, 1953, **45,** 143–149.

Underwood, B. J. An evaluation of the Gibson theory of verbal learning. In C. N. Cofer (ed.), *Verbal learning and verbal behavior.* New York: McGraw-Hill, 1961.

Underwood, B. J. Laboratory studies of verbal learning. In E. R. Hilgard (ed.), *Theories of learning and instruction.* Sixty-third Yearbook. Chicago: National Society for the Study of Education. Part I, 1964 (a).

Underwood, B. J. The representativeness of rote verbal learning. In A. W. Melton (ed.), *Categories of human learning.* New York: Academic Press, 1964 (b).

Underwood, B. J., and Schulz, R. W. *Meaningfulness and verbal learning.* Philadelphia: Lippincott, 1960.

UNESCO. *The teaching of modern languages.* New York: Columbia University Press, 1955.

Watson, J. B. *Psychology from the standpoint of a behaviorist.* Philadelphia: Lippincott, 1919.

Watson, J. B., and Rayner, R. Conditioned emotional reactions. *J. exp. Psychol.*, 1920, **3,** 1–14.

Wertheimer, M. *Productive thinking.* New York: Harper & Row, 1945.

White, R. W. Motivation reconsidered: The concept of competence. *Psychol. Rev.*, 1959, **66,** 297–333.

Wilson, A. B. Class segregation and aspirations of youth. *Amer. Sociol. Rev.*, 1959, **24,** 836–845.

Woodworth, R. S. *Dynamics of behavior.* New York: Holt, Rinehart and Winston, 1958.

Worthen, B. R. Discovery and expository task presentation in elementary mathematics. *J. educ. Psychol. Monogr. Suppl.*, 1968, **59,** No. 1, Part 2.

Author Index

Subject Index

Acquisition, as phase of learning, 73–74
Action, as learning factor, 8
Apprehending, attending, 72
  coding, 73
  perceiving, 72
  and perceptual learning, 73
  as phase of learning sequence, 72–73
Assessment, procedures in instruction, 339–342
Association, basic learned capability, 6
  and contiguity, 8
  in modern learning theories, 11
  and repetition, 8
  in single trial, 11
  Thorndike's views, 8–10
Associationist tradition, 7–8
Associationists, British, 7–8
Attention, in apprehending phase of learning, 72
  as event of instruction, 305–306
  as readiness for learning, 279–281
Attentional sets, as readiness for learning, 280–281

Basic learning types, in foreign language instruction, 265–266
  in science instruction, 257
Behavior modification, 119, 121

Capability, acquiring of, 73–74
  as learning prerequisite, 66–67
  and performance change, 5–6
Chaining, 122–154
  conditions, 128–131
  in learner, 128–129
  in situation, 129–131
  contiguity in, 130
  description, 42–45, 124–128
  and discrimination, 132
  examples, 124
  extinction of, 131–132
  and forgetting, 133
  and generalization, 132
  in instruction, 68
  in mathematics, 248
  and maze learning, 127–128
  order, in learning, 129
  and procedures, 133–134
  and reinforcement, 131
  and repetition, 130–131
  uses of, 133–134
  and verbal instructions, 125–127
Classification, as result of concept learning, 174